The Revolution within the Revolution

NANCY GINA BERMEO

THE REVOLUTION WITHIN
THE REVOLUTION

Workers' Control in
Rural Portugal

PRINCETON UNIVERSITY PRESS • PRINCETON, NEW JERSEY

Copyright © 1986 by Princeton University Press

Published by Princeton University Press, 41 William Street,
Princeton, New Jersey 08540
In the United Kingdom: Princeton University Press, Guildford, Surrey

All Rights Reserved

Library of Congress Cataloging in Publication Data will be found
on the last printed page of this book
ISBN 0-691-07688-X

Publication of this book has been aided by the Whitney Darrow Fund
of Princeton University Press

This book has been composed in Linotron Times Roman

Clothbound editions of Princeton University Press books are printed
on acid-free paper, and binding materials are chosen
for strength and durability

Printed in the United States of America by Princeton
University Press, Princeton, New Jersey

TO THE MEMORY OF MY FATHER

Carlos Bermeo

CONTENTS

I

The Emergence of Workers' Control in Agriculture

II

The Consequences of Workers' Control in Agriculture

III

Workers' Control and the Problem of Articulation

LIST OF ILLUSTRATIONS

LIST OF TABLES

PREFACE

In May 1954, a small group of farmworkers assembled in a remote town in southern Portugal. They came together to protest the sunup to sundown schedule that had been the lot of local workers for generations. Men and women, young and old filled the town square for a peaceful demonstration in support of the eight-hour day. Landowners and local officials panicked. Someone called the Civil Guard. They came and fired into the crowd, leaving a young mother named Catarina Eufémia dead.

In September 1979, another group of farmworkers assembled in another remote area of southern Portugal. Men and women of all ages, they looked much like their counterparts in the time of Catarina Eufémia. Two of them were to share her fate. António Casquinha and João Caravela were shot and killed by the Civil Guard.

Both of these incidents involved an open and tragic confrontation between farmworkers and armed agents of the Portuguese state. But much had changed in the years between the shootings. The fall of the Salazar-Caetano regime, in April of 1974, had given rise to massive transformations in rural property relations and a certain transformation of the farmworkers themselves. Catarina Eufémia died petitioning for an eight-hour day, a demand that had been accepted throughout the primary sector in most, if not all, of capitalist Europe. António Casquinha and João Caravela died in a different context. They died in an attempt to stop the Civil Guard from breaking up an agricultural cooperative—a cooperative that their fellow farmworkers had formed through the occupation of large estates. In the first instance, the Portuguese state had exercised its coercive power against reformers, in the second, against revolutionaries.

This study is an analysis of reform and revolution in the Portuguese countryside. It focuses on the issue of workers' control, by which I mean the collective management and usufruct of productive property. The inquiry addresses three interrelated questions. First, what moved the farmworkers of the South to challenge property relations and establish worker-controlled farms in the first place? Second, what was the microlevel impact of the worker-controlled cooperative units once established? Finally, what was the nature of the interaction between the cooperatives and the state system in which they were imbedded? How did they fare in the postrevolutionary state?

Devoid of any other pretense, the answers to these questions would add up to the story of the Portuguese agrarian reform. Although one of my aims is simply to tell a story that merits telling, I also aim to address theoretical issues of interest to an academic community that extends beyond Portugal and beyond the group of scholars interested in Portugal per se. Raised to a higher level of abstraction, each of the questions posed bears on a heated theoretical debate. The question of why the farmworkers seized the land provides a practical format for addressing the issue of revolutionary mobilization—i.e., when do poor people act in concert to change relations of power and property? The question concerning the microlevel impact of cooperative units serves as a context for studying the effects of "power at the point of production," or more neutrally put, the effects of democratization of the workplace. The final question to be addressed—the question relating to the interaction between the worker-controlled cooperatives and the state—derives directly from the debate about the viability of combining liberal democracy and socialism. What is the fate of socialist experiments in a liberal democracy? Can democracy at the national level and democracy at the base be combined? The study of Portugal's agrarian reform brings us closer to answering all of these larger theoretical questions and closer to an understanding of the long-suffering people of the Portuguese countryside as well.

PORTUGAL proved an ideal place to research the questions outlined above. When I began my fieldwork there in 1977, memories of the 1974 revolution were still vivid. Workers and owners had clear visions of what had happened when land was seized and of what had preceded the change in property relations. The question of how the worker-controlled farms emerged could thus be researched not only through archives but through the reports of witnesses and participants.

The consequences of workers' control unfolded before my eyes in the nearly three years I spent in Portugal. By 1980, when I ended my research, the experiment with worker-controlled farms was a full five years old and both the microlevel and macrolevel consequences of changes in property relations were readily observable. Studies of the long-term effects of workers' control will come only in the future, of course, but the short-term effects had enough scope and weight to merit a study of their own.

The feasibility of combining workers' control and national democracy was one of the most important issues on the Portuguese political agenda when I arrived. The abstract questions that had perplexed me on one side of the Atlantic were very real ones on the other. Now that a national democracy had been consolidated, what should be done with the legacy of the revolution? Can one new set of "democratic structures" stand beside another? The fact that the nation was a liberal democracy enabled me to ask these questions openly and to do my work with a minimum of inter-ference. Though some of the drama involving the farms and the state was played out behind closed doors, there was a rich, public debate about just what should be done. The very frailty of the two democratic experiments—the one at the national level and the other at the base—meant that the risks of any particular action were great and thus that options were debated earnestly and at length. I benefited greatly from the sincerity and patience with which people expressed their views to me.

The place of workers' control in Portugal's liberal democracy has prob-ably not been permanently fixed, but at the time of this writing, worker-controlled farms were clearly on the decline. They did not fare well in the aftermath of the revolution, and this book helps to explain why.

The explanation is complex, as are the three major theoretical questions I deal with, so both a summary of what happened and an outline of the study itself are in order before the book begins. What happened, condensed to its essentials, is this. On April 25, 1974, a group of middle-ranking military men, seeking to put an end to the colonial wars, overthrew the forty-eight-year-old Salazar-Caetano regime in a bloodless coup. Unable to agree on how the war should be ended or, indeed, on what specific direction the revolution should take, the officers broke into competing factions and, along with civilian politicians, wrestled for hegemony in the state apparatus. Six provisional governments (lasting from April 1974 to July 1976) were formed as a result.

The first three were essentially liberal democratic. The fourth and fifth (lasting from March to September 1975) were essentially radical. But the sixth (lasting until July 1976) was much like the first. The revolution thus reached its crescendo in the spring and summer of 1975, as the fourth and fifth governments embarked on massive nationalizations and initiated a social revolution. The sixth provisional government reversed this trend and began a period of consolidation. When the Socialist party formed the First Constitutional Government after winning the national elections of April 1976, it faced the legacy of both a political and social revolution.

Worker-controlled farms were a very important part of the revolutionary legacy. The farms, and the land seizures that made them possible, emerged during the moderate third provisional government and continued after the radical fourth and fifth governments had been ousted, but they were con-sistently identified with the radical period of the revolution and with the party that led it: the Communist party (PCP). As Part I of this book illustrates, this identity was *initially* a false one. The land seizures emerged with much more autonomy than non-Communists believed and with more autonomy than many Communists desired. However, the equation of the cooperatives with the Communist party had great political ramifications anyway. The diverse and largely positive consequences of worker-controlled farms (discussed in Part II of the book) were overshadowed by partisan issues because aiding the cooperatives became equated with aiding the PCP. The Socialist party was loathe to do either. Instead, as it struggled to consolidate democracy at the national level, it battled against what it alleged to be an "undemocratic" party at the base.

The scene of the battle was the Alentejo—the southern region where the land was seized—and the principal casualty was the rural experiment in workers' control. The farms (as I argue in Part III) were not the victims of mismanagement but of a partisan struggle. The Socialist party sealed their fate in July 1977 with legislation that restored large sections of occupied property to former landowners. By 1977, the cooperatives really *were* identified closely with the Communist party, but this had not always been the case and it had proved much more of a liability than an asset.

The experiment with worker-controlled farms was extensive—over five hundred cooperative farms were established on some 25 percent of the nation's arable land—but it was short-lived. Though the dismantling legislation has been applied only irregularly, the worker-controlled sector is clearly on the decline. Many farms have disappeared altogether, many have been greatly weakened by the devolution of their best lands, and only a minority survive.

The theoretical questions that bear on this drama provide the organizational framework for this study. Part I relates the emergence of workers' control to literature on peasant mobilization. It concludes that the participants in the land seizures acted more autonomously than either the existing literature on rural mobilization or the literature on Portugal would lead us to believe.

Part II deals with the consequences of workers' control at the microlevel. It examines four hypotheses emerging from social science literature. The section begins by investigating the hypothesis that the formal establishment of workers' control leads to fully participatory management and concludes that management is not fully participatory but is still democratic. The study then moves on to address the idea that workers' control leads to increased productivity and finds strong evidence which suggests that worker-controlled farms are at least as productive, if not more productive, than their private counterparts. In its second half the section analyzes the assertions that control of one's work environment makes one a) more inclined toward participation elsewhere and b) more radical. Here the study corroborates both ideas but suggests that the association is due to factors that previous analysts have not foreseen.

Part III explores the interaction between worker-controlled farms and the postrevolutionary state. Beginning with theoretical writings that advocate the articulation of democratic structures at the national level and the base, the study concludes that the problems of articulation are more grave and more related to party competition on the left than certain analysts have realized. It suggests that future research on the feasibility of articulation should investigate *party* relations rather than simple, bipolar class relations.*

I have chosen to work with three bodies of literature in sequence because neither the emergence, nor the consequences, nor the articulation of workers' control can be understood in isolation. The emergence of workers' control affected its consequences, and both affected the fate of the experiment in the larger political system.

IN the long course of doing the research described above, I said thank you hurriedly to hundreds of people, and I take satisfaction in finally recording my gratitude in a more permanent way. This project began as a dissertation at Yale University, and I am indebted to many scholars there as a result, namely, David Apter, Robert Dahl, Juan Linz, and Alfred Stepan. My greatest debt in New Haven is to David Cameron whose scholarship and personal decency inspire a whole generation of comparativists at Yale.

My debts in the United States extend beyond Yale to Dartmouth College, where my former colleagues in the Government Department provided a fine environment for writing up my results, and to Princeton University, where my new colleague Ezra Suleiman read and commented on the manuscript, where Elizabeth Doherty and Teresa Sanchez assisted with some last-minute research, and where Julie Bengochea put it all together in typed form. Joyce Reiglehaupt of Sarah Lawrence College was very generous with both her research material and her time, and the project is much better as a result. My study would probably not have been possible at all without the financial assistance of the Fulbright Doctoral Research Committee, the Social Science Research Council, the Yale Concilium, and the Centre National de la Recherche Scientifique of France.

My academic debts abroad begin with the working people of the ministries, offices, and libraries in Portugal and extend to Mário Bacalhau, Afonso de Barros, Tom Bruneau, Michel Drain, Manuel Cabral, José Girão, Virginie Laffon, Nelson Lourenço, the Instituto Gulbenkian, and the Instituto António Sergio, among others. Special gratitude goes to the workers and farmers of the Alentejo who shared their world with me, to

* The term *articulation* is awkward but difficult to replace. It is widely used by European and Latin American scholars to connote the joining and coordination of social, economic, or political structures. The straightforward synonym might be "meshing," but the original term is so common in the literature cited here that I have decided to use it myself.

Eleanor Bermeo who contributed to this project in a variety of ways, and to the Câmara family of Lisbon, whose own struggles and unflagging friendship enabled me to keep my scholarly setbacks in perspective. Last and most, I thank my husband Richard Thypin for both his friendship and his insights as a political scientist.

LIST OF ABBREVIATIONS

ALA   Associação Livre de Agricultores
                  Free Association of Farmers

CAP   Confederação dos Agricultores de Portugal
                  Confederation of Portuguese Farmers

CDS   Centro Democrático Social
                  Social Democratic Center

COPCON   Commando Operacional do Continente
                  Operational Command for the Continent

CRRA   Centros Regionais da Reforma Agrária
                  Regional Agrarian Reform Centers

MAP   Ministério de Agricultura e Pescas
                  Ministry of Agriculture and Fishing

MDP   Common name for MDP-CDE

MDP-CDE   Movimento Democrático Português-Comissões Democráticas
                    Eleitorais
                  Portuguese Democratic Movement-Democratic Electoral
                    Commissions

MFA   Movimento das Forças Armadas
                  Armed Forces Movement

MIR   Movimiento de la Izquierda Revolucionária (Chilean)
                  Movement of the Revolutionary Left

PCP   Partido Comunista Português
                  Portuguese Communist Party

PPD   Common name for PPD-PSD

PPD-PSD   Partido Popular Democrático-Partido Social Democrata
                  Popular Democratic Party-Social Democratic Party

PSP   Partido Socialista de Portugal
                  Portuguese Socialist Party

UCP   Unidades Collectivas de Produção
                  Collective Production Units

I

The Emergence of Workers' Control
in Agriculture

INTRODUCTION

LATE in the evening of April 24, 1974, Portugal's state-run radio station broadcast a song entitled "Grândola." Named for a southern agricultural town known as a center of resistance to the dictatorship, the song glorified a sun-baked "land of fraternity" where "the people ruled." For those who knew that "Grândola" had been banned, the broadcast provoked some puzzlement, but for a small group of middle-ranking military officers, it provoked a frenzy of activity. For these men, stationed at strategic points throughout Portugal, the song was a secret signal to begin a revolution. Troops converged on major government centers, and within thirty-six hours the Portuguese military toppled a dictatorship that had lasted nearly half a century. In posters, speeches, books, and banners, the military action would be known as the 25th of April, and its leaders would be known as the MFA, the Armed Forces Movement.

The MFA had emerged from a series of professional frustrations associated with Portugal's colonial wars in Africa. The captains and majors who organized the movement were convinced that they were involved in a war they would not win and were distraught at what the conflict had done to the military as an institution.[1] The officers agreed on two issues: first, that the war should be ended, and second, that this could not be accomplished without a change of regime. Once the officers brought down the regime, the ideological differences that had always been present rose to the surface. Linked with civilian allies in a broad spectrum of political parties, factions of the military continuously jostled for power at the top of the state system, forming six provisional governments in eighteen months. Table 1.1 provides a chronology.

Between April 1974 and July 1976, when the first constitutional government assumed power, the country underwent radical transformations. During the first three provisional governments, multiparty, largely civilian

---

[1] Career military officers were frustrated with their low prestige in colonial and metropolitan society and relatedly with their level of remuneration. Captains fighting in rural areas of Mozambique are reported to have earned less than barbers in Luanda. Professional frustrations were exacerbated in the early seventies, when college-trained draftees were given the same privileges as career officers and when the prestigious General Spínola published a book in which he argued that the colonial problem could not be solved militarily. See António Spínola, *Portugal and the Future* (Johannesburg: Perksor, 1974), and Avelino Rodrigues, Cesário Borga, and Mário Cardoso, *O Movimento dos Capitães e o 25 de Abril* (Lisbon: Morães, 1974).

TABLE 1.1
Chronology of Postrevolutionary Provisional Governments

Government	Prime Minister	Government's Political Image	Beginning Date
I	Adelino Palma Carlos	Moderate	May 16, 1974
II	Col. Vasco Gonçalves	Moderate	July 19, 1974
III	Gen. Vasco Gonçalves	Moderate	October 1, 1974
IV	Gen. Vasco Gonçalves	Radical	March 26, 1975
V	Gen. Vasco Gonçalves (replaced by Admiral Pinheiro de Azevedo on August 29)	Radical	August 8, 1975
VI	Admiral Pinheiro de Azevedo	Moderate	September 19, 1975

cabinets laid the foundations for a liberal democratic state. Political prisoners were released, political parties were formed, freedom of expression was guaranteed, and union activity was finally liberated from state control.

The largely political revolution launched in April gave way to a social revolution in March of 1975, when right-wing forces staged an unsuccessful coup. Arguing that moderates had underestimated the strength of counterrevolutionary forces, left-wing officers gained the ascendancy in the MFA and set about making major changes in property and power relations. Personnel purges, known as *saneamentos*, were set in motion to ensure that the revolution would not be jeopardized by "reactionary" forces in schools, universities, and public institutions. More important, the government decided to destroy the economic base from which a counterrevolution might be launched. Accordingly, it nationalized all Portuguese banks and insurance firms and began a massive nationalization of basic industries. It also witnessed the first stage of the largest popular land seizures in European history. The land occupations and the system of workers' control that grew out of them continued well into the tenure of the moderate sixth provisional government and thus outlasted the state-directed social revolution itself.

The system of workers' control that grew out of the land occupations was probably the most dramatic of all the changes following the 25th of April, for it began with a popular, rather than a state, initiative. While the nationalization of banks and industries was engineered by the national government in Lisbon, the collectivization of land emerged from the direct and dramatic actions of the masses themselves.[2]

___

[2] Direct seizures of property took place in the industrial sector as well but to a lesser extent. Small worker-controlled factories and service firms were established throughout the

The drama began south of the Tejo River in the first months of 1975. It was then that groups of cultivators—with no legal backing from the state—began to occupy local lands and to establish collective farms. More than 152,000 hectares of land were seized prior to the publication of the first land expropriations law. Following the law's publication on August 1, 1975, more than one million additional hectares were seized.[3] More than 23 percent of Portugal's farmland changed hands in less than twelve months, and every occupied hectare was farmed and managed collectively.[4]

The occupation and expropriation of lands involved virtually no loss of life. Thus, this revolutionary experience differed from many others. But the drama in the Alentejo was unquestionably "revolutionary" in that it brought about rapid and radical changes in property relations.

The land seizures were concentrated almost exclusively in the southern half of Portugal in a latifúndia region where grain crops, olives, cork, and grazing animals sustained an ever-decreasing population. The occupations were most extensive in an area known as the Alentejo, the area "beyond the Tejo" encompassing the districts of Évora, Portalegre, Setúbal and Beja. Map 1.1 illustrates the location and the extent of the land seized.[5]

Who were the cultivators who seized the land? Why did they act when they did and why did they initiate worker-controlled farms? These questions are important not only in the context of Portugal but in the context of the general literature on rural mobilization. Unfortunately, the questions are not easily answered by the existing literature.

As I shall discuss in detail in the chapters that follow, occupied lands were located exclusively in those areas of Portugal where a rural proletariat was numerically dominant. By a rural proletariat I mean cultivators who earned money wages, owned little or no land, made purchases from merchants, and were employed by entities with whom they did not have

---

nation, but they often emerged from bankruptcies and abandonments rather than from the deliberate revolutionary efforts of workers. For more on workers' control in industry, see Nancy Gina Bermeo, "Worker Management in Industry: Reconciling Representative Government and Industrial Democracy in a Polarized Society," in Lawrence S. Graham and Douglas L. Wheeler, eds., *In Search of Modern Portugal: The Revolution and Its Consequences* (Madison: University of Wisconsin Press, 1983).

[3] Figures are from unpublished documents from the Centros Regionais da Reforma Agrária and the Lisbon offices of the Ministry of Agriculture.

[4] One hectare equals 2.47 acres. Farm land totaled approximately 4,983,000 hectares as the seizures began. See the Instituto Nacional de Estatística's *Inquérito às Explorações Agrícolas do Continente* (Lisbon: INE, 1968) for the most recent data available.

[5] The district of Setúbal is unlike the other districts of the Alentejo in that it contains a major industrial city (Setúbal) and a significantly different mix of crops. The analysis that follows focuses on the other three districts, where the most land was seized.

MAP 1.1
Hectares of Land Occupied,
December 1974 to December 1975

Castelo
Branco
4,173

Santarém
74,340

Portalegre
233,911

Lisbon
5,500

Évora
430,691

Setúbal
95,101

Beja
316,201

Faro
500

SOURCES: Ministério de Agricultura e Pescas, staff members of the Regional Agrarian Reform Centers, and Afonso de Barros, *A Reforma Agrária em Portugal* (Oerias: Instituto Gulbenkian, 1979). Figures for Portalegre are estimates.

continuous personalized relations. The vast majority of the individuals who seized property came from this group.

Compared with that of other sorts of cultivators, the rebellious potential of the rural proletariat is generally thought to be quite low. The views expressed by Eric Hobsbawm are widely shared:

Peasants, however unrevolutionary, want land, and lack of land is against natural justice. The remarkable characteristic of the proletarianised labourer was that he no longer wanted land but higher wages and good employment.[6]

Essentially, the political ambitions of rural proletarians are thought to be trade unionist rather than revolutionary. Sidney Mintz argues that the rural proletariat is usually given only to reformist activities.[7] Other scholars argue that, regardless of their ambitions, farmworkers have an especially restricted capacity to rebel. Eric Wolf asserts that rural proletarians live "completely within the power domain of [their] employers" and are "unlikely to pursue the course of rebellion, *unless* they are able to rely on some external power to challenge the power which constrains them."[8] James Scott argues similarly that these laborers may seem susceptible to socialist ideals but that "their social organization makes them less culturally cohesive and hence less resistant to [state] hegemony."[9] Theda Skocpol adds her argument to a growing consensus and writes:

> Agricultural regimes featuring large estates worked by serfs or landless laborers tend to be inimical to spontaneous, self-organized peasant rebellions. . . . Rentier agrarian systems, where smallholder peasant families possess and work the land on their own, are notoriously more susceptible to peasant revolts.[10]

The image that emerges from these and other studies is that rural proletarians, or landless laborers and farmworkers as I shall sometimes call them here, are rather helpless creatures, wholly dependent on the creative and organizational resources of other groups. On the rare occasions when they do rebel, they do so as the lesser party in a group alliance. Their demands, moreover, are not for land or for any radical changes in property relations but for higher wages and more job security.

The writers just cited are careful scholars. Their conclusions are justified with concrete evidence and they might indeed be valid for the nations studied, but they do not hold in the Portuguese case. In fact, they lead us in precisely the wrong direction. One of the few scholars who leads us in

[6] Eric Hobsbawm and George Rudé, *Captain Swing* (London: Lawrence and Wishart, 1969), p. 66.

[7] Sidney Mintz, "The Rural Proletariat and the Problems of Rural Proletarian Consciousness," *The Journal of Peasant Studies* (April 1974), p. 319.

[8] Eric R. Wolf, *Peasant Wars of the Twentieth Century* (New York: Harper and Row, 1973), pp. 290-291. Emphasis in original.

[9] James Scott, "Hegemony and the Peasantry," *Politics and Society* (Fall 1977), p. 289.

[10] See Theda Skocpol, *States and Social Revolutions* (Cambridge: Cambridge University Press, 1979), p. 116. It must be noted that Skocpol was concerned with explaining the general origins of social revolution and that this point about the landless was not central to her argument.

the right direction is Jeffrey Paige. After comparing various types of cultivators engaged in the production of third world export crops, he concludes that the group with the greatest potential for rebellion is that which earns its living "from wages in cash or kind."[11] He is referring specifically to migrant laborers and sharecroppers, but his point can be extended. Though the farmworkers of the Alentejo were generally not engaged in export agriculture and were neither sharecroppers nor migrant laborers, they started a revolution within the revolution. Contrary to what many previous analysts would lead us to expect, these cultivators rebelled with a high degree of autonomy, and their rebellion led, not to trade unionist demands, but to extensive land seizures and to the emergence of the largest network of worker-run farms in Western Europe.

The chapters that follow analyze the process of the land seizures and the concomitant emergence of workers' control in agriculture. The first chapter discusses how the history and the social structure of the South fostered a potential for radicalization long before the revolution came about. The second chapter illustrates how this potential was activated by the political revolution in Lisbon. The third chapter deals with the relationship between the occupations and the social revolution, and the fourth chapter, presenting questionnaire research, explains the emergence of the occupations in a single county.

Taken as a whole, this section will illustrate why the rural proletarians of the Alentejo had no need to be tutored either in collective action or in class consciousness. Both emerged, almost inevitably, from the historical, sociological, and political characteristics of the Alentejo itself.

[11] Jeffrey M. Paige, *Agrarian Revolution* (New York: Free Press, 1975), p. 26.

ONE

The Preconditions for Radicalization

IN order to understand the emergence of workers' control in agriculture,
one must understand those aspects of rural social structure that fostered
radicalization. Most are rooted deep in regional history.

LANDHOLDING AND LOW PRODUCTIVITY IN THE PAST

The Prerepublican Period

The patterns of landholding that the rural proletarians of the South sought
to obliterate were established in the twelfth century at the time of the
Reconquista. It was then that Afonso III ended more than five hundred
years of Moorish domination, ceding huge tracts of territory to military
leaders as defense posts against the Moors. When the battles were over,
the Christian victors were rewarded with permanent possession of the lands
on which they fought. Joined by the religious orders (who had scored an
important victory of their own), the new regional elites came to possess
"most of the land" in the South.[1]

The new and very large landholdings were concentrated in the South
because it was there that the struggle with the Moors really focused. The
Moorish penetration of the North had been seriously hampered by the
region's Atlantic climate, hilly terrain, and relatively strong nobility. The
Tejo was thus, for generations, the boundary between the Moorish and
Christian worlds.

The new elites of the South organized their lands as latifúndia for the
cultivation of cereal crops just as the Roman conquerors in the same area
had done centuries before. In Roman times, the region was known as "the
granary" of the empire,[2] but its productive capabilities had changed markedly by the thirteenth century because the slaves who had worked the lands
for first the Romans and then the Moors were gone. In fact, the whole
region had become depopulated due to the destruction and danger of the

---

[1] Luiz Augusto Rebello da Silva, *Memória sobre a População e a Agricultura de Portugal
desde a Fundação da Monarchia até 1865* (Lisbon: Imprensa Nacional, 1868), p. 24. This
and all other translations are mine unless otherwise noted.

[2] Joseph James Forrester, *Portugal and Its Capabilities* (London: John Weale, 1856), p.
101. Julius Caesar is said to have called the Alentejo the Sicily of Spain.

9

war.[3] If the land were to be worked, the new owners would have to both attract and secure the labor to do it. They failed in this, as they failed in restoring the Alentejo to its former productive position. In fact, the low productivity of the region was to plague heads of state for centuries.

Underutilization was the root of the problem. But monarch after monarch failed to coerce the local landed elite into either more extensive or more intensive farming. Royal decrees demanding the immediate cultivation of southern lands were issued as early as 1362, but the calls went unheeded and the Alentejo remained a rugged wasteland.[4] Seventeenth-century accounts bemoan the "indifference" of the area's landowners[5] and note that "without investment" the miserable and "half-cultivated countryside" could not support even its own "shrinking population."[6]

The nationalization of religious properties in the 1820s and the elimination of feudal obligations in 1832 were to have improved the productivity of the area but were disappointing in effect. Land was now a commodity bought up by an urban bourgeoisie, but its productivity remained problematic. Since small farmers could not hope to outbid the urban bourgeoisie at the public auctions where the land was sold, a nouveau riche simply replaced the older landed elite, holding properties as large or even larger than those of their predecessors.

More land was cleared,[7] and productivity did indeed begin to rise by the middle of the nineteenth century (due in large part to government investment in railroads and roads), but the region's potential remained untapped. Personal reports from the latter half of the century describe the area as a deserted region that "never fully recovered" from the wars against the Moors.[8] An account by a nineteenth-century English nobleman gives us a vivid picture of the region and its problems:

[3] The Christian armies burned crops and properties in their efforts to drive the Moors south. Not surprisingly, natives fled the area as well. See Edgar Rodrigues, *Breve História do Pensamento e das Lutas Sociais em Portugal* (Lisbon: Assírio and Alvim, 1977), p. 53.

[4] The decrees began with Pedro I in 1362 but the most famous was the 1375 Law of Sesmarias whereby King Fernando declared that all uncultivated land would be expropriated by the crown. The application of these laws was extremely limited. See Julião Soares de Azevedo, *Condições Económicas da Revolução Portuguesa de 1820* (Lisbon: Básica Editora, 1976), pp. 64-70, and Eugénio de Castro Caldas, *A Agricultura Portuguesa no Limiar da Reforma Agrária* (Oeiras: Instituto Gulbenkian, 1978), p. 40.

[5] The quotation is from a government report dated 1615. See Rebello da Silva, *Memória*, p. 309.

[6] Luiz Augusto Rebello da Silva, *História de Portugal*, 4 vols. (Lisbon: Imprensa Nacional, 1869), 4: 426.

[7] Writing in 1875, Gerardo Pery estimated that the amount of land under cultivation had increased by two-thirds in the previous forty years. See Gerardo A. Pery, *Geographia e Estatística Geral de Portugal e Colónias* (Lisbon: Imprensa Nacional, 1875), p. 115.

[8] Oswald John Frederick Crawfurd [John Latouche], *Travels in Portugal* (New York: Putnam's Sons, 1875), p. 209.

With the exception of the small properties in the immediate vicinity of the principal towns, agriculture appears to be unknown in the Alem-Tejo. . . . People of substance [have organized] extensive estates, these have descended from father to son and, through mismanagement and neglect, are at this moment so many waste lands in the possession of proprietors who themselves have not the means of cultivating them, and who will not allow others to do so.[9]

The region that had once been a fertile granary served neither the cereal needs of an ever-expanding urban population nor the employment needs of the dwindling local populace. A vicious circle emerged whereby the underutilization of land produced out-migration, out-migration raised the price of labor, and "high" wage bills discouraged utilization even further.[10] Periodic attempts to break the cycle with guaranteed grain prices had unforeseen negative consequences. The infamous Wheat Law of 1899 guaranteed domestic wheat growers protection from imports and a price that was two times the international market rate.[11] This stimulated a twofold increase in Alentejan wheat production,[12] but the nation was still forced to import half its wheat and a third of all its cereals.[13] More important, perhaps, was the fact that the problem of the underutilization of land had still not been solved. Much of the increase in wheat production came not from clearing land but from changing crops. Moreover, the absenteeism and low investment that had created the crises of production in the first place still remained. The laws, and indeed the whole state, would change radically with the birth of the First Republic in 1910, but the problems of production in the South would continue.

The First Republic, 1910-1926

Portugal's First Republic was racked with troubles, but few were as perplexing and far-reaching as those that emanated from the Alentejo. The problems of production that had plagued previous leaders were made more salient by the politicization that accompanied the establishment of the

[9] Forrester, *Portugal and Its Capabilities*, p. 102.

[10] When wage demands rose, landowners simply switched to using land for pasture or forestry. See Manuel Villaverde Cabral, *Materiais para a História da Questão Agrária em Portugal, Século XIX e XX* (Porto: Editorial Inova, 1974), p. 62.

[11] Fernando Medeiros, *A Sociedade e a Economia Portuguesa nas Origens do Salazarismo* (Lisbon: A Regra do Jogo, 1978), p. 50.

[12] Jaime Reis, "A 'Lei da Fome': As Origens do Proteccionismo Cerealífero, 1889-1914," in Afonso de Barros, ed., *A Agricultura Latifundiária na Península Ibérica* (Oeiras: Instituto Gulbenkian, 1981), p. 315.

[13] From Eça de Campos, *Riqueza Nacional*; as cited in George Young, *Portugal Old and Young: An Historical Study* (Oxford: Clarendon, 1917), p. 314.

Republic. The class divisions that lay at the base of this politicization were deep and enduring—so enduring that they would reemerge as the stimulus for radicalization sixty years later.

Predictably, the most important class division was between those who owned land and those who worked it. Agricultural wage workers were numerically dominant in most of the Alentejo by the mid-nineteenth century. In Beja, for example, some 60 percent of the agricultural work force was wage labor as early as 1845.[14]

Though reports of politicization among southern farmworkers date from at least the 1800s,[15] it was the founding of the Republic that precipitated the emergence of farmworkers' unions and agricultural strikes. There were literally none of the former before 1910, but by 1914 there were 110 union locals for farmworkers. Each of these lay south of the Tejo.[16] All the counties in Évora contained a local as did 70 percent of the counties in Beja and 75 percent of the counties in Portalegre.[17]

Strike activity followed closely on the organization of the unions. In the district of Évora alone, seventy farmworkers' strikes erupted between 1910 and 1925.[18] Most, if not all, of these strikes were prompted by a desire for higher wages. But rural workers' congresses issued demands that went beyond what could be characterized as merely "trade unionist." In 1925, for example, the National Congress of Rural Workers' Unions demanded the "integral and complete socialization of agricultural property" and proposed that the agricultural work of the future be organized exclusively by unions.[19] Neither of these demands were met, of course, but they were reflective of a widespread belief that property relations in the South should change.

A whole series of Republican ministers struggled with the problems of production in the South, but their efforts were as fruitless as those of their predecessors. Republican leaders were compelled to act by newly organized and politicized workers' groups but, like their pre-Republican counterparts, they were also moved by the belief that the Alentejo held the key to Portugal's future. Many hoped that the region "could play the role of the

[14] See Cabral, *Materiais*, p. 17.

[15] Albert Silbert, *Le Portugal Méditerranéen à la fin de l'Ancien Régime: XVIIIe—Début du XIXe Siècle* (Paris: SEVPEN, 1966), p. 831. Citing a landowner who lamented his inability to contract workers at a reasonable wage in the 1830s, Silbert concluded that the farmworkers of the South "represented an active social force" well before the twentieth century.

[16] A. H. de Oliveira Marques, *História de la República Portuguesa: As Estruturas de Base* (Lisbon: Iniciativas Editoriais, 1978), p. 322.

[17] Ibid., p. 59.

[18] Castro Caldas, *A Agricultura Portuguesa*, p. 61.

[19] Rodrigues, *Breve História*, pp. 227-228.

American Far West''[20]—if, like the West, it were properly colonized. Thus, in 1911, Agricultural Minister Ezequiel de Campos proposed that all uncultivated land in the South be nationalized and then sold, on credit, to family farmers. The scheme was to improve production in the South and to rechannel the wave of emigration to Brazil, giving Portugal its own frontier. This, and even other less radical schemes to alter land tenure, failed to become law.[21] In fact, the distorted size of the southern properties was actually accentuated during the Republican period.

With absenteeism largely unchanged and the structural distortions of the region growing worse, it is perhaps not surprising that the fields of the Alentejo failed to meet the domestic demand for wheat. Production rose irregularly and never managed to keep pace with demand: the difference between the two was as great in the first five years of the Republic as it was in the last.[22]

Grain production problems and the resultant balance of payments crises helped to bring the Republic itself to an end in 1926.[23] As António Salazar became minister of finance in 1928, and then prime minister in 1932, Portugal entered a period in which yet another new state would make fruitless attempts to improve the agriculture of the South.

The Alentejo Under the Salazar-Caetano Regime, 1932-1974

Salazar was an extraordinary man and he created an extraordinary regime. Its uniqueness derived in part from its origins. Mussolini and Hitler rose to power as heads of national movements. Franco fought his way to power in a civil war. Salazar was simply handed power by the military officers who overthrew the Republic. He was a professor of economics at the

[20] *Revista da Exposição Agrícola de Lisboa*, May 24, 1885; as cited in Reis, ''A 'Lei da Fome,' '' p. 99.

[21] Failed schemes included João Gonçalves' attempt to disentail and then sell the Companhia das Lezírias, Afonso Costas' 1913 attempt to force use of publicly held lands called *baldios*, and various attempts to compel landowners to employ an increased number of farmworkers. See Oliveira Marques, *História de la República*, pp. 72-88, and Douglas Wheeler, *Republican Portugal: A Political History, 1910-1926* (Madison: University of Wisconsin Press, 1978), p. 66.

[22] Freppel Cotta, *Economic Planning in Corporative Portugal* (London: P.S. King and Son Ltd., 1937), p. 28. Part of the new imbalance was due to urbanization and the related increase in demand.

[23] Although this is not the place to discuss the complexities of the tumultuous First Republic, its last seven years were marred by such divisions that the average cabinet lasted only three months. For an excellent English language study of the period, see Wheeler, *Republican Portugal*. A brief discussion is also available in A. H. de Oliveira Marques, ''The Portuguese 1920s: A General Survey,'' *Revista de História Económica e Social* (January-June 1978), pp. 87-103.

University of Coimbra and almost unknown outside the academic community. The fiery oratory and the spectacular displays of mass support that were intrinsic to the emergence of other dictatorships were absent in the Portuguese case. Salazar was stoic, devoutly religious, and inward-looking, and he expected the nation he dominated to be the same.

At the level of organization, this implied a deliberate attempt to forge an apolitical society where conflicting interests would not have free expression. Political parties and free trade unions were banned, the press was censored, and a secret police force came to permeate all levels of society from the ministries to the neighborhood cafes. In these respects, Salazar's regime resembled the other interwar dictatorships, but there were important differences as well. First of all, Salazar's "party," the União Nacional, was not a mass-mobilizing agency. Membership was small, activities were few, and association was not mandatory—even for cabinet members. Second, Portugal was not a developmentalist regime. Mussolini and Hitler linked industrialization to military expansion and had elaborate plans for both. Franco had no plans for military expansion but adopted an ambitious and successful industrialization program after 1959. Salazar remained suspicious of industrialization and was reluctant to follow suit. His primary aim was to right the disequilibrium brought on by the Republic: to crush the left, to balance the budget, and to restore the balance of trade.[24] His policies in the Alentejo were an important component of these goals.

In many respects, Salazar faced a more serious problem in the Alentejo than any of his predecessors. Urbanization was at an all-time high, and demand for bread—and thus wheat—showed no signs of decreasing.[25] Yet, the foreign supply that had satisfied this demand in the past was proving increasingly costly. In the last years of the Republic, the importation of approximately 150,000 tons of wheat annually "was one of the heaviest charges" the nation had to meet,[26] comprising a weighty 22 percent of its balance of payments deficit.[27]

Yet, if imports were curtailed, how would domestic demand be met?

[24] Longer English language discussions of the Salazar regime are available in Tom Gallagher's *Portugal: A Twentieth-Century Interpretation* (Manchester: Manchester University Press, 1983), and António de Figueiredo, *Portugal: Fifty Years of Dictatorship* (New York: Holmes and Meier, 1976).

[25] The population of the Alentejo grew at a rate superior to that of the rest of the country. See A. H. de Oliveira Marques, *História de Portugal* (Lisbon: Palas Editores, 1981), p. 293.

[26] Great Britain, Department of Overseas Trade, *Report on the Trade, Industries, and Economic Conditions in Portugal* (London: His Majesty's Stationery Office, July 1924), p. 23.

[27] Joel Frederico da Silveira, "Alguns Aspectos da Política Económica do Fascismo: 1926-1933," in *O Fascismo em Portugal* (Lisbon: A Regra do Jogo, 1982), p. 372.

Republican leaders had argued that production would only be increased with the restructuring of property relations. Salazar himself, while still a student of economics, had drawn a similar conclusion,[28] but the leaders of the post-Republican state were hardly likely to antagonize the landed elites with redistribution schemes. Mobilized since the 1860s and extremely active in the anti-Republican movement, the latifundiários were among the new regime's most important allies.[29] If domestic production were to be increased, it would be increased through a process that would leave the properties and the interests of the landed elites unscathed.

The Wheat Campaign of 1929 was the answer to the new regime's dilemma. The Portuguese program was modeled on Mussolini's campaign in Italy and was intended to stimulate production through a combination of guaranteed prices and bonuses. The latter, called *prémios de arroteia*, were awarded for seeding previously uncultivated land with wheat. Coupled with the increased use of fertilizers, these bonuses did, in fact, stimulate production. Average annual wheat production rose 70 percent over the Republican average, and the nation's wheat import bill plummeted, dropping 95 percent between 1929 and 1933.[30]

Though the Wheat Campaign seemed to solve the import problem, it exacerbated other problems. In their zeal to take advantage of their cultivation bonuses, latifundiários cut down thousands of trees and precipitated a soil erosion crisis.[31] Moreover, the campaign had been so poorly designed that a great deal of the increased production merely rotted because of insufficient infrastructural support. Roads and transportation were among the worst in Europe but the most serious problem was that of storage. Only the largest and most modern estates had their own storage facilities, and the state had no storage facilities of its own. Proposals for county-level warehouses and silos were being studied by 1932, but in the years before they were built, grain was stored precariously in homes, schools, and even Évora's municipal theater.[32]

---

[28] See António de Oliveira Salazar, *A Questão Cerealífera: O Trigo* (Coimbra: Imprensa da Universidade, 1916).

[29] In 1860, businessmen who had purchased farm land from landed aristocrats joined with the latter in organizing the Central Royal Association of Portuguese Agriculture. See Castro Caldas, *A Agricultura Portuguesa*, p. 62.

[30] Great Britain, Department of Overseas Trade, *Report*, p. 32.

[31] V. Xavier Pintado, *Structure and Growth of the Portuguese Economy* (Geneva: European Free Trade Association, 1964), p. 85

[32] The Teatro Garcia Resende was literally filled to the roof during this period. See José Machado Pais, Aida Maria Valadas de Lima, José Ferreira Baptista, Maria Fernanda Marques de Jesus, and Maria Margarida Gameiro, "Elementos para a História do Fascismo nos Campos: A 'Campanha do Trigo,' 1928-1938 (II)," *Análise Social* (April-June 1978), p. 367.

The final and perhaps the major problem with the Wheat Campaign was that it did not produce a genuine modernization of agriculture. This was one of its official goals, but while there was indeed an increase in the use of fertilizers and machinery during the campaign, Portuguese agriculture remained what many believed to be the most backward in all of Europe.

Part of the problem with the modernization of agriculture in the South derived from Salazar's own romanticization of rural life. He even ran a contest for the "Most Portuguese Village in Portugal," rewarding the most "traditional" village in the nation for "combatting foreign ideas" in dress, music, and life style.[33] This excerpt from a 1932 interview illustrates how his appreciation for the spiritual values of rural life was tainted with a certain hostility to technological change.

> We are not seduced by or satisfied with the acme of technique, or the machinery that lessens the man, or the delirium of the mechanical . . . if the wings of the spirit do not touch them. The ideal is to flee from the materialism of today: to make the fields more fertile without silencing therein the merry songs of the girls.[34]

The "girls" of the Alentejo's fields were surely not as merry as Salazar maintained and were even less so after the Wheat Campaign came to an end. Thousands of families had been attracted to the area through a government internal colonization program. The project was a redistribution of people rather than property, for it aimed only at the provision of additional labor for the more intensive cultivation brought on by the campaign. Sharecroppers and seeders grew in number as the campaign progressed, but they were forced into much more precarious proletarian positions when it ground to a halt. As a result, the proletarianization that had begun centuries earlier and then decreased now increased, both rapidly and greatly. Table 1.2 illustrates the dramatic trend.

Between the end of the Wheat Campaign and the 1960s the members of this enlarged proletarian class suffered greatly as the landowners around them no longer required their labor. Some landowners turned toward mechanization, but most merely returned to the practices of the past, leaving huge tracts of (now depleted) soil unused and thousands of people unemployed.

The existence and continuing growth of this large and underemployed proletariat was potentially detrimental to the security of the new regime.

[33] For a description of this unique contest, see Joaquim Pais de Brito, "O Estado Novo e a Aldeia Mais Portuguesa de Portugal," in *O Fascismo em Portugal* (Lisbon: A Regra do Jogo, 1982).

[34] From an interview in the *Diário de Notícias*, April 15, 1937, p. 2; as cited in Cotta, *Economic Planning*, p. 185.

TABLE 1.2
Farmworkers as a Percentage of All Cultivators

District	1930	1940	1950
Beja	53.2%	68.5%	83.3%
Évora	50.8	75.0	89.2
Portalegre	39.3	72.1	87.5
Setúbal	48.3	76.2	82.5

SOURCES: For 1930, *Recenseamento Geral da População de 1930* (Lisbon, Imprensa Nacional, 1934), 3: 17, 32, 47. For 1940, *Recenseamento Geral da População de 1940* (Lisbon: Imprensa Nacional, 1943), 3: 15, 8: 14, 13: 15, 15: 15. For 1950, *Recenseamento Geral da População 1950* (Lisbon: Tipografia Portuguesa, 1952), tome 3, vol. 2, pp. 164-167.

Continued poverty and increasing frustrations among the people of the rural South were bound to fuel political conflict and thus disturb the order that Salazar had so solemnly promised to preserve. Eventually he decided that the solution for the problem of the South, and indeed for the nation as a whole, was corporatism.[35] As a philosophical perspective, corporatism was rooted deeply in Portuguese political culture and tradition. Based on the premise that hierarchy is natural, that the state is natural, and that the role of the state is to ensure social harmony *despite* hierarchy, corporatism implies a powerful and autonomous state apparatus.

When institutionalized, the corporatist perspective implies a system of interest representation in which potentially conflictual groups are discouraged from organizing independently and channeled into state-sponsored organizations instead. Freedom of association is sharply restricted for the alleged good of the organic whole.

Salazar himself expressed the rationale behind the corporatist system openly and often. Denying the inevitability of class conflict he stated, "We do not accept the strife of the productive classes as a historical fact."[36] Social harmony was possible because the interests of "all . . . productive elements *can* and *ought* to be subordinated to the higher interests of the community."[37] The agent of subordination would of course be the state.

[35] For a systematic and detailed discussion of corporatism in Portugal, see Howard J. Wiarda, *Corporatism and Development: The Portuguese Experience* (Amherst: University of Massachusetts Press, 1977).

[36] António de Oliveira Salazar, *Salazar Says* (Lisbon: SPN Books, 1939), p. 52.

[37] António de Oliveira Salazar, *The Road for the Future* (Lisbon: SNI, 1963), p. 15. Emphasis mine.

Though in reality the interests of workers were consistently subordinated to the interests of owners, there was at least a superficial social welfare component in specific corporatist institutions.[38] The notion that certain corporatist organizations might perform some charitable functions was not at all alien to Portuguese paternalistic traditions.

Both the paternalism and the restrictions on free association that lay at the base of Portuguese corporatism were embodied in institutions called *Casas do Povo*—The Houses of the People. These organizations were to be established in all the rural parishes in Portugal. Throughout the nation, they were to function as social welfare institutions providing sickness benefits, old age pensions, unemployment subsidies, and low-cost drugs. They were also to serve the additional function of "representing" the professional interests of farmworkers. In typical corporatist fashion, farmworkers were deprived of independent trade unions and offered representation in these state-sponsored organizations instead.

The dual functions of the *Casas do Povo* were especially important in the Alentejo where social assistance was most needed and where farmworkers were most numerous. In fact, it was argued that the *Casas* were conceived especially for the South.[39] Ironically, neither their social welfare nor their representational function was well served there—or, indeed anywhere else.

Part of the explanation came from the fact that many parishes simply had no *Casas do Povo* at all. As late as 1967, a full 70 percent of the nation's parishes had no such institution.[40] Though the *Casas* were more numerous in the Alentejo than elsewhere,[41] many Alentejanos were simply unable to gain access to them—whatever their function.

However, the real problem with the *Casas* was that so few people actively desired access. Southern villagers resented having to seek assistance from the state and saw themselves "morally damaged"[42] by what they regarded

[38] Wiarda raises this point in his *Corporatism and Development* and in so doing properly distinguishes Portuguese corporatism from other experiments in corporatism that focus more explicitly on controlling the organization of potentially conflictual groups.

[39] From the Colóquio Nacional do Trabalho, 1961, as reported in Manuel de Lucena, *A Evolução do Sistema Corporativo Português*, vol. 1, *O Salazarismo* (Lisbon: Perspectivas e Realidades, 1976), p. 249.

[40] Wiarda, *Corporatism and Development*, p. 247.

[41] This is another indication that the *Casas* were created with the Alentejo in mind. In 1959, there were 62 in Beja, 51 in Portalegre, 42 in Évora, and 36 in Santarém. See Manuel de Lucena, *A Evolução*, p. 248.

[42] Joyce Reiglehaupt makes this point in "Peasants and Politics in Salazar's Portugal: The Corporate State and Village 'Nonpolitics,' " in Lawrence S. Graham and Harry M. Makler, eds., *Contemporary Portugal: The Revolution and Its Antecedents* (Austin: University of Texas Press, 1979), p. 178. See also José Cutileiro, *A Portuguese Rural Society* (Oxford: Clarendon Press, 1971), pp. 75-76.

as institutional charity. Though regime officials described the *Casas* as "famílias de famílias,"[43] farmworkers saw them instead as "simply another instrument for serving the interests of landowners."[44]

There is no doubt that the *Casas* did serve the interests of the landed elite. Their very structure ensured this, for each *Casa* president was elected by the large landowners of the parish.[45] Farmworkers had no role in the selection process, or indeed in the operation of the *Casas* themselves. They were under legal obligation to become members and to pay dues (just as local landowners were), but they received very little in return. Decades after the Portuguese constitution declared the creation of a "corporatist state," social services for workers in Portugal were still the worst in Europe.[46] Those services that did exist were meager and were largely restricted to skilled urban workers. The regime's weak commitment to using the *Casas* as social welfare institutions is well illustrated by the fact that their social welfare function was not written into law until seven years after the Houses were created.[47]

Though the social service function of the *Casa do Povo* was rather ambiguous, their repressive role was patently clear. The *Casas* were to be the sole bargaining agents for farmworkers, and the *Grémios de Lavoura*, or Landowners Guilds, were to be the sole bargaining agents for those who hired labor. No real bargaining took place, however, for the same landed interests controlled both organizations. If a radicalized worker succeeded in being elected to a *Casa*'s governing board, the *Casa* was, typically, labeled as subversive and shut down altogether.[48] Generally, landowners "representing" rural workers were called on to "bargain" with landowners representing landowners.[49]

---

[43] Manuel de Lucena, *A Evolução*, p. 247.

[44] José Cutileiro, *A Portuguese Rural Society*, p. 155. Cutileiro's generalization was valid far beyond the area he studied. In a northeastern parish of Beja, a worker described the *Casas* to the author as *Casas do Fascismo*—Houses of Fascism.

[45] Manuel de Lucena, *A Evolução*, p. 257. The *Casas* were run by an individual elected by the "*sócios protectores*" of each House. These were the major landowners in the area, whose modest but mandatory contributions to the *Casas* entitled them, in theory, to complete control. The very name of these individuals, i.e., the "protector members," illustrates the paternalistic base of the institution.

[46] Wiarda, *Corporatism and Development*, p. 211.

[47] The *Casas* were created on paper in 1933. In 1938, they were declared "representational bodies of rural workers." In 1940, they were declared "agents of social assistance." See ibid., pp. 246-248.

[48] This occurred after the election of PCP leader Dinis Miranda. See José Pacheco Pereira, *Conflitos Sociais nos Campos do Sul de Portugal* (Lisbon: Publicações Europa América, 1982), p. 134.

[49] Philippe Schmitter, "Corporatist Interest Representation and Public Policy-Making in Portugal," Paper presented at the Annual Meeting of the American Political Science Asso-

Responding to government reports on the inefficiency of these structures, Marcelo Caetano attempted to make the *Casas* more potent when he succeeded Salazar in 1969.[50] Though their social services did increase under new national leadership, their repressive role in the realm of labor relations remained more or less the same. The *Casas* were, in the words of one Alentejano, "a joke: no, worse. . . . a pile of shit." They clearly occupied the organizational space a real union might have occupied and merely served, even through their feeble and paternalistic social services, as agencies for social control. They were a critical part of a system that "actively encouraged the political apathy of [the rural] population."[51] To work within them was fruitless; to act outside them was foolhardy. What mattered in the rural South was not structures or institutions but "the personal intervention of powerful men."[52] The landless simply had no power.

By the 1960s, the precarious position of the southern landless worker was alleviated somewhat. The decade brought Caetano to power, but it also brought earlier changes as the central government in Lisbon turned toward a more growth-oriented economic policy. The expansion of domestic industries, the influx of foreign capital, and the beginning of major civil construction projects, such as the bridge across the Tejo in Lisbon, opened up new employment for the men of the rural South.

As thousands left the Alentejo to seek employment in Lisbon and Setúbal, the pressures for farmwork in the rural South diminished. Yet, while the new development orientation provided some relief for the problems of farmworkers, it also underscored the backward state of the existing agricultural sector. As the nation's economists and policy planners looked more and more toward northern Europe as both a model and partner for growth, Portugal's low agricultural productivity became increasingly problematic. Negotiations for entrance into the European Economic Community stumbled on this point immediately,[53] but government policy makers either would not or could not initiate major programs for change.

The government's intransigence cannot be attributed to an absence of stimuli. For years, OECD reports maintained that the land tenure of the South was "one of the most serious obstacles to the development of

ciation, Washington, D.C., September 1972; as cited in Wiarda, *Corporatism and Development*, p. 145.

[50] Marcelo Caetano became head of the regime when Salazar became incapacitated after a fall from a deck chair. Caetano was thought to be more liberal than Salazar but never succeeded in controlling forces and personalities to his right.

[51] Reiglehaupt, "Peasants and Politics," p. 183.

[52] Cutileiro, *A Portuguese Rural Society*, p. 199.

[53] Castro Caldas, *A Agricultura Portuguesa*, p. 89.

agriculture."[54] Analysts from other international agencies also argued consistently for alterations in policy, ranging from penalties for absenteeism[55] to an elimination of cereal subsidies.[56] Yet, in its third and final economic plan, the Salazar regime adopted a policy of "deliberate non-intervention" in agriculture.[57]

Despite more than forty years in power, the Salazar-Caetano regime left the Alentejo little changed. The region's farmworkers had not been coopted by corporatism, and the longstanding problems of productivity remained. Through monarchy, republic, and dictatorship, the rural world of Portugal remained divided in three parts, with an area of small- and medium-sized farms in the North, an area of large latifúndia in the Alentejan South, and areas that included both types of property elsewhere.[58]

SOUTHERN SOCIAL STRUCTURE ON THE EVE OF THE REVOLUTION

Land Tenure and Class Consciousness

Table 1.3 illustrates the distribution of farming property on the eve of the revolution. The contrast between the size of properties in the Alentejo and the North is striking. While nearly 75 percent of all northern land was held in properties of less than twenty hectares, only 10 percent of the properties in the Alentejo fit this description. For large properties the situation was reversed. In the northern districts, less than 8 percent of all land was held in units of more than one hundred hectares. In the Alentejo, nearly 78 percent of farm units were this large. These landholding patterns

---

[54] Organization for Economic Cooperation and Development, *Economic Survey: Portugal* (Paris: OECD, 1963), pp. 9-12.

[55] Pintado, *Structure and Growth*, p. 114.

[56] Castro Caldas, *A Agricultura Portuguesa*, pp. 91-92.

[57] Ibid., p. 90.

[58] It is interesting to note that differences in property relations did not lead to dramatic differences in social welfare. The small-holding peasantry of the North did not live better than the landless workers of the South. Cultivators throughout the nation lived badly. A comparison of social welfare measures for southern rural and northern rural districts yields mixed results. In terms of health and health care, inhabitants of southern rural districts were better off than their northern counterparts: life expectancy was longer (indeed it was longer than the national average), there were more physicians per capita, and although child mortality was slightly higher than the national average, it was significantly lower than in most northern rural districts. The evidence is somewhat ambiguous on the question of housing. Southern rural districts had a lower proportion of ill-housed families than the North (or the nation as a whole). However, these districts had a higher proportion of "substandard" dwellings. In education, the picture for southern rural districts was more negative, with lower literacy and lower school enrollment than in either the northern rural districts or the nation as a whole. See International Labour Organization, *Employment and Basic Needs in Portugal* (Geneva: International Labour Organization, 1979), pp. 45, 47, 49, 68.

TABLE 1.3
Percentage Distribution of Farm Land by Size of Holding (in hectares)

	Less than 4	4-19	20-49	50-99	More than 100
Southern districts					
of the Alentejo					
Beja	1.9	9.2	8.5	7.7	72.7
Évora	1.4	5.2	3.6	2.9	87.0
Portalegre	2.7	6.9	5.7	5.4	79.2
Setúbal	4.6	9.1	7.8	6.0	72.6
Average	2.6	7.6	6.4	5.5	77.9
Other southern					
districts					
Faro	11.3	32.4	18.3	11.0	27.2
Lisbon	30.7	32.3	9.2	6.4	21.4
Average	21.0	32.3	13.7	8.7	24.3
Central districts					
Castelo Branco	10.2	22.0	10.7	7.0	50.1
Coimbra	49.1	33.7	5.9	2.6	8.7
Leiria	42.6	32.1	7.7	3.8	13.9
Santarém	15.7	23.8	8.9	6.5	45.2
Average	29.4	27.9	8.3	5.0	29.5
Northern districts					
Aveiro	44.8	31.5	7.2	3.6	12.9
Braga	38.3	47.9	8.8	2.8	2.1
Bragança	7.4	45.0	23.8	8.7	15.1
Guarda	16.0	47.9	19.7	7.0	9.5
Porto	38.7	43.3	11.4	4.2	2.5
Viana do Castelo	54.3	29.0	5.0	2.3	9.3
Vila Real	25.3	50.3	15.6	4.1	4.6
Viseu	39.1	40.6	9.5	5.2	5.5
Average	33.0	41.9	12.6	4.7	7.7

SOURCE: Instituto Nacional de Estatística, *Inquérito às Explorações Agrícolas do Continente* (Lisbon: INE, 1968).

had obvious implications for regional class structures. Holdings in the northern region were numerous enough and small enough to be worked as family farms; holdings in the southern region were not. Southern landowners required extra labor, and this perpetuated the existence of a rural proletariat.

Table 1.4 illustrates the concentrations of family farmers and rural proletarians in the two regions. As would be predicted, a sharp contrast emerges. In the northern region, family farmers comprised more than 45

TABLE 1.4
Distribution of Agricultural Labor Force by Type of Activity

	Employers	Farmers	Family Workers	Paid Workers
Southern districts				
of the Alentejo				
Beja	1.7%	17.3%	3.7%	77.3%
Évora	1.0	10.8	0.7	87.5
Portalegre	1.6	14.3	1.2	82.9
Setúbal	1.5	17.2	2.1	79.2
Average	1.4	14.9	1.9	81.7
Other southern				
districts				
Faro	2.2	38.6	6.6	52.6
Lisbon	3.2	33.3	3.2	60.3
Average	2.7	35.9	4.9	56.4
Central districts				
Castelo Branco	2.2	32.0	6.6	59.2
Coimbra	1.8	45.7	7.5	45.0
Leiria	2.2	47.5	9.1	41.2
Santarém	1.9	22.3	3.2	72.6
Average	2.0	36.8	6.6	54.5
Northern districts				
Aveiro	2.3	56.1	14.7	26.9
Braga	1.4	41.0	27.1	30.5
Bragança	1.7	44.7	14.9	38.7
Guarda	2.0	49.3	8.0	40.7
Porto	1.8	46.3	27.1	30.8
Viana do Castelo	0.6	50.3	28.1	21.0
Vila Real	3.5	37.8	14.6	44.1
Viseu	2.0	41.4	16.7	39.9
Average	1.9	45.8	18.9	34.1

SOURCE: Instituto Nacional de Estatística, *Recenseamento Geral da População de 1970* (Lisbon: INE, 1970).

percent of the active agricultural population. The comparable figure for the Alentejan South was less than 15 percent. In the Alentejo more than 81 percent of those involved in agricultural work were wage and salaried laborers, while in the North these farmworkers comprised only 34 percent of the agricultural labor force. Thus, property relations were markedly different in the two areas. In the North, property owners comprised the largest grouping within the active agricultural population. In the South, farmworkers outnumbered property owners by nearly five to one. Since only

15 percent of the economically active agricultural population could thus identify with landed employers as fellow proprietors, the likelihood of cooptation in the South was relatively low.

Social divisions were no less radical than differences in property relations. Though the levels of absenteeism and class interaction varied somewhat from region to region, kinship relations between landowners and farmworkers were nonexistent, and many dayworkers had no personal contact with landowners at all. The words of an old man interviewed after the revolution in the Alentejo tell the story: "There were landowners in this area but they never set foot here. I am seventy-two years old and I can tell you frankly that I never knew the owners of these properties and I've always lived here."[59]

The upper and lower classes were usually so distanced in structural space that even patron-client relations were rare. With no competitive elections and no union activity, landless laborers were so lacking in resources that being a patron was usually not worthwhile.[60] From the workers' perspective, being a client had disadvantages as well, for hostilities toward a given *agrário*, or landowner, were often so intense that they threatened anyone associated with him. A woman in the district of Évora related a story that exemplifies this. Her husband was apparently one of the tallest and strongest men in the area and an eager worker. Through familial connections with a servant and a series of chance encounters, he caught the attention of a local landowner and was promoted from seasonal to permanent farmhand. Though the family was ecstatic with their new security, they paid a social price. The son was ridiculed in school and nicknamed the "landowner," and the wife lost several friends.[61]

This sort of class-conscious behavior was a predictable by-product of local labor conditions. Employment was seasonal, and until the mid 1960s workers were contracted in a manner that sharply underscored class differences. The process involved *praças de jorna*, large weekly gatherings in town squares where capital and labor came face-to-face in an outdoor version of a hiring hall. Workers would assemble at dawn on Mondays or on Sunday afternoons to wait and hope that a local landowner or farm foreman would offer them a week's work. Laborers who were older, weaker, or truculent came away with nothing. The drama of the *praça de jorna*, enacted again and again, year after year, is described in the words of a foreman, or *capataz*, from the district of Santarém:

[59] António Modesto Navarro, *Memória Alentejana* (Amadora: Orion, 1977), p. 52.

[60] My observations confirm the points made by Joyce Rieglehaupt in "Peasants and Politics."

[61] The story was recounted to me by the woman herself, Montemor-O-Novo, October 1977.

24

The *capataz* arrives and looks at the workers who await him. He evaluates who looks best, those who are the strongest, those who look like they can handle the task. . . . When he sees a weak one with less strength than the others, he passes him by. He doesn't speak with him. It's exactly like a cattle market. . . . Sometimes an unhappy worker would come to me and say, "If you don't mind, I'll go with you," and I'd respond, "Hey man, I already have so many people, too many, it's impossible." But I was just lying and I'd continue to look over the others.[62]

The colonial wars, along with urban and foreign emigration, relieved much of the agony of rural unemployment by the late sixties, and fewer and fewer men left the *praças de jorna* with no work. But the memory of the recent past remained. Anyone who journeys to the latifúndia region today and asks questions about the prerevolutionary period will hear descriptions of the hiring method first, for its effects on the workers' consciousness were profound. The thoughts of an underground labor organizer—written decades before the revolution—illustrate the point. The "*praça*," he wrote,

is useful for the unity of the farmworkers. . . . On the patio of an employer, or in a [landowner's] house, a worker feels weak because he is isolated. He'll be silenced with a glass of wine; hurt his own interests and those of his comrades. . . . [But] it is well known that unity makes strength. And the *praças de jorna* prove the saying. There, the worker feels the strength of the union of his fellow workers.[63]

Other aspects of the laborers' work lives also enhanced their group consciousness. After gathering in groups in village squares, workers traveled in groups to landowners' fields, where they worked in groups until sundown. Then they returned home, not to isolated cottages, but to relatively large villages, where even their houses were grouped together behind long, whitewashed facades. The interactive nature of the southern dayworker's life differed markedly from that of the small peasant farmer or even the permanent farmhand, who spent his days toiling alone and was often geographically isolated from his neighbors.

The rural proletariat of the South did not have to wait until 1974 to be tutored in class consciousness. As early as 1909, a foreign observer studying the Alentejo noted that "the salaried workers are very demanding and

[62] Francis Pisani, *Torre Bela* (Coimbra: Centelha, 1978), p. 68.

[63] The citation is from a fascinating essay by Soeiro Pereira Gomes. It was written and published underground in August 1946 and reprinted by the Portuguese Communist Party (PCP) in 1976. See Soeiro Pereira Gomes, *Praça de Jorna* (Lisbon: PCP, 1976), p. 9.

difficult to control."[64] Decades later, but still years before the revolution, another observer wrote that the local workers maintained "an entrenched conviction of the unfairness of the society in which they live" and "a deep if rarely articulated hatred of the latifundists."[65]

Secularity

The extreme and marked class division in southern agricultural society is only one aspect of the southern social structure that contributed to the radicalization of landless laborers. The secular nature of the latifúndia region was also an important contributing factor. Religion did not provide the sort of cross-cutting cleavage that would obviate the growth of class consciousness.

The people of the Alentejo are notorious for their disinterest in organized religion. Indeed, the Catholic Church classifies the region as a "missionary area"—a distinction usually reserved for non-Christian areas in Africa and Asia. During the time of the Spanish occupation, most of the priests in the southern region were Spanish Jesuits. When the Spanish left, the priests left too, but they were never replaced.

In the Alentejo priests do not act as a link between classes, as they are said to do in other societies and in other parts of Portugal. Sermons from the pulpit are likely to fall on deaf ears or no ears at all. In *A Portuguese Rural Society*, José Cutileiro describes a priest-parish relationship that is typical of the latifúndia region:

> Mass is celebrated . . . every morning at eight o'clock, but only two or three old women bother to attend, and even these, particularly in winter, may stay away. The priest and verger (always a young boy) are often alone in the Church. Afternoon Mass is said every Sunday and is attended by school children of both sexes who are taken by their schoolteacher, and by a few women, mostly young girls, who treat it as a social occasion for dressing up. . . . Attendance by married women is . . . infrequent. . . . Men spend Sundays in the taverns.[66]

The Catholic Church and its representatives are generally held in low esteem. Anyone who spends time in the latifúndia region today is treated to a diverse range of jokes about priests in general and to gossip about the nearest priest's private life. For example, the priest in a town I visited was

---

[64] Leon Poinsard, *Inquérito à Situação das Classes Laboriosas* (Lisbon, 1909), p. 30. See also Leon Poinsard, *Portugal Ignorado: Estudo Social, Económico, e Político* (Porto: Magalhães e Moniz, 1912).

[65] Cutileiro, *A Portuguese Rural Society*, p. 289.

[66] Ibid., p. 251.

TABLE 1.5
Population to Priest Ratio for Portuguese Dioceses, 1974

Southern dioceses		Northern dioceses	
Beja	3,969:1	Aveiro	1,677:1
Évora	1,988:1	Braga	998:1
Faro	3,418:1	Bragança-Miranda	1,326:1
Lisbon	3,258:1	Guarda	1,077:1
Average	3,132:1	Porto	2,128:1
Central dioceses		Vila Real	1,215:1
Coimbra	1,889:1	Viseu	1,386:1
Leiria	1,119:1	Average	1,416:1
Portalegre-Castelo Branco	1,637:1		
Average	1,609:1		

SOURCE: *Annuário Pontificio Per L'Anno 1976* (Città del Vaticano: Tipografia Poliglotta Vaticana, 1976).
NOTES: Figures published in 1976 were collected in 1974. Boundaries of dioceses do not correspond with boundaries of government districts. The diocese of Portalegre-Castelo Branco extends into the south but lies principally in the center of the nation, parallel with Leiria.

nicknamed "O Pior" instead of "O Prior"—that is, he was called "The Worst One" instead of "The Prior."

As Cutileiro's study illustrates, the secular nature of southern society predates the revolutionary period. The conclusion drawn from his impressionistic account is confirmed by statistical evidence. Long before the 25th of April, baptisms and church marriages were less frequent in the Alentejo than in any other rural region. Table 1.5 helps to explain why by illustrating the weak institutional penetration of the Catholic Church. For the four major southern dioceses the ratio of residents to priests is extremely high. In Beja, the ratio is nearly 4,000 to 1. This is not only the highest figure in Portugal, it is the highest figure in Western Europe. The figure for the South as a whole falls well below the European average.

Military Service

Though the institutional church played a minimal role in the shaping of southern society, the South was not immune to influence from other outside institutions. One such institution was the national armed forces. As the colonial wars escalated, more and more men were taken from their homes and sent to Guinea, Mozambique, and Angola. Others were merely sent as far as Lisbon or the northern city of Porto.

As is ususally the case, the burden of military service and combat fell

27

disproportionately on the lower classes, and the younger laborers of the southern districts were greatly affected.[67] Though military service is certainly not a radicalizing experience in itself, it did provide younger rural workers with exposure both to workers and intellectuals who *were* radicalized and to new information of all sorts. Military service also subjected rural workers to new levels of danger and gave their families an additional reason to oppose the state.

Emigration

Emigration patterns were a fourth aspect of the southern social structure that contributed to radicalization. In the thirteen-year period preceding the revolution, economic stagnation forced more than 1.5 million Portuguese to seek employment abroad. Hundreds of thousands of other Portuguese were forced to leave rural areas and seek employment in the nation's major cities. The pressures to leave home were especially great for the landless laborers of the South. The crops of the latifúndia area required a large labor force during the planting and harvest seasons, but a very small labor force during the rest of the year. In most of the southern region, agricultural work was virtually paralyzed between November and March.[68] Even when southern laborers could obtain work, they were paid less than agricultural workers elsewhere, as is illustrated in Table 1.6.

Clearly, southern rural workers had ample material incentive to leave the land. But when they did, they usually went to the Lisbon area rather than to a foreign country.[69] Table 1.7 illustrates that an annual average of only 438 individuals emigrated legally from the Alentejo region between 1960 and 1975. This is less than 17 percent of the average for the nation and only 29 percent of the average for the northern region.

These emigration patterns had important political ramifications. When landless laborers of the South migrated, they did not become members of a foreign work force where linguistic and cultural isolation could inhibit politicization; they became members of the manual labor force of Lisbon

[67] The author knows of one case in which a wealthy youth assigned to combat duty in Angola "bought" himself another assignment in continental Portugal and had a working-class youth sent in his place.

[68] Carlos Almeida and António Barreto, *Capitalismo e Emigração em Portugal* (Lisbon: Prelo Editora, 1970), p. 197.

[69] This impression was gathered from personal interviews and confirms the observations of Caroline B. Brettel in "Emigration and Its Implications for the Revolution in Northern Portugal," in Lawrence S. Graham and Harry M. Makler, eds., *Contemporary Portugal: The Revolution and Its Antecedents* (Austin: University of Texas Press, 1979), p. 283.

TABLE 1.6
Agricultural Workers' Wages, 1973 (in 1973 escudos)

	Wages for Full-time Unspecialized Work
Southern districts of the Alentejo	
Beja	80.6
Évora	78.7
Portalegre	79.9
Setúbal	86.7
Average	81.3
Other southern districts	
Faro	108.2
Lisbon	130.1
Average	121.2
Central districts	
Castelo Branco	78.5
Coimbra	97.9
Leiria	114.8
Santarém	97.6
Average	96.6
Northern districts	
Aveiro	95.9
Braga	83.6
Bragança	88.9
Guarda	84.9
Porto	97.8
Viana do Castelo	99.0
Vila Real	99.6
Viseu	94.4
Average	93.4

SOURCE: Instituto Nacional de Estatística, *Anuário Estatístico do Continente e Ilhas Adjacentes, 1973* (Lisbon: INE, 1974), 1: 279.
NOTE: All averages are weighted.

or Setúbal instead.[70] Their opportunities for politicization were great, for they were, in essence, members of *both* a rural and an urban proletariat. They were part of an urban wage-earning class but still closely associated with their lives as landless laborers.

A questionnaire study conducted by the government in 1971 illustrates the dual nature of these workers' positions. Only 27 percent of the rural

[70] Manuel Villaverde Cabral makes the same point about an earlier period in "Situação do Operariado nas Vésperas da Implantação da República," *Análise Social* (April-June 1977), p. 427. Setúbal is a large industrial center in the district of the same name, which lies to the northwest of the heartland of the Alentejo. The city stands just across the Tejo from Lisbon and has been an important center of left-wing organization for decades.

TABLE 1.7
Legal Emigration, 1960-1975

	Average Annual Emigration	Emigration Rate per 1,000
Southern districts of the Alentejo		
Beja	584	2.4%
Évora	205	1.0
Portalegre	153	.9
Setúbal	811	1.9
Average	438	1.5
Other southern districts		
Faro	1,503	5.1
Lisbon	3,668	2.5
Average	2,585	3.8
Central districts		
Castelo Branco	1,728	6.0
Coimbra	1,829	4.4
Leiria	3,348	8.5
Santarém	1,640	3.7
Average	2,136	5.6
Northern districts		
Aveiro	3,958	7.4
Braga	3,950	6.5
Bragança	2,016	9.7
Guarda	2,596	10.5
Porto	4,509	3.6
Viana do Castelo	2,381	9.0
Vila Real	2,180	7.4
Viseu	3,285	7.3
Average	3,109	7.7
Adjacent islands	9,707	17.1
PORTUGAL	5,033	5.7

SOURCE: *Boletim Anual da Secretária de Estado da Emigração, 1975* (Lisbon: INE, 1976).

workers taking jobs in the Lisbon area did so with the intention of staying. A full 39 percent of these rural workers left their wives and children in the countryside and were presumably accustomed to making regular trips home. Nearly 60 percent of these workers *preferred* to live in the country,[71] but the overwhelming majority felt compelled to leave because of the nature of their rural work life. Table 1.8 describes the reasons rural migrants used

[71] Carlos Fernandes de Almeida , Flávio Henrique Vara, and Isabel Faria Martins, *Adaptação do Trabalhador de Origem Rural ao Meio Industrial e Urbano* (Lisbon: Ministério de Economia, 1971), p. 124. Emphasis mine.

TABLE 1.8

Rural Workers' Reasons for Emigrating to Lisbon

Why did you leave your rural life?

To get work that paid more	45%
To get nonagricultural work	5
To get work with a better schedule	6
To get work with more security	12
To get work that would be less taxing	7
To avoid unemployment in rural areas	2
To learn a trade	1
To have a better life	13
To have excitement	1
To educate their children	1
Others	7

SOURCE: Carlos Fernandes de Almeida, Flávio Henrique Vara, and Isabel Faria Martins, *Adaptação do Trabalhador de Origem Rural ao Meio Industrial e Urbano* (Lisbon: Ministério de Economia, 1971), p. 49.

to justify their move to Lisbon. The reasons cited are overwhelmingly negative—reflecting a dissatisfaction with the opportunities in rural Portugal rather than an attraction to Lisbon per se.

If life in a new environment had satisfied the material goals that had stimulated emigration in the first place (as was the case so often for the relatively well-paid emigrants to France and Germany), rural workers might have undergone some form of embourgeoisement. But material goals were not met. By and large, rural migrants to Lisbon were disappointed in their wages and unable to garner the savings they had expected. In answer to the question "Is your salary sufficient for your needs?" only 13 percent of the workers surveyed responded affirmatively. When asked "Do you manage to put any money aside?" only 6 percent of the workers said "yes." A full 94 percent of the workers said they would choose a different job "if they had a choice."[72]

Caught up in two proletariats and disappointed with the material rewards of even city life, these workers were hardly likely to identify with the middle class. They were unlikely to identify with any class group but their own—for their frustration is the stuff from which class consciousness is made.

There is evidence to suggest that many of these semiurban, semirural proletarians were in fact radicalized years before the revolution. When

[72] Ibid., pp. 92, 94, 104.

asked if wage differentials were "just," a full 26 percent of these workers responded "no," and an additional 27 percent said that differentials were only just under certain conditions.[73] Clearly these workers were thinking along egalitarian lines. The fact that they would voice these thoughts in 1971 to a government employee is testament to the strength of their conviction.

In addition to reinforcing material frustrations, urban migration provided rural workers with exposure to labor unions. Though these unions were never free from government control, they provided a forum for organizational action unavailable to agricultural workers. Lisbon and Setúbal (where migrants concentrated) contained 105 different labor unions with over 350,000 members and an additional 350,000 associates.[74] When Marcelo Caetano loosened government reins on union elections in 1968, union leadership turned leftward and a wave of strikes followed, peaking in 1969 and then again in 1973. Involving more than 100,000 workers in 1973 alone,[75] these strikes served to illustrate the potential of class-based activity and were no doubt an important part of the migrant worker's urban experience.

Urban migration also provided the rural worker with exposure to more communications media. Though only 27 percent of the migrants surveyed had read newspapers regularly before coming to Lisbon, a full 37 percent did so afterwards. Exposure to television increased as well. While only 23 percent of all workers watched television regularly in the countryside, a full 41 percent did so in the city.[76]

Traveling regularly between urban and rural areas, these workers were important carriers of information and a crucial link between two proletariats. Though they earned their meager livelihood in urban civil construction jobs or in labor-intensive factories, many of these workers remained linked to the land. Despite the long hours, the uncertainty, and the physical strain of agricultural work, a full 55 percent of the migrant workers surveyed said that they would definitely return to their rural jobs "if the pay were the same." An additional 8 percent said that they might return.[77]

As the revolution unfolded, the differential between rural and urban wages narrowed and the conditions for the emigrant workers' return improved. An agricultural workers union was formed, and wages in southern

[73] Ibid., p. 94.

[74] Mário Pinto and Carlos Moura, *As Estruturas Sindicais Portuguesas: Contributo para o Seu Estudo* (Lisbon: Gabinete de Investigações Sociais, 1973), pp. 19, 37.

[75] Álvaro Cunhal, *A Revolução Portuguesa: O Passado e o Futuro* (Lisbon: "Avante!" 1976), p. 43.

[76] Fernandes de Almeida et al., *Adaptaçaõ*, p. 141.

[77] Ibid., p. 143.

FIGURE 1.1
Convergence of Wages: Lisbon Construction Workers
and Évora Farmworkers, 1974-1975

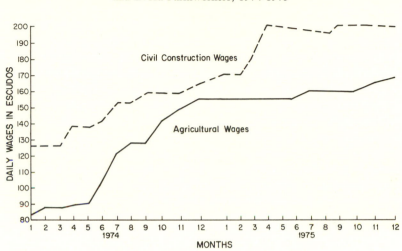

SOURCE: Instituto Nacional de Estatística, *Anuário Estatístico* (Lisbon: INE, 1976).

rural areas rose dramatically. Figure 1.1 contrasts monthly wage levels for agricultural and civil construction workers in Évora and Lisbon respectively. The differential between the two clearly decreased over time, becoming smallest in the last months of 1974. As this occurred, more and more migrant workers returned to their original homes in search of permanent work and higher wages. They returned with a memory of frustrated expectations, with an exposure to union activity, and with a relatively high level of sophistication. In a rural environment with a high radicalization potential of its own, these workers came to play an important role in the occupation of land and in the organization of workers' control.

IN a well-known article on European land tenure and voting behavior, Juan Linz outlines seven factors that facilitate the radicalization of farmworkers. Each of these factors is present in the situation just discussed. The southern latifúndia system fostered employment in considerable numbers on large farms in nonisolated work, as well as the growth of large villages. The crops produced locally required a minimum of internal occupational differentiation and led to large-scale seasonal or permanent unemployment. The colonial wars exposed workers to new communications that eroded traditional legitimacies, and urban migration provided workers with both

33

a minimum of economic independence and contact with an urban labor movement and protest ideologies.[78]

A final factor not mentioned by Linz but of some importance is a local tradition of resistance. Despite the presence of secret police and the denial of both the right to strike and the right of free association, the people of the Alentejo managed to engage in a significant amount of collective protest activity during the years of the dictatorship. The farmworkers of the South illustrated their capacity for resistance through strikes for higher pay in the 1940s, through demonstrations for employment in the 1950s, and through demonstrations for an eight-hour day in the 1950s and 1960s.[79] Workers' demands often went unsatisfied, but the struggles themselves produced long lists of local heroes and martyrs. Workers who were shot during peaceful strikes or sent to prison for other acts of resistance provided both the models and reasons for further opposition to the regime.[80] The myths that grew up around these local martyrs combined with all the factors discussed above to produce a rural proletariat with a high potential for radicalization.

[78] Juan Linz, "Patterns of Land Tenure, Division of Labor, and Voting Behavior in Europe," *Comparative Politics* (April 1976), pp. 365-430.

[79] There is surprisingly little public information on the nature of collective action in the South during the dictatorship. The only major study available is José Pacheco Pereira's *Conflitos Sociais nos Campos do Sul de Portugal*. See pages 188 to 220 for his chronology of strikes.

[80] It is significant that many worker-controlled farms chose to name themselves in honor of local and (less frequently) national martyrs such as Catarina Eufémia, Germano Vidigal, Maria Machado, Pedro Soares, José Bernardino, Bento Gonçalves, and Humberto Delgado.

TWO

The Political Revolution as a Prelude
to the Occupations

So far this discussion has focused only on the potential for radicalization in the rural South. But one must explain how this potential was realized in order to understand the seizure of property and the resultant emergence of workers' control. What forces prompted the rural proletariat to abandon its previous patterns of behavior and forcibly seize the land? What, in other words, were the forces that made this class *in* itself a class *for* itself?

The best place to begin is to look more closely at the seizures themselves. The chronology in Table 2.1 illustrates the rate of land occupation in the three districts where the most property was seized.

TABLE 2.1
Hectares of Land Seized, 1975-1976

	Beja	Évora	Portalegre
January	775	132	—
February	—	3,567	2,392
March	1,502	711	3,020
April	—	8,629	1,541
May	—	5,776	1,066
June	4,891	4,105	18,617
July	19,422	30,441	13,508
August	37,016	99,719	6,756
September	20,611	113,379	3,154
October	186,467	144,681	29,872
November	36,279	19,551	153,985
December	9,238	—	—
January	—	—	—
Total	316,201	430,691	233,911
Land in large holdings	450,000	500,000	300,000

NOTE: The figures for the number of hectares seized are from the Centros Regionais da Reforma Agrária. The figures for the amount of land in large holdings are estimates made by António Lopes Cardoso, Minister of Agriculture for the sixth provisional government.

35

TABLE 2.2
Percentage of Land Seized, 1975

	Beja	Évora	Portalegre
January	.2%	.03%	—
February	—	.8	1.0%
March	.5	.2	1.3
April	—	2.0	.6
May	—	1.3	.5
June	1.5	1.0	8.0
July	6.1	7.1	5.8
August	11.7	23.2	2.9
September	6.5	26.3	1.3
October	59.0	33.6	12.8
November	11.5	4.5	65.8
December	2.9	—	—
Total	100.0	100.0	100.0
Total hectares	316,201	430,691	233,911

SOURCES: Ministério de Agricultura, Gabinete de Investi-
gações Sociais. Centros Regionais da Reforma Agrária and
Afonso de Barros, *A Reforma Agrária em Portugal: Das
Ocupações de Terras à Formação das Novas Unidades de
Produção* (Oeiras: Instituto Gulbenkian, 1979), p. 70.

Occupations peaked in the fall in Beja, Évora, and Portalegre, and then
dropped off sharply after November, but the similarities between the districts end there. Each district had its own peculiar pattern of seizures,
having markedly different percentages of land transferred each month.
Table 2.2 depicts the contrast in the rate of seizures across the districts.

Why did the rate of seizures vary so markedly prior to October? Why
did the seizures peak at that time and then end abruptly in December? An
accurate answer must explain the irregular pattern described above.

Working consciously or unconsciously with the same assumptions as
scholars who have written on the revolutionary potential of landless laborers
elsewhere, many analysts of revolutionary Portugal assume that the land
occupations were not the result of local workers' initiatives but the result
of the machinations of the Portuguese Communist Party instead. In separate
studies and from a variety of political perspectives, Ian Rutledge, H. V.
Livermore, John Hammond, Ana de Vale Estrela, and Manuel Villaverde
Cabral reach similar conclusions.[1] Their line of reasoning is easy to unravel:

[1] See, for example, Ian Rutledge, "Land Reform and the Portuguese Revolution," *The
Journal of Peasant Studies* (October 1977), p. 91; H. V. Livermore, *A New History of*

the occupations were concentrated almost exclusively in the Alentejo; the Alentejo is the rural stronghold of the Communist Party; the Communists were bent on making massive changes in property relations and therefore organized the occupations as a means toward this end. The rural proletariat, incapable of independent action, merely followed the party's lead.

The real explanation for the occupations is much more complex. It derives from a complicated series of structural changes related to different phases of the revolutionary process. These changes did not affect all poor cultivators in the same way, and they did not have the same impact in all districts. Different sorts of people were affected at different times. Variations in the timing of the seizures and in the proportion of land seized can be explained by the differential impact of structural change.

Chapter One illustrated how, long before the revolution, the social structure of the latifúndia region gave rise to a rural proletariat with a high potential for radicalization. This chapter will illustrate how a first set of structural changes—new laws, new organizations, and new roles for old organizations—made the potential for radicalization manifest. It will illustrate that the radical behavior embodied in the land seizures was not the result of a single party's master plan but, rather, the result of a complex series of structural changes associated with the political phase of the revolution.

No political party predicted that the occupations would occur, and none could control them once they did. Instead, the unions, parties, leagues, and military groups created by the political revolution were forced into a particular form of social revolution by the landless laborers themselves. New and renovated organizations *followed* the landless onto the land because they sought to establish constituencies and expand support in an extremely competitive environment.

Portugal (Cambridge: Cambridge University Press, 1976), p. 384; John L. Hammond, "Electoral Behavior and Political Militancy," in Lawrence S. Graham and Harry M. Makler, eds., *Contemporary Portugal: The Revolution and Its Antecedents* (Austin: University of Texas Press, 1979), p. 272; Ana de Vale Estrela, "A Reforma Agrária Portuguesa e os Movimentos Camponeses: Uma Revisão Crítica," *Análise Social* (April–June 1978), p. 241; and Manuel Villaverde Cabral, "Agrarian Structures and Recent Rural Movements in Portugal," *The Journal of Peasant Studies* (July 1978), p. 426. Cabral argues that the occupations were "controlled" by the unions but also concedes at another point that the PCP was not "fully dominant"; see p. 424. Though all of these authors argue that the Communist party played a dominant role, they vary greatly in their evaluation of that role's legitimacy. For example, Hammond implies that the party's role was legitimate, writing that the workers took part in the occupations "under the inspiration—if not the control—of the same party for which they had voted" (p. 272). Livermore adopts a more negative position, contending that "the communist groups who had *snatched* power after the revolution encouraged the seizure of land" (p. 384; emphasis mine).

37

STRUCTURAL CHANGE AND THE POLITICAL REVOLUTION, APRIL 1974 TO MARCH 1975

As stated previously, the first phase of the Portuguese revolution was a "political revolution." A political revolution is a revolution that affects only the distribution of formal political rights. New elites take charge of the national government, new political organizations develop, systems of accountability are expanded, but property relations remain fundamentally unchanged.

Portugal's political revolution began when the Armed Forces Movement overthrew the Salazar-Caetano regime in April 1974. It ended when conservatives organized an unsuccessful countercoup and provoked a reaction from the left in March 1975. The three provisional governments that ruled Portugal between these dates dedicated their efforts to political rather than economic change. While almost no property was nationalized or collectivized, political structures altered dramatically. The foundations of a liberal democracy were laid through structural changes such as the assumption of new roles by the military, the organization of a competitive party system, and the formation of new class associations. The discussion that follows illustrates that these structural changes served as catalysts for the occupation of land, though they were certainly not initiated with this intention.

New Roles for the Military

The military officers who controlled the first three provisional governments denied any interest in establishing a military dictatorship. Immediately after they ousted the Caetano regime, the officers published a program promising the restoration of civilian rule as soon as a president and legislative assembly were elected.[2] There was a great deal of favorable discussion of socialism, but there was a general consensus that socialism, whatever it was, was to be built upon the foundations of a liberal democracy. As late as October 1974, it was widely thought that the majority of the MFA's leaders sought "a system of social democracy on the Swedish model."[3]

Though there was little indication that the MFA might be the forerunner of a military dictatorship, it was obvious that the armed forces would now

[2] See "O Programa do MFA," released April 1974. An English translation of the program is available in Douglas Porch, *The Portuguese Armed Forces and the Revolution* (Stanford, California: The Hoover Institution Press, 1977), pp. 244-258.

[3] *Povo Livre*, October 1974. Interview with Otelo Saraiva de Carvalho, in Avelino Rodrigues, Cesário Borga, and Mário Cardoso, *Abril nos Quartéis de Novembro* (Lisbon: Livraria Bertrand, 1979), p. 377.

assume a variety of new roles. Structural changes within the military were to have an indirect, but important, effect on the rural population. The first such change was the establishment of the Cultural Dynamization Campaign. The campaign emerged from revolutionary revelry and from fears of what a liberal democracy might bring. Progressives inside and outside the military feared that the largely illiterate rural population would be manipulated by right-wing forces and vote the right back into power. To ensure against this possibility, the military government began its dynamization campaign in October 1974. Although civilian singers and artists often participated, the campaign was run wholly by military men.

According to one of its organizers, the campaign's "Sessions of Enlightenment" were nonpartisan, focusing on issues such as decolonization, the mechanics of the upcoming elections, and the role of the Armed Forces Movement. But some discussion of party politics was unavoidable. Officers usually explained that the military could not have assumed its new role without the activities of underground political parties,[4] and sessions sometimes ended with the audience asking, "For which parties should we vote?"[5]

The advent of the Cultural Dynamization Campaign was a structural change of great importance, for it meant a new role for the military. Not only were officers and enlisted men going to oversee the establishment of a democracy, they were going to guide this democracy in a particular direction. They were going to ensure, in essence, that the bourgeois democracy was not too bourgeois. The hearts and minds of the lower classes in rural areas would have to be won, and this necessitated new levels of interaction between civilians and military men. The men in the dynamization campaigns eventually brought their program to more than one-and-one-half-million peasants, workers, and shopkeepers.[6]

Another structural change of great importance was the founding of COPCON, the Operational Command for the Continent. According to the law that brought COPCON into existence on July 8, 1974, the new organization was to concern itself with the "maintenance and establishment of order"

---

[4] This was an indirect reference to the Communist party, since it was the only major opposition party to function underground throughout the entire Salazar-Caetano regime.

[5] *Diário de Notícias* (Lisbon), January 24, 1975. Interview with Ramiro Correia, organizer of dynamization campaigns.

[6] Andreu Claret Serra, *Hablan los Capitanes* (Barcelona: Ariel, 1975), p. 151. It is important to note that the dynamization campaigns often met with mixed success. They were frequently organized by people who knew nothing of rural life. Teams would travel long distances to show films only to learn that their target town had no electricity. Daytime meetings sometimes drew no one but aged men and children, for everyone else was hard at work. The small-holding peasantry of the North was the real focus of the campaigns, but they were often the most inaccessible and skeptical.

in all situations in which existing coercive forces were "insufficient, inappropriate or inaccessible." It was to guarantee the public peace, "safeguarding people and goods" and maintaining order in all public and private institutions deemed "essential to national life."[7] In essence, the men of COPCON were to be the policemen of the revolution.

It was inappropriate for the despised and discredited national police to take on the task of maintaining order, and yet challenges to order—to people, to property, and to public and private institutions—were becoming increasingly common. COPCON was the answer to the dilemma, but as such it represented a very new sort of military institution, for its main concerns were nonmilitary. The spheres in which it operated, the disputes it was designed to resolve, were primarily, if not exclusively, civilian. Like the units concerned with cultural dynamization, COPCON was an organization that bridged two worlds. It brought military men into constant contact with civil society and compelled them to assume the political functions of adjudication and allocation.

The man chosen to lead COPCON was Brigadier Otelo Saraiva de Carvalho, a charismatic individual who relished political activity and did not need to be compelled to take political action. His own political views were to have a dramatic effect on the nature of COPCON and on the course of the entire revolution.[8]

COPCON's very creation was both proof and prophecy of the inadequacy of the provisional governments, for it was charged with tasks that ministries and police forces would have assumed in a nonrevolutionary situation. In the long run, the delegation of political authority to a military body was to have a dramatic effect on the emergence of workers' control in agriculture, but in the short run, it was merely viewed as a means of safeguarding the birth of a democracy dependent on the maintenance of order.

A New Party System

Of course, the foundation of the nation's new liberal democracy would be a free electoral system with universal suffrage and a broad array of competing parties. By late fall, more than twenty-two such parties had registered for the April elections, the most prominent being the Communist party (PCP), the Socialist party (PSP), the Popular Democratic party (PPD), and the Social Democratic Center (CDS).[9]

[7] Decree Law 310/74, parts a and b.

[8] See Rodrigues et al., *Abril*, p. 371, for more details. For Carvalho's own views on the revolution, see Otelo Saraiva de Carvalho, *Alvorada em Abril* (Lisbon: Livraria Bertrand, 1977).

[9] Elections for the Constitutional Assembly were scheduled for April 1975. According to the election law of October 31, a party had to register five thousand members to be on the

With 74 percent of the national electorate living in rural areas, it is not surprising that the Portuguese countryside was the scene of intense party competition. In the rural South, the main competitors were the Communists and the Socialists.

The competition was especially important for the PCP, for the Communists realized that they stood little chance of winning many electoral battles in other parts of the nation. The PCP's leaders predicted that their success would rest largely on their ability to attract the support of voters in greater Lisbon and the Alentejo. Accordingly, the party invested a great deal of effort in local organization. By the time of the April elections, Beja, Évora, and Portalegre hosted 105 Communist party centers: one for every 3.6 thousand voters.[10] This network of local organizations, duplicated on a lesser scale by the Socialist party, was, in the short run, simply another step in the preparation for a liberal democracy. In the long run, the network was to provide an infrastructure for the advancement of workers' control and the onset of a much more radical structural change.

The Emergence of Class Associations

Of the many structural changes affecting the Portuguese countryside, the emergence of class associations had the strongest impact. The corporatist organizations of the Salazar-Caetano regime were the very negation of class organizations. The owners' associations (the *Grémios de Lavoura*) included wealthy latifundists as well as peasants earning only subsistence incomes. The workers' associations (the *Casas do Povo*) included wealthy landowners as well as rural proletarians. Indeed, as stated previously, the whole corporatist system was based on the denial that there was a need for organization along class lines.

The political revolution brought "freedom of association" and with it the immediate emergence of peasant leagues and farmworkers' unions. These organizations were a logical part of any liberal democracy and not intrinsically "revolutionary" in themselves, but in the context of Portugal's latifúndia system, they became the catalysts for major alterations in property relations.

Peasant Leagues. As was illustrated in the previous discussion of rural social structure, class divisions were clearly drawn long before the 25th of April. But the divisions were not merely bipolar, involving only wage

---

ballot. The parties are listed in the text as they would be on a left-right spectrum, with the Socialist party and the Popular Democratic parties representing the center left and center right respectively.

[10] Figures compiled from lists published in October 1975 in the PCP's monthly magazine *O Militante* (Lisbon), p. 10.

workers and *patrões* (i.e., employer-landowners). A very large sector of the agricultural population lay outside both of these categories. These individuals were officially categorized in the census as *isolados*, individuals who were not wage workers and did not make "habitual use" of hired labor but who gained most, if not all, of their income from farming.[11] More than 328,000 Portuguese classified themselves as *isolados* in the 1970 census. They comprised over 11 percent of the nation's working population and more than 36 percent of those engaged in farming. In the latifúndia region, they comprised approximately 15 percent of the farming population.

Isolados were neither part of the proletariat nor part of the dominant class but part of a much more amorphous group that might best be described by the term peasantry. Situated between two classes, and comprising nearly 40 percent of the national electorate, the Portuguese peasantry became the focus of great political attention. Their support was sought by proletarians and landowners alike. This was predictable, for the peasantry shared similarities with both groups. Like wage workers, many peasants maintained barely more than a subsistence standard of living.[12] But, like the latifundists, most peasants were, in fact, owners of land. Would peasant leagues act independently, or would they align with the organizations of other classes? Since the peasantry was a heterogeneous group encompassing individuals with various relations to the means of production, the answer to this question depended very much on which sorts of "peasants" controlled the leagues.

There were several important subcategories within the peasantry. First, there were the semiproletarianized peasants who owned plots of land that were large enough to require attention throughout the year but too small to sustain the owner's family. Semiproletarianized laborers were forced to hire themselves out as wage laborers on a seasonal basis to supplement the income that their own farms produced. They were most likely to align with the farmworkers' unions, for the farmworkers' gains were their gains as well.

Other sorts of peasants were in a different position. First, there were two sorts of landless peasants: *seareiros* and *rendeiros*. *Seareiros* rented land on a short-term basis for the planting and harvesting of single crops. Like wage workers, they lived in villages and had no permanent relationship to any particular parcel of land. *Rendeiros* rented land for years at a time and lived (often for generations) on the plot they worked. In certain re-

---

[11] The definition is from the census form itself. Unfortunately, the term "habitual use" was never clearly defined.

[12] World Bank, *Portugal: Agricultural Sector Survey* (Washington, D.C.: World Bank, 1978), p. 8.

spects, their position was much like that of the peasant who actually owned land, for they worked and lived in relative isolation, and even made occasional use of hired labor.

Finally, there were the independent peasants—the farmers who cultivated their own land and earned enough by so doing that they avoided wage work themselves and also made occasional use of hired labor. In many respects, the interests of the independent peasant were opposed to those of the farmworker. A minimum wage, a wage increase, a new list of worker benefits would all decrease what little resources the independent peasant had at his command. If independent peasants took charge of peasant leagues, an alliance with rural proletarians and the farmworkers' union would be highly improbable.

Of course, peasants were not only economic actors but political actors as well, and the party affiliation of peasant leaders had an important effect on the public image of the leagues. In most areas, the founders of the leagues were either sympathetic to or members of the Socialist party.[13] Their ranks included members from each of the subgroups in the peasantry. During the earliest days of the leagues, it seemed that the organizations would strike a political position independent of both large landowners and farmworkers—defending interests that were particular to the peasantry itself—but the situation soon changed.

Peasant leagues were growing up alongside political parties (and before a critical election), and it was perhaps inevitable that parties take an active interest in their formation. The Communist party's interest was the greatest, for the party leadership fervently believed that the success of the revolution would depend on the alliance between poor peasants and unionized workers. As early as 1943, Álvaro Cunhal wrote that the success of even a bourgeois revolution would depend on whether "the workers' movement would attract the peasantry into its ranks" or allow it to be seduced by a "reactionary bourgeoisie."[14] An "independent" peasant league could easily be seduced into an alliance with landowners, for the line between landowners and rich peasants was not clearly drawn. Seeking to avoid this scenario, and seeking to expand its own sphere of influence in the South, the Communist party set about trying to reorganize the peasantry in the fall of 1974. The targets for reorganization were the peasant leagues themselves.

An important step in the new campaign was the funding of the First

---

[13] António Lopes Cardoso, *Luta Pela Reforma Agrária* (Lisbon: Diabril, 1976), p. 46. Cardoso's impressions were confirmed by the author in conversations with peasants in Évora, Beja, and Portalegre.

[14] Partido Comunista Português, *O PCP e a Luta Pela Reforma Agrária* (Lisbon: "Avante!" 1975), p. 12.

Conference of Southern Peasants in January 1975. More than two thousand small farmers and farmworkers attended the meeting, along with Álvaro Cunhal and the Communist Minister of Labor Avelino Gonçalves. The party's message to the conference participants was clearly expressed by Cunhal himself. Two themes were salient. First, peasants should be assured that the party sought only to represent their interests. As Cunhal put it, the PCP wanted ''to be the voice of the small- and medium-sized farmer.'' Second, the peasantry should recognize the merits of a peasant-proletarian alliance. Cunhal underscored the similarities of interest that could bind the two groups together:

> We all know that those who work in the countryside are not all in the same situation. But in our view, there is not a great contradiction between a small landowner and a salaried worker. There is no animosity, all are exploited when all is said and done. The major enemies are the large landowners.[15]

These messages were aimed directly at the peasant leagues and were repeated continuously at smaller conferences organized throughout the South.

The response to the party's drive for a peasant-proletarian alliance was mixed, and peasant leagues varied from district to district as the political revolution wore on. In Beja, the peasant leagues came closest to conforming to the party's ideal, for they came to be dominated by semiproletarianized peasants whose interests lay as much with wage workers as with the peasantry itself.[16]

In other districts of the latifúndia region, the position of the leagues was much more ambiguous. Faro, Castelo Branco, Lisbon, Setúbal, and the north of Santarém had no leagues at all, and the leagues of Évora and Portalegre, even after the party's conferences in January and February, were controlled by *seareiros* and *rendeiros* who were less than enthusiastic about becoming an ''arm of the trade unions.''[17]

This reluctance to enter into a permanent alliance with trade unions eroded by the spring of 1975, but it was still evident as the first lands were occupied in February and March and does much to explain the pattern of occupation that finally emerged.

Agricultural Workers' Unions. The farmworkers' unions that emerged with the Peasant Leagues in the summer of 1974 were also class organizations of great importance. More than 510,000 Portuguese classified themselves as wage- and salary-earning agricultural workers and were thus

[15] *Diário de Notícias*, January 6, 1975.
[16] Personal interview, Beja, February 1978.
[17] Personal interview, Lisbon, March 1978.

potential union members. This meant that nearly one-sixth of the nation's active population might be integrated in the new structures once created. In the latifúndia region of the Alentejo, the importance of salaried agricultural workers was unmatched. In Beja, farmworkers were 78 percent of the agricultural work force; in Portalegre, 83 percent; in Setúbal, 81 percent; and in Évora, 88 percent.[18]

Farmworkers had been prevented from forming labor unions for nearly forty years. From 1938 until 1974, the only legal "representative organs" of the salaried agricultural workers were the *Casas do Povo*. In fact, as stated previously, these organizations fulfilled no representative function at all. Though responsible for collective bargaining and for the defense of "the moral, economic and social interests of all enrolled workers,"[19] the *Casas* functioned almost exclusively in the interests of the large landowners who controlled them. As late as 1969, a government report conceded that the primary sector was "almost untouched by collective bargaining," and the few collective contracts that were signed were binding upon all workers but not binding on all employers.[20] Even if some *Casas* had been able to escape the control of the local landed elite, the work lives of landless laborers would have been little changed, for nearly 90 percent of those that did exist functioned only as charitable institutions.[21]

Though the Salazar-Caetano regime had kept industrial unions under tight control, it had at least permitted their existence and had even allowed them a limited degree of autonomy in the early 1970s. Thus, while industrial unions could be merely "rebuilt," agricultural unions had to be built from scratch. The *Casas do Povo* could not even provide the framework for a future structure.

Given the complexity of the organizational task, it is not surprising that union organization varied from place to place. There was no single apparatus that could be seized at the top and then manipulated from above. Unions were established at different times and under different circumstances. Once established, new unions attracted very different proportions of the eligible populations. The districts with the greatest union penetration were Beja and Évora. Less than one year after the 25th of April, more than 62 percent of Beja's eligible workers were unionized. The comparable

[18] *Instituto Nacional de Estatística, Estatísticas Agrícolas do Continente* (Lisbon: INE, 1976).

[19] Decree Law 28859 from July 18, 1938, as recorded in Manuel de Lucena, *A Evolução do Sistema Corporativo Português*, vol. 1, *O Salazarismo* (Lisbon: Perspectivas e Realidades, 1976), p. 254.

[20] Ibid., p. 255.

[21] Howard J. Wiarda, *Corporatism and Development: The Portuguese Experience* (Amherst: University of Massachusetts Press, 1977), p. 245.

percentage for Évora was still quite high at 53 percent, but other union structures were far less successful. The unions of Portalegre included less than 20 percent of all workers. The unions of Setúbal and Santarém included only 15 percent. The unions of Faro and Lisbon attracted even fewer members, and the union of Castelo Branco did not even come into existence until 1976.[22]

Social differences within the rural proletariat itself hampered the growth of trade unions and help to explain the pattern of penetration just described. The most important differences were those between permanent and temporary workers, or *trabalhadores permanentes* and *jornaleiros*. Both sets of workers had the same relation to the means of production, for both were landless and forced to sell their labor to live, but the similarities often ended there. Permanent workers generally lived outside the temporary workers' villages, on the latifúndia themselves, where they often kept their own livestock and their own small garden. Equally important in a social sense was the fact that permanent workers often had highly personalized relations with landowners and managers. It was not uncommon for landowners to become godparents to permanent workers' children and to send them Christmas, wedding, and other gifts. As stated previously, patron-clientism was not common in the Alentejo. That which existed was between landowners and permanent workers. In interviews, landowners often described their maids, shepherds, and foremen as "members of the family" and spoke with pride about "treating them well." I interviewed a landowner near Redondo who was typical in his eagerness to illustrate his generosity. He described the amenities in his foreman's house and related how he had even paid for the schooling of the worker's children. Concluding what sounded, objectively, like the description of a genuinely caring relationship, the landowner added, "the more he owes me, the more I get in return": a classic description of a patron's motivation.

Good treatment was, in fact, often rewarded with heartfelt fidelity. A case in point was a former worker in Portalegre who described with pride how he had defended his *patrão*'s property at gunpoint and how he had refused an offer of employment from the "rabble" who had occupied the farm. With the help of his boss, the man had become a taxi driver, but he was anxious that the farm be returned and was a vociferous supporter of the Popular Democratic party—the largest party that lobbied toward this end.

These differences in political loyalties combined with differences in

[22] The figures for Beja, Évora, Setúbal, and Santarém are from different issues of *Alavanca* (Lisbon), the main publication of Intersindical. See May 7, 1975; March 21, 1975; and April 23, 1975. Information on other districts was collected at the headquarters of Intersindical in Lisbon. Figures are estimates.

training to distinguish permanent workers from *jornaleiros*. The former were often shepherds or hunters or tractor drivers,[23] while the latter were rarely skilled in a formal sense at all. For all of these reasons, permanent workers did not always identify with *jornaleiros* and were less likely to join labor unions. This too was to have an effect on the course of the property seizures.

Like the peasant leagues, the farmworkers' unions became quickly embroiled in party politics. In the eyes of the public, the unions were almost immediately associated with the Communist party, and indeed it is true that they were more influenced by the PCP (and its ally, the MDP-CDE) than by any other party. Though critics of the party insist that this influence was due to coercion and manipulation, the historical factors previously discussed offer a more compelling explanation. The PCP's position of influence was as much the result of its structural position before the revolution as of any alleged machinations afterward.

To state that the farmworkers' unions were more influenced by the PCP than by any other party is not to state that the unions comprised a monolithic organization under complete party control. For at least a year after their formation, the unions, like the peasant leagues, differed from district to district. Other political groups, especially ultraleftists who were often hostile to the PCP, were highly influential in all district unions, with the possible exception of Beja. Indeed, even observers who were most critical of the PCP concede that the party's "control" of the unions was not assured until well after the "political" revolution came to an end.[24]

Employers' Associations. The organization situated opposite the unions on the class spectrum was the *Associação Livre de Agricultores,* the Free Association of Farmers, known as ALA. ALA was organized to protect the interests of all employers, regardless of the size of their property holding. As such, it was similar to the *Grémios de Lavoura* organized by Salazar, for it incorporated small, medium, and large landowners. However, ALA's leaders attempted to give their new organization a more democratic public image. ALA spokesmen insisted that they were defenders of private property but not defenders of the old regime. They also claimed to support the MFA program and insisted that no individuals with institutional links to the old regime were eligible for leadership positions within

[23] Tractor drivers held a high position within the proletariat, for they were always literate. This was a requirement for a driver's license.

[24] In *Portugal Socialista* (Lisbon), a periodical of the PSP, a January 7, 1976, article states that the PCP and the far left disputed "control" of the unions until after the passage of the land expropriations law on July 30, 1975.

their new organization.[25] Despite these public pronouncements, ALA's leadership never succeeded in disassociating itself from the Salazar-Caetano regime. The minister of agriculture during the fourth and fifth governments, for example, believed that the men who led the ALA were essentially "the same men who headed the *Grémios de Lavoura.*"[26]

ALA's problems of image combined with problems of recruitment. Shortly after its founding in Beja in May 1974, the organization had county representatives in every district of the center and South, but its geographic spread was greater than its actual penetration. Membership figures are unavailable, but reports at the time suggest that the organization had difficulties securing the active participation of a large constituency. This is not surprising, given that the peasant leagues seemed to offer an organizational alternative to a substantial portion of ALA's would-be members and that many large landowners associated with the old regime were withdrawing from political activity altogether and even leaving the country.

Whatever the reason, ALA's weak penetration was extremely problematic, for the organization was viewed, by the government at least, as the only legitimate representative of farming employers and their sole negotiator in the upcoming collective bargaining sessions. The fact that ALA was lacking in representational authority was to contribute to the turmoil and indirectly to the land occupations in the aftermath of the contract negotiations.

THE emergence of class associations related to the seizure of property in an indirect but unmistakable way. The relationship began with the collective bargaining process initiated in rural areas in the early summer of 1974. Farmworkers were, understandably, eager to work under a binding labor contract and to make the contracts operable before the harvest season when the most work was available. This meant that contracts had to be negotiated during the early summer. This presented a serious problem because the negotiating partners were not yet organized. The establishment of unions was to be initiated by *pro-sindicatos*, or union formation committees, but even these initiating bodies were hardly in place when negotiations began. Unions had few members and no elected officers. ALA was still very much

[25] Little information is available on ALA today. One of the few newspaper articles dedicated to the organization appears in *Expresso* (Lisbon), February 22, 1975. The organization seems to have failed to solicit much attention even in the mid 1970s. Joyce Rieglehaupt reports that a well-off peasant family near Lisbon had not even heard of ALA in the summer of 1976.

[26] Fernando Oliveira Baptista, *Portugal 1975—Os Campos* (Porto: Edições Afrontamento, 1978), p. 16.

in the organizational stage as well and did not involve more than a small fraction of regional employers.

Contract negotiations went ahead anyway, with the nascent ALA bargaining on behalf of employers and the *pro-sindicatos* bargaining on behalf of workers. The contracts that emerged from the bargaining sessions varied somewhat from district to district but typically involved a 40 percent pay increase, time and a half for anything beyond a forty-five-hour week, paid holidays, and a two-week vacation.

None of these benefits seemed extraordinary by Western European standards, but one aspect of the new agreements was. Each district's contract stated: "The farmers whose properties are found to be partially or totally underutilized will be forced to accept the number of workers necessary for the profitable and proper exploitation of their holdings."[27] The new contracts thus went beyond regulating how employers related to workers by also attempting to control how employers used land.

Land use was a serious problem for the economy as a whole. Portugal had the least productive primary sector in all of Western Europe, and this was largely due to the fact that huge tracts of land were left to lie fallow year after year. The underutilization of land meant few employment opportunities, low wages, and a low standard of living. Wage increases brought by new contracts would be an improvement, of course, but the benefits would not be widely shared until more workers were employed.

The special clause in the new contract addressed this problem directly. Worker placement commissions, comprised of government and union officials, would determine first if properties were properly utilized and then the number of workers that an underutilized property could support. The unions negotiated the contracts, and the commissions guaranteed that the maximum number of workers enjoyed the benefits.

ALA evaluated these first collective agreements with less hostility than might be predicted. Spokesmen for the organization insisted that the agricultural sector "does not have the capacity to absorb all the labor which exists" but also conceded that the "contracts echoed the just demands of the working class."[28]

Individual employers viewed the contracts in a much less favorable light. Though many landowners "complied with regularity,"[29] there were also flagrant cases of noncompliance. Unions reported scores of contract violations to government officials and publicly denounced landowners for not

---

[27] Sindicato de Trabalhadores Agrícolas, *Convenção de Beja*, clause 3, mimeographed.
[28] João Garin, *Reforma Agrária: Seara de Ódio* (Lisbon: Edições do Templo, 1977), p. 44.
[29] *Expresso*, February 8, 1975.

49

"respecting what they themselves had signed."[30] Charges of economic sabotage became commonplace. Owners were accused of letting livestock starve, of slaughtering whole herds at once, and of letting crops rot unattended. ALA denied most of the charges and called upon the Ministry of Justice to undertake an in-depth investigation.[31]

Conflict was inevitable since workers' expectations were higher than ever and employers' resources were lower than ever. Due to inflation, production costs had soared in the ten months following the revolution. In addition to a 100 percent increase in labor costs, the price of fertilizers rose 98 percent and that of equipment fuels 100 percent. Only a portion of these new costs was absorbed by the market, for the grain crops that formed the basis of the southern rural economy rose only 20 percent in price, due to government controls.[32]

The emergence of new forms of regulation and organization shattered the foundations of an economic sector that had been frail from the start. Rural class associations were now in open confrontation and were calling increasingly for government intervention.

THE INADEQUACY OF THE REVOLUTIONARY STATE

The structural changes that had been integral to the political revolution were now provoking an imbalance that the provisional governments could not set right. The governments were constrained in several ways. One set of constraints derived from the structure of the state itself. The Ministry of Agriculture (MAP) had been eliminated in 1934, and the revolutionary governments had not yet set up a replacement. Agricultural policies were set by a secretary of state in the Ministry of Finance, just as they had been under the Salazar-Caetano regime. This meant that no cabinet-level official dealt exclusively with agricultural affairs. Though channels for the articulation of demands had been expanded, there was still no structural guarantee that information would filter through to the very top of the state apparatus. Pressures from the base thus built up with no release.

The provisional governments had other problems in responding to new demands. The secretary of state for agriculture employed 7,500 professionals, but more than 45 percent of them worked in Lisbon. Rural staffs were hardpressed to cope with the roles that structural change had thrust upon them.

To begin with, many, if not most, of the government's agricultural

---

[30] Albano Lima, *Sindicatos e Acção Sindical* (Lisbon: "Avante!" 1976), p. 31.

[31] *Diário de Notícias*, February 11, 1975.

[32] *Expresso*, February 22, 1975. For more information on price changes, see World Bank, *Portugal: Agricultural Sector Survey* (1978), pp. 5-7, 106-111, 301-323.

experts in rural areas were native to the regions in which they worked, and connected, through family or friendship, to the wealthy landowning class.[33] Their new responsibilities as servants of a "revolutionary" state were not always easily or willingly assumed. But even staff members with the most flexible views were faced with difficulties. In addition to providing the technical services they had furnished in the past, staff members were forced to arbitrate continuously in conflicts between workers and employers. Arbitration was an especially difficult task, for legal guidelines were either nonexistent or fraught with ambiguities.

The judgments of the placement commissions are a case in point. Labor contracts were clear in specifying that land could not go "totally" or even "partially" underutilized, but how would the term "underutilized" be defined? Ambiguities inevitably emerged. For example, a rotational field system had been used for generations throughout the South as a means of soil conservation. Even on working farms, at least a quarter of the arable land was sometimes left to lie fallow, not out of disinterest, but as part of an outmoded farming technique. Would the rotational field system now be unacceptable? If so, what would replace it, and who would pay the cost? If trees were planted on lands that could support a labor-intensive crop, was the planter guilty of underutilization? These are but a few of the questions that faced the local agricultural officials.

Charges of economic sabotage were also problematic. When was the sale of animals justified, and when was it not? What percentage of an owner's herd could be slaughtered at the same time and not merit the charge of sabotage? The regional bureaucracy was unable to resolve all the questions that emerged, and hostilities between landowners and farmworkers increased. Government officials had to deal with these and other questions on a local level, for the provisional government in Lisbon had not yet produced sufficient legislation to be used for national guidelines. During a period of eleven months, three provisional governments had produced only a handful of laws relevant to the agricultural sector. The first emerged on August 14, 1974, and opened up private game preserves to local hunters and owners of livestock. A second forced minor tax penalties for uncultivated lands. Another established liquidation commissions for the *Grémios de Lavoura*. A fourth decreed that *rendeiros* should be reimbursed for all investments on rented property, and two others guaranteed the automatic renewal of land rental contracts. A final piece of legislation gave a government agency the right to rent abandoned property.

The provisional governments that orchestrated the political revolution had not ignored the agricultural sector, but they had not made any major

---

[33] Interview with Fernando Oliveira Baptista, *Diário Popular*, February 12, 1975.

effort to transform it either. No law relevant to expropriation had emerged, and a law regulating land rental was still languishing in committee. The closest the government came to a concrete move toward agrarian reform involved the publication of the "Social and Economic Program" of February 20, 1975. Though vague regarding the actual nature of the agrarian reform, the plan did state that properties over five hundred hectares would eventually be expropriated and that owners would be compensated with government bonds.[34]

The slow pace of government intervention was partially the result of the outmoded bureaucracy and personnel deficiencies previously discussed, but it was also the result of a conscious decision on the part of key government officials. As the first winter of the revolution approached, a surprising range of MFA leaders argued that any major reform of the agrarian sector be postponed until other issues were resolved. The moderate Captain Melo Antunes presented this position to the MFA on December 28, 1974. He stated:

> Personally, I reject the rapid and radical transformation of the primary sector through what one might call the agrarian reform. . . . Everyone speaks of an agrarian reform, but no one knows what it is. Similar experiments in Latin America have been too costly in financial and human resources. . . . Our greatest immediate concern is to increase our industrial production.[35]

The radical General Vasco Gonçalves expressed a similar position in another address to the MFA Assembly on January 4, 1975. He said:

> Are we, at this moment, in the condition to adopt measures like an agrarian reform? . . . Do we not know that there have been agrarian reforms in various countries that have created many, many problems? . . . Are rural workers already sold on the idea of cooperatives? Are small farmers? . . . We run grave risks politicizing ourselves so rapidly: we can inadvertently fall into left-wing adventurism. That is to say [we run the risk of] taking positions and attitudes that are absolutely correct from a moral point of view . . . but are inappropriate to the practical realities of the moment.[36]

The argument for postponing the agrarian reform was rejected by other officers within the MFA. While Antunes and Gonçalves were urging that

---

[34] Ministério das Finanças, *Programa Económica e Social*, February 20, 1975.

[35] MFA Assembly, December 28, 1974, as recorded in Ramiro Correia, Pedro Soldado, and João Marujo, *MFA e Luta de Classes* (Lisbon: Ulmeiro, n.d.), p. 80.

[36] MFA Assembly, January 4, 1975, in ibid., p. 100.

the state *not* initiate "the rapid and radical transformation of the agrarian sector," the editors of the *Boletim MFA* were writing:

> It is necessary and *urgent* that agrarian structures be transformed. . . . Landowners, especially owners of latifúndia, should be obliged to meet minimum levels of production established by the government. . . . All absentee landlords should be replaced by public administrators who can either work the land directly or give the land to cooperatives and family farms.[37]

Arguing for immediate and substantial government intervention, the *Boletim* took a position quite distinct from that of either Antunes or Gonçalves. The public could only guess at which direction policies might take, for the provisional government was simply too divided to speak with one voice. The *Boletim* was controlled by the chiefs of staff of the famous Fifth Division and was closely associated with the ultraleft. But the urge to initiate an agrarian reform immediately was shared by individuals from other parts of the political spectrum as well. Henrique de Barros, an agrarian scholar who eventually became the elder statesman of the Socialist party, voiced fervent concern about the government's inaction in a January editorial entitled "Where Is the Agrarian Reform?"[38] The Communist leader Álvaro Cunhal demanded immediate action as well. On February 9, he addressed the Southern Agricultural Workers' Conference, stating: "Right now, without any more waste of time, it is necessary that all uncultivated or poorly cultivated lands be handed over to unemployed workers."[39]

The groups and individuals who called for immediate measures of agrarian reform were not strong enough to force the passage of any major legislation, but they were strong enough to guarantee that the coercive apparatus of the state would remain neutral in the event of an extralegal initiative from below. This is precisely what happened when the early occupations took place, and this is what gave them an importance that far exceeded their size and extent.

The Introductory Phase of the Occupations

As tensions between employers and unionized workers continued unabated, the latter assumed a more radical tactical position. After months of private

---

[37] *Boletim MFA* (Lisbon), November 16, 1974; also in Serafim Ferreira, *MFA: Motor da Revolução Portuguesa* (Lisbon: Diabril, 1975), p. 385.

[38] The editorial appeared first in the newspaper *República* (Lisbon), on January 18, 1975, and was published once again in *Diário de Notícias* on January 19, 1975.

[39] See *Diário de Notícias*, February 9, 1975, for the text of the conference in Évora. Note that this is not a call for occupations but a call for government action.

lobbying, public demonstrations, and even strikes, the unions began to use the decisions of the worker placement commissions as a justification for the seizure of lands. Near the end of September, the workers announced that they would soon proceed with the occupation of "all underutilized properties" in order to "do away with the large landowners" and to "guarantee the productivity of the land."[40] The threat was carried out on December 4 in Beja on a property called Monte de Outeiro. Twenty unemployed workers were placed on the property by the union committee but never paid. They continued working until the property was transferred from the owner's control under the provisions of the Decree Law 660/74.[41] The workers maintained control of the property and started the first postrevolutionary farming cooperative.

Shortly after the incident at Monte de Outeiro, the farmworkers of the lower Alentejo issued what came to be known as the Declaration of Beja. Beginning with the claim that four thousand men and ten thousand women were now unemployed, the declaration stated that the workers "recognized the need to generalize the occupations as a form of struggle."[42]

The Declaration of Beja served as an instigation for the first occupations but not in the manner one might expect, for most of the earliest occupations were carried out by individuals outside the union organizations. The second group of people to actually seize land were the landless *seareiros* and *rendeiros*.

The position of the *seareiros* was probably worse than that of any other class group in the agricultural sector. Being outside the union structure, *seareiros* did not enjoy the benefits of wage increases or placement commissions. Nor did they enjoy much attention from the central government. In late November 1974, the state had ruled that it had the right to rent underutilized property to landless farmers. This law might have served the interests of the *seareiros,* but two months had passed and it had not yet been put into effect. Now unionized workers were announcing that *they* would take control of the underutilized property and (presumably) put only their fellow members to work. The *seareiros* feared that they would not benefit from this plan either. The situation was especially bad for those who had earned enough in the past to purchase their own farming equipment on credit. If they could not secure planting contracts, they would be unable to meet their loan payments, thus losing their entire investment and their only means of earning a living.

Pressed by inflation and fearful of the future, landowners were refusing

[40] *Alavanca*, October 1, 1974.

[41] Decree Law 660/74 held that the state had the power to take control of any productive property that was not functioning in the national interest. At the time of its passage, the Council of Ministers assumed the law would apply only to failing industrial firms.

[42] *Alavanca*, February 7, 1975.

to provide *seareiros* with contracts. Panicked by the thought of having no income at all, small groups of *seareiros* moved onto properties and began to prepare for planting.

The *seareiros* were quickly joined by *rendeiros* who had been ousted from properties and were equally impatient with government inaction. The first phase of the occupations had begun. It was to last until the end of March and to involve approximately five thousand hectares.

The first occupation that was typical of the introductory phase occurred in January in Graça do Divor when a small group of *seareiros* seized a property of 132 hectares that had been the beneficiary of a state-funded irrigation project but had been left uncultivated. *Seareiros* in Beja followed suit, seizing approximately 750 hectares. In February, the pace of occupations quickened, and more than twenty properties were seized. Nine of these were in the district of Évora. Most of these lands were seized individually, several days apart, and all were occupied by small groups of landless peasants. Properties varied between 174 and 690 hectares in size.

The district of Lisbon was also affected by the February occupations. Two properties were seized in the county of Azambuja. One seizure was organized by *rendeiros* who had been expelled from a 500-hectare property six years earlier. Another involved the occupation of a 150-hectare farm that had been inactive for fifteen years.[43] The largest occupations of the month occurred in the district of Portalegre, in the county of Avis. There, on February 23, *seareiros* and *rendeiros* of the small farmers' league formed a caravan of forty-three tractors and occupied five properties totaling approximately 3,000 hectares.[44]

The right-wing coup attempt that precipitated the fall of the third provisional government on March 11 did not dramatically affect the pace of the seizures, which continued in March at a slightly decreased rate. But for the first time since the early occupations in Beja, reports of seizures led by farmworkers rather than landless peasants began to filter back to Lisbon. These reports were a portent of things to come.

The Meaning of the Early Occupations

The landless men and women who initiated the early occupations stressed that they merely wanted to protect their own livelihood. A spokesperson for the peasant leagues of Évora explained that the leagues' members were not "stealing" property. As he put it, "We only want to work the unfarmed lands and we want to pay rents for them."[45] José Soeiro, president of the farmworkers' union of Beja, denied that the early property seizures con-

---

[43] *Expresso*, March 22, 1975.

[44] *Diário de Notícias*, February 24, 1975.

[45] Ibid., March 6, 1975.

stituted occupations at all. During the second week of February he stated flatly:

> *There have been no occupations.* . . . The workers are just doing the work that the owners refuse to do. . . . They take action because the state is too slow to intervene. . . . It is obvious that as soon as the workers are paid, *we are not interested in the ownership of the land.* The land belongs to [private owners]. Let them keep it, but with the certainty that they will farm it properly.[46]

Though participants and allies tried to stress that the early seizures were not attacks on property relations per se, the actions did in fact have a revolutionary content. The class organizations that had formed as a seemingly innocuous part of a political revolution were now undertaking the redistribution of resources that the state itself had failed to introduce. This meant that individuals were assuming a role that the state had, at least formerly, reserved for itself. Most meaningful of all, the individuals involved had been successful in their actions. They had met with little resistance from landowners and, most importantly, no resistance from the state. Not a single participant in the occupations was either arrested or detained. The coercive apparatus of the state had remained passive in the face of a popular initiative.

The political revolution had had repercussions that forced the Portuguese nation beyond the bounds of a "bourgeois democracy." The structural change embodied in the formation of class organizations enabled the needy to articulate demands that the existing structure of property relations could not meet. When the state failed to right the imbalance and to change property relations itself, the landless took their own initiatives. One set of structural changes had led to another.

The early seizures were thus an important encroachment on both private property and the powers of the state. They illustrated that landless cultivators could take control of the land they needed without invoking any sanctions from the armed forces. This had a demonstration effect that was to influence more rural proletarians as the fourth provisional government initiated a social revolution.

Rethinking the Role of the Communist Party

Analyzing the land seizures in the context of the revolution as a whole, it becomes clear that the role of the Communist party has been misunderstood. The PCP was the only party to survive the fall of the democratic Republic

---

[46] Ibid., February 15, 1975; emphasis mine.

and the decades of dictatorship, but its longevity did not ensure its hegemony, in the Alentejo or anywhere else. To view the occupations as
products of the PCP's orchestration is to overestimate the party's unity
and power.

Years of clandestine activity had left the party with advantages and
disadvantages in the rural South. On the positive side, the party had a
longstanding reputation as a defender of workers' rights. Throughout the
Salazar-Caetano period party members and sympathizers were involved in
nearly every protest and strike activity. No other political party could claim
so many martyrs and so many years of dedication to the betterment of
farmworkers' lives. The party's prerevolutionary role gave its candidates
a distinct advantage when competing with new parties in local elections.

The PCP's role in Intersindical provided another advantage. Intersindical
was a federation of labor unions created by progressives in 1970 after
Marcelo Caetano liberalized state controls on the corporative union structure. The federation grew quickly, encompassing forty-one unions in only
two months.[47] In fact, the federation's growth was so rapid that its leaders
decided that future members would have to be sponsored by representatives
already inside the organization.[48] This exclusionary ruling ensured that the
federation did not fall into the hands of government stooges, but it also
guaranteed that the organization remained in the hands of its original
founders. Since most of the original founders were sympathetic to the
Communist party, the party came to have a strong influence on the organization long before the 25th of April.

After the 25th of April, the federation was charged with the responsibility
of choosing the organizers of the future farmworkers' union. Intersindical's
appointees organized *pro-sindicatos* to perform the functions of unions
until membership could be recruited and elections could be held. As would
be expected, these individuals were sympathetic to the PCP.

The Communist party thus had important advantages when the political
revolution opened up organizational competition in the South, but history
had left the party with important disadvantages as well. The PCP was
neither as powerful nor as monolithic as outsiders imagined. Part of the
party's problems derived from its origins. At its founding in 1921, the
party was basically a small, urban organization rooted in Portugal's industrial and service sectors. Only a small percentage of the party's mem-

[47] Albano Lima, *Movimento Sindical e Unidade no Processo Revolucionário Português*
(Lisbon: "Avante!" 1975), p. 12.

[48] The original unions in the federation were the Cashiers, Metalworkers, Woolworkers,
Bank Workers, and Medical Advertising Workers.

bership was engaged in agricultural work.[49] This was not surprising given that isolation and illiteracy discouraged rural residents' association with any party at all, but it left the party's leadership with an especially difficult problem during the years of the dictatorship. If the rural base of the party had been relatively weak under the democratic regime how could it possibly be expanded under the repressive conditions of the dictatorship?

The answer depended in large part on the activities of the party's leadership, but here, too, the PCP encountered a major disadvantage, for the party's leaders were the primary targets of the nation's secret police. Few escaped capture, torture, and imprisonment. It is significant that the members of the Central Committee that emerged in the aftermath of the revolution had spent an average of fourteen years each in jail.[50] Their long years of confinement (and typically exile) sharpened their resolve and solidarity but weakened their contact with what might have been the party's base. The secret police had succeeded in creating an atmosphere of such fear and suspicion that party leaders could not confidently estimate how many would-be sympathizers existed. They could guess that the structural conditions of the South would provide them with a solid base of support, but there was no way of being certain how deeply the support went or of estimating how other left-wing parties might divide it.

A third problem for the party in the South derived from the peculiar nature and history of southern rural employment. With no freedom of association, the party had to promote both itself and its social goals through participation in illegal activities related to employment. From the thirties through the early sixties, this is exactly what the organization did, but by the mid-sixties, the employment situation had changed. Migration had greatly eased the region's employment problems and reduced the party's potential rural base. The *praças de jorna* became less and less frequent and deprived the party of the closest thing it had to a collective association. The change was demographic and not ideological, but the effects were damaging nevertheless: the people who were most likely to furnish the party with an active base of support were earning a living elsewhere.

The question of the party's true strength in the Alentejo was therefore a rather open one in the early seventies. José Pacheco Pereira has even argued that the PCP had only a "residual" presence there by the late sixties, inasmuch as strikes and other acts of opposition had decreased.

---

[49] Pacheco Pereira estimates that rural workers comprised less than 6 percent of the party's 1921 to 1926 membership. Of these, less than 5 percent lived in the Alentejo. See José Pacheco Pereira, "O PCP na I República: Membros e Direcção," *Estudos sobre o Comunismo* (September-December 1983), pp. 6-10.

[50] Tom Gallagher, *Portugal: A Twentieth-Century Interpretation* (Manchester: Manchester University Press, 1983), p. 112.

His conclusion seems hasty, however, for this particular trend was more likely the result of the easing of the employment crisis than a direct measure of the party's support. Yet it does demonstrate the difficulty of evaluating the party's popularity in such a controlled society. The critical point is that the party's leadership had no means of evaluating its popularity either. After living in clandestinity and exile longer than any other set of communists in Europe, the PCP leadership was uncertain about its level of support and, quite properly, unwilling to take the South for granted.

This uncertainty led to a cautious but changing sort of behavior in the South. Like all the other institutions left over from the old regime, the Communist party was to be shaped and altered by the structural changes associated with the political revolution. The chapters that follow will illustrate that its position vis-à-vis the land seizures changed from ambivalence to opposition to direct involvement according to the stages of the revolution itself.

Did the party play a role in the occupations? The answer is unquestionably yes—but it was not a vanguard role.[51] The PCP followed the landless onto the land because it sought to (and had to) respond to the needs of this extremely important constituency. The organizational need to be responsive was greatest after September 1975, when the party had lost all hope of capturing state power. It was not until then that the organization tried wholeheartedly to assume a leadership role. But the movement had started at the base and had proceeded for months as a local response to multifaceted structural change. The nature of this change is analyzed in the following pages.

[51] The party's inability to play a vanguard role in the revolutionary period is a repetition of a pattern established years earlier. Ana de Vale Estrela wrote of the workers' protests under Salazar: "Although the PCP was politically active [in the rural South] it definitely did not lead the protests." Similarly, José Pacheco Pereira writes that the party and its newspaper, *O Camponês*, joined the movement for the eight-hour day *after* the workers themselves. See Ana de Vale Estrela, "A Reforma Agrária Portuguesa," p. 236, and José Pacheco Pereira, *Conflitos Sociais nos Campos do Sul de Portugal* (Lisbon: Publicações Europa América, 1982), p. 151.

THREE

The Social Revolution and Mass Mobilization
in the Countryside

THE officers who engineered the April coup were united in their belief that the colonial wars should be ended but were of greatly varied opinion on other important political issues. As the participatory institutions that emerged during the political revolution began to articulate citizens' demands and to solicit an immediate government response, the political differences within the military became more public and more marked.

The moderate third provisional government (lasting from October 1974 to March 1975) confronted more serious internal conflicts than any of its predecessors. Three related factors explain why. First, the simple passage of time made it more and more difficult to postpone the controversial issues that previous governments had avoided. Second, the parties that comprised the government became more and more competitive as the spring electoral campaign approached. Third, the MFA became more divided as individual officers began to vote in assemblies according to particular party positions or to follow the initiative of particular military leaders.

One of the third government's most serious internal conflicts was a controversy over union federations. Intersindical's unofficial association with the PCP was a source of great consternation for non-Communist parties. The PSP, the PPD, and many other parties argued that the Communists had a structural monopoly on the labor movement and insisted that multiple union federations be permitted. The Communists countered with the argument that multiple federations would only divide the working classes and serve the interests of reactionary forces. After prolonged and bitter debates, the government ruled in favor of a single union federation on January 22, 1974.

The move was viewed as proof that the Communist party had gained the ascendancy in the coalition of forces at the head of the state and that the whole character of the revolution would soon change. One could not be certain that this were true, but the idea that the revolution was veering leftward was sufficiently widespread and sufficiently alarming to provoke a right-wing reaction. On March 11, troops loyal to the ousted General Spínola attacked the barracks of an artillery regiment outside Lisbon, killing one and wounding eighteen others.[1] The revolt was put down within a matter of hours, and 111 people were arrested.

The failed coup illustrated what certain individuals on the left had been saying all along: the political revolution had not gone far enough. Reactionaries in the armed forces and in the private sector still posed a threat to the MFA and to the political changes that it was trying, albeit slowly, to bring about. As long as the classes that benefited most from the old regime were left intact, the revolution would be threatened by a reactionary civilian-military alliance. If a new wave of reaction were to be prevented, property relations would have to be altered and the armed forces would have to be further reformed.

The MFA was the first institution to be changed by the failed coup. After an all-night meeting on March 12, the two-hundred-member MFA Assembly ruled that a Revolutionary Council be established as a permanent part of the executive body of the government. The council was composed of twenty-four officers representing the army, the navy, and the air force. The emergence of the Revolutionary Council marked the abandonment of previous plans for a European-style liberal democracy, for it implied that civilian government would not be supreme even after elections were held.

The composition of the fourth provisional government also confirmed that the revolution had changed its tone. The government was still a coalition of diverse political parties, but the coalition was now weighted in favor of the Communist party and its ally, the Movimento Democrático Português (MDP).[2] The PCP and the MDP directly controlled four out of eighteen ministries, including the all-important Ministry of Finance, which had been previously controlled by a moderate Socialist named Ruí Vilar.

Party affiliation was not the only aspect of the government's composition that made it different from its predecessors. The ministries themselves had changed. The fourth government created a Ministry of Agriculture and selected as its head a young man named Fernando Baptista. A former student of Charles Bettelheim, Baptista was one of many young professionals who were decidedly on the left but not affiliated with the Communist party. Baptista's role would be a difficult one as the revolution wore on.

---

[1] António Spínola was the leader of the first provisional government. Though he was not active in the MFA before the 25th of April, he was handed power by the movement's leaders because he was thought to be the highest-ranking officer sympathetic to the coup. By the summer of 1974, however, it was clear that Spínola was more conservative than the majority of the MFA leaders. He resigned under pressure on September 30, 1974, after arguing that decolonization was proceeding too quickly and that the Communist party was leading the country toward "new forms of slavery."

[2] The MDP-CDE (MDP) was legally an independent political party with no formal links to the PCP, but there were no major policy differences between the groups and they eventually formed an electoral alliance in 1976.

In less than a month, the forces controlling the Portuguese state had altered radically, and the country was soon submerged in a new wave of change. The social revolution had begun.

THE SECOND PHASE OF THE OCCUPATIONS

The emergence of the fourth provisional government provoked a new wave of structural change in the agricultural sector. Although some of the changes were the desired result of deliberate government policies, many were the undesirable by-products of events that the government could not control. Both sorts of changes played a determining role in the emergence of a new phase of land occupations.

Economic Crisis and Pressure on the Land

The Revolutionary Council initiated the redistribution of private property on March 14, 1975, when it nationalized all domestic banks and insurance firms. Shortly afterward, most basic industries were nationalized.[3] These moves threw private businessmen into a panic, and investments in nearly all endeavors dropped off sharply.

The civil construction industry was one of the first affected. The industry had been troubled since the early months of the revolution when housing starts began to drop off, but labor pressures had forced wages to rise steadily anyway. In April, shortly after the fourth government came to power, wages reached an average of nearly two hundred escudos a day—a 60 percent increase in a twelve-month period. Such a rapid rise in labor costs would have been difficult to support in even an ideal investment climate, and the new situation was certainly less than that. Building starts nearly came to a standstill, and projects in progress were halted unfinished.

The collapse of the civil construction industry had immediate ramifications in the Portuguese countryside, especially in the district of Évora, which had furnished so many of the industry's workers. Migrant laborers had begun to return to their homes voluntarily in November and December to take advantage of increased agricultural wages, but now they returned involuntarily, unemployed, and in great numbers.

Regional unemployment was also increased by the European recession. The industrialized countries that had provided employment for hundreds of thousands of Portuguese in the past were experiencing their own economic crises and accepting fewer and fewer of their poorer neighbors'

---

[3] Electricity and oil companies were nationalized on April 16, 1975. The cement, cellulose, beer, and tobacco industries were nationalized on May 14.

workers. A government employment expert estimated that fifty thousand Portuguese workers were forced to remain in their home country because of the change.[4] Thousands more were compelled to return home unexpectedly after layoffs and dismissals.

Another structural change that contributed to unemployment and to the pressure on the land was the demobilization of troops. At the time of the April coup, Portugal's armed forces employed approximately 250,000 men. More than half of these were stationed overseas in the African colonies. By the time the fourth provisional government came to power, each of the former colonies had negotiated its independence, and the dismantling of the colonial army was sending thousands of men into the labor market every month. The demobilization meant still more unemployment and more pressure on the primary sector. The servicemen who risked their lives in the colonial wars, only to return home and face unemployment, were understandably the target of special concern.[5]

The demobilization, the European recession, and the civil construction crisis combined to cause a rapid increase in rural unemployment, and this increase in turn brought on a second wave of occupations. Just as the prospect of no income had led *seareiros* and *rendeiros* to occupy land during a first phase of seizures, it now forced unemployed wage workers to do the same. This second phase of the occupations lasted from the end of March to the beginning of July. The occupations in this phase differed from previous occupations in that they were more frequent and involved more people and property, but they were similar in that they were not orchestrated from outside the workers' communities. They were usually the result of a local initiative directed at the solution of a local problem of unemployment.

The Role of Formal Organization

To state that the first- and second-phase occupations were largely local initiatives is not to deny the role of formal organizations. The land seizures were autonomous, but they were not necessarily spontaneous nor were they devoid of organizational associations. Formal organizations played a part in the occupations, though they did not initiate action from above.

The most important organization in the second phase of the occupations was the farmworkers' union. Union delegates and committee members participated in scores of land seizures. This fact does not detract from the

[4] *Alavanca* (Lisbon), interview with Dr. Maria do Carmo Nunes, Ministry of Labor, May 28, 1975.

[5] The demobilization of troops helped to precipitate land occupations in revolutionary Russia and in post-World War I Italy as well.

autonomy of the seizures in general, for the farmworkers' unions—at that time at least—were *local* organizations headed by local leaders responding to local pressures. Neither a national union leadership nor a national party leadership could afford to ignore local leaders or local demands because both unions and parties were trying to build support.

The role of the farmworkers' unions is especially relevant to the debate about the role of the Communist party because union presence was often mistaken for party presence. Outsiders believed that the farmworkers' unions were simply conduits for Communist party policy, but the real role of the *sindicatos* was more complex.

As was stated in the last two chapters, the PCP had access to the farmworkers' unions through Intersindical and the *pro-sindicatos*, but access did not guarantee control. Even if the party leadership had wanted to manipulate the unions for its own ends, it would have been unable to do so. To begin with, the PCP had operated legally for just over one year, and it simply did not have the manpower to staff every union local. Even if this had been on the agenda, urban organizers would have had great difficulty being accepted on the local level, for the people of the South are notoriously suspicious of outsiders. The party's connection with the *pro-sindicatos* may have yielded a network of local union candidates who expressed sympathies with the PCP, but this network was far from homogeneous and its members were primarily responsive to the petitions of those in their immediate surroundings.

The preceding point can be illustrated through a comparison of the unions in Évora and Beja. Union leaders in Évora faced a more troubled situation than their counterparts in Beja, for unemployment was higher and contract compliance was lower. As a consequence, workers in Évora were more desperate and more anxious to take action than their counterparts in the South. Évora's union leaders responded to their constituents' needs with verbal and concrete support for property seizures. The following statement is representative of the union president's position: "We see only one possibility in the Alentejo. We must *take* the large properties from the big landowners and form cooperatives."[6]

This was not a vague endorsement of a future agrarian reform nor a call for the support of government-led expropriations. It was an unambiguous call to take control of property immediately. It was also a response to local conditions and grass-roots initiatives. It came from a man named Manuel Vicente who had worked on the estates of Évora since the age of eight. He was truly representative of the men who elected him, for like them

[6] *Alavanca*, February 21, 1975. Emphasis mine.

neither he, nor his father, nor his grandfather had ever owned "even a handful of land."[7]

Responding to a different local situation, the district leader of the Beja union took an approach more in keeping with Communist party policy in Lisbon. He stated:

> During this first phase, we are not very supportive of the formation of cooperatives. [People should beware] of the appearance of opportunists who seek to involve workers in the occupation of farms. They create insecurity and confusion among the workers and lead them toward actions that are not, by any means, the most advisable.[8]

The difference in the union leaders' positions illustrates the diversity within the farmworkers' movement and helps to explain the marked contrast between the second-phase occupations in Beja and Évora. As the occupation chronology indicates, the workers in Beja seized no property at all in April and May, while the workers of Évora seized nearly 14.5 thousand hectares. In one case the workers' organization supported the occupations, in the other it did not. In both cases, the union's position was determined by local conditions.

Just as the likelihood of seizures was heightened by the support of trade unions, so was it heightened by the changes within the military. The new roles that the military assumed during the political revolution took on added meaning as the social revolution unfolded. COPCON and the dynamization campaigns still provided networks for constant civilian-military interactions, but the nature of the interaction changed, and the changes contributed to the likelihood of seizures.

The campaigns lost one of their principal raisons d'être with the elections for the Constitutional Assembly on April 25. The fear that the elections would be dominated by reactionary forces was put to rest with the publication of the electoral results. The Socialist party polled 38 percent of the vote, the Communist party polled 12.5 percent, and the PPD (which was reformist, though not actually socialist) polled 26.4 percent. The nation seemed "safe" for some kind of socialism.

Ironically, the electoral results had negative implications for the leaders of the dynamization campaigns. Arguing that the legacy of the dictatorship was still too strong to permit enlightened voting, the far-left leaders of the campaigns had urged that the elections not be held. When the Revolutionary Council, after long debate, decided that the elections would be held as

[7] Vicente explained this in a personal interview in October 1980. He repeated the phrase about the land in another interview published in António Barreto, *Memória da Reforma Agrária* (Lisbon: Publicações Europa-América, n.d.), p. 11.

[8] *Alavanca*, May 7, 1975.

planned, the campaign leaders urged that people cast blank ballots in support of the MFA itself and against the "bourgeois" party system.[9] Less than 6.9 percent of the electorate followed the suggestion. The elections were thus an unambiguous endorsement of major social change but also an embarrassment to the far left. The "hearts and minds" of the people remained with the "bourgeois" party system.

The new political context demanded a reorganization of the campaigns. A new emphasis was put on "civic action" aimed at building both the physical and social structures that officials found lacking during the earlier phase of the campaigns. Roads would be constructed and sanitation facilities expanded, but more overtly political projects would be undertaken as well.

The campaigns were reorganized into various departments, including a Department of Agriculture that focused primarily on the "agrarian reform" and on the extension of "agricultural credit."[10] In this and all other departments, the new emphasis was on "the support of direct democracy organizations at the base, such as residents' associations, workers' commissions, and cooperatives."[11]

The emphasis on civic action created a stimulus for the seizure of land by sometimes providing a political infrastructure through which the rural poor could mobilize. The campaigns' "Sessions of Enlightenment" never concluded with a march onto a particular owner's land, but they sometimes ended with the formation of a workers' commission or a village council that organized a seizure months later.

COPCON's connection with the seizure of land was much more direct. As was mentioned previously, COPCON was started during the political revolution to mediate disputes that the overburdened government and the disassembled police force were unable to resolve. Since the political revolution was, by definition, a period of minimal property transfer, the disputes that COPCON first mediated did not normally involve a challenge to property relations. During the social revolution, on the other hand, challenges to property relations became more and more common, and COPCON was drawn into an increasing number of struggles over factories, houses, and farms.

The political ideology of COPCON's leader assumed a new importance as the stakes of the property struggles grew higher. Otelo Saraiva de

[9] Avelino Rodrigues, Cesário Borga, and Mário Cardoso, *O Movimento dos Capitães e o 25 de Abril* (Lisbon: Morães, 1974), p. 194.

[10] *Boletim MFA* (Lisbon), May 20, 1975.

[11] Ramiro Correia, Pedro Soldado, and João Marujo, *MFA e Luta de Classes* (Lisbon: Ulmeiro, n.d.), p. 177.

Carvalho, or Otelo, as he was best known, was a proponent of *poder popular*: people's power. The term was seldom defined, but it was essentially a shorthand for a decentralized social system based on units of direct democracy in neighborhoods, schools, and places of work.

As the revolution progressed, Otelo was faced with more and more opportunities to transform *poder popular* from a political blueprint to a real-world phenomenon. The cooperatives that emerged from the seizures could well form the cornerstone of the sort of self-managing society that the far left proposed. Thus, when workers sought the "neutrality" or passivity of coercive forces for a given occupation, Otelo cooperated regardless of what other elements of the MFA or the government advised. The organization that was founded to assist the government in maintaining order in the political revolution began to impose an order of its own.

COPCON's role in the support of land occupations is nicely illustrated by Otelo's own description of the seizures and the reaction they engendered.

> Was there resistance to the idea of the agrarian reform within the MFA? It is quite evident that there was. A ferocious resistance. I remember when the first occupations . . . took place. There was a tremendous scandal, and right away my comrades on the *Conselho dos Vinte* . . . came to me with a photograph of an occupied farm in which there appeared . . . a rural worker shouldering a rifle in defense of the occupied farm. They said "Have you seen this? It is impossible. You have to send troops, our troops, to get those people out of there." I said, "No, no, if anyone goes and tries to take that away . . . I'll go there and defend the land with the workers." So there was immediately a profound disagreement, . . . and this disagreement existed always, throughout the process.[12]

Otelo was not the only far-left officer who played a role in the second phase of the land occupations. An active unit commander named Rodrigues in Vendas Novas, Évora, is reported to have lent military support to several occupations in the surrounding region, and it is no coincidence that such a high percentage of the land invasions occurred in the geographic area adjoining his unit.

The support that far-left military men furnished was usually of a practical rather than a coercive nature—that is, they provided transportation rather than guns. Transportation was of critical importance in the second phase

---

[12] The Conselho dos Vinte was a council of twenty officers chosen to lead the MFA. The quotation is from an Associated Press interview with Otelo Saraiva de Carvalho, as recorded in Otelo Saraiva de Carvalho, *O Povo é Quem Mais Ordena* (Lisbon: Assírio e Alvim, 1977), p. 149.

of the occupations. Whereas *seareiros* and *rendeiros* seizing single properties in small groups could usually furnish their own transportation, wage workers often could not. As was stated previously, the second-phase occupations began as a response to massive unemployment, and as a consequence, second-phase occupations typically involved scores if not hundreds of individuals—too many to be accommodated on single farms. Large numbers of people had to be transported to several properties, often situated miles apart. Vehicles had to be commandeered from somewhere, and the local military unit provided a ready option.

Thus, the political leaning of the local unit commanders came into play when occupations were being planned, but it is important to emphasize that the absence of sympathetic officers did not prevent the workers from moving ahead with a seizure. This is illustrated by Map 3.1, which details the location and political orientation of Portugal's military units during the first year of the land seizures. Although the map categorizes the units as simply left, right, or neutral and does not distinguish between the Communist left and the far left, even with these general categories, it is possible to see that occupations were not limited to areas dominated by leftist units. The district of Portalegre, for example, contained no leftist units but was the scene of many second-phase occupations.

Military support was not by any means a necessary precondition for the occupations, though it was, in some cases, an important contributing factor. The rural poor usually acted independently, requiring only the "neutrality" and not the overt support of the local coercive forces.

The Meaning of the Second-Phase Occupations,

Like their earlier counterparts, the second-phase occupations were a challenge to both property relations and the existing state. Unlike the first-phase occupations, however, these later occupations had a special meaning because they were a challenge to a state that was attempting to orchestrate its own social revolution. The fourth provisional government was indisputably in favor of land *expropriation*, but its policy toward land *occupation* was ambiguous, if not actually hostile. This is where simplistic generalizations about Communist orchestration break down. Less than three weeks after the fourth government emerged, its Council of Ministers announced that it would soon expropriate irrigated properties over fifty hectares and dry land properties over five hundred hectares. The announcement was tempered, however, by another important government proclamation:

The Council of Ministers reaffirms that the true beneficiaries of the

MAP 3.1
Political Character of Military Units:
Southern Portugal, 1975

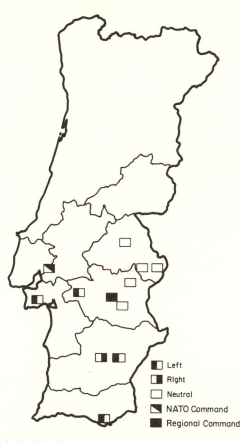

SOURCE: Diniz de Almeida, *Ascensão, Apogeu e Queda do MFA*, 2 vols.
(Lisbon: Edições Sociais, 1976), 2: 20.

agrarian reform must be the rural agricultural workers and the small-
and medium-sized farmers. Toward this end, the council appeals to
the workers' sense of self-discipline. *From this moment on, land
occupations will no longer be tolerated, as they are damaging to the
agrarian reform and therefore reactionary.*[13]

[13] Government proclamation as printed in *Jornal Novo* (Lisbon), April 19, 1975. Emphasis
mine.

The following day the Communist party published a statement supporting the ministers' proclamation.[14]

Why would a revolutionary government oppose these seemingly revolutionary attacks on existing property relations? There are several reasons. First, the left-wing leaders of the fourth provisional government feared—quite rightly—that the spontaneous seizure of property would panic small- and medium-sized farmers and drive them into the ranks of reactionaries. They also recognized that the success and longevity of the social revolution depended very much on economic performance and that extralegal redistribution of property would provoke fear and eventually economic chaos.[15]

The leaders also recognized that any cooperatives formed before the harvest season would encounter severe capital-flow problems, for occupations involved only the seizure of land and not bank assets. Occupiers who seized land early would have no means of support until crops could be marketed. The earlier the seizure took place, the more grave the problem.

A fourth reason for the radical provisional government to object to the seizures was the recognition that spontaneous seizures would jeopardize the particular agrarian reform that the ministers themselves were trying to design. If the individuals involved in the seizures took control of properties the government did not want seized or if they organized cooperatives with what officials believed were too few members, a most uncomfortable situation would arise. The government would be forced to either disassemble the structures and incur all the political costs involved or allow the structures to continue, unchallenged, but in obvious contradiction to the national plan. The greater the number of seizures, the more difficult the government's future role. There were thus many reasons for the government to oppose the land seizures, but it could not pay the high political price of putting them to an end.

The continuation of the occupations illustrates a great deal about the internal problems of the revolutionary state. That the preceding paragraphs have focused on government policy rather than state policy is due to the fact that no state policy existed. The revolutionary state had no single policy toward occupations because its disparate elements could not concur.

[14] Partido Comunista Português, "Manifesto de Apoio," April 16, 1975, mimeographed. The government statement was released on April 15.

[15] There are other cases in which left-wing parties opposed spontaneous seizures of property. Most relevant to the Portuguese case was the opposition that the Unidad Popular expressed toward the land seizures in southern Chile. See Chapter Eight for a discussion of the Chilean case. For a discussion of the Spanish Communist party's opposition to anarchist farm cooperatives during the Spanish Civil War, see Edward Malefakis, "Peasants, Politics, and Civil War in Spain, 1931-1939," in Robert Bezucha, ed., *Modern European Social History* (Lexington, Massachusetts: Heath, 1972).

The government had a policy, but the government was only part of the state. It could not control what other factions of the state apparatus did. Sections of the state's coercive apparatus acted in direct contradiction to the government decree. Not only did far-left officers tolerate the occupations, they often lent them active support.

The side of the fourth provisional government was riddled with thorns, but few cut as deeply as the presence of Otelo, who was simultaneously critical of government policy, independent of government control, and wildly popular. Stopping him coercively would invoke the hostility of thousands, but allowing him to operate without restraint compromised the very foundation of the government's political program.

The struggle between Otelo and the fourth provisional government was essentially a dispute over two plans for socialism. The far left's plan, emphasizing maximum decentralization and autonomy, conflicted with the PCP's plan, emphasizing centralized planning and top-down coordination. The PCP in the government and the Gonçalves wing of the MFA were skeptical about the feasibility of the far-left plan. Complete decentralization might seem appealing from a moral perspective, but it could lead to inequities and chaos, especially in situations of scarcity.

These two perspectives were as old as socialism itself, but they became particularly volatile during the social revolution, for they were held by different factions within a single state. Conflicts within the state itself provided the ideal environment for autonomous popular action, because as long as the government and the armed forces failed to act in concert, government policy decisions were unenforceable. The second-phase occupations were thus an illustration of a crisis in state authority. The fourth provisional government had sought to lead a social revolution but found itself being led instead.

July 1975: A Period of Transition

The month of July marked a period of transition in the capital and in the countryside. By the end of the month, both the central government and the movement for the occupation of farms would assume new forms. The dynamic behind the transition derived from two sets of structural change, one that the government initiated and another that it was unable to control.

Government-Initiated Changes

In an attempt to meet the needs of an increasingly vocal rural proletariat and to reestablish state authority in the countryside, the cabinet of the fourth provisional government passed a land expropriations law on July 5,

1975. The government recognized that structural conditions in the latifúndia region made the transfer of land in the South almost inevitable and that the conditions of the transfer could only be controlled with the passage of a law. But producing a land expropriations law in the spring of 1975 was no easy task.

Though much has been made of the Communist party's ascendancy in the fourth provisional government's cabinet, it is important to remember that the cabinet was a coalition of forces and that the Communists, like all other groups, were constrained by the coalition. "Even the Communists," as a PPD leader put it years later, "could not do what they pleased."[16] The Communists could not pass a law which was so radical that the more moderate parties would leave the government, for this would exacerbate an already obvious crisis of legitimacy and possibly bring down the government altogether. On the other hand, they had to endorse a law that would legitimate as many of the existing occupations as possible or face the difficult task of dismantling structures that the working class itself had already created—a task any revolutionary party would seek to avoid.

The July expropriations law was very much a child of these constraints, with aspects to placate both the moderate parties in government and the radical workers of the occupied farms.

The first aspect of the law that placated moderates was the concept of an "area of intervention." The legislation stated that properties would be subject to expropriation only if they were located in "an area of intervention to be defined by law." In other words, land expropriations would not take place throughout Portugal but in a limited area to be defined at a later date. Regardless of the size of their holdings, certain landowners would be immune from expropriation.

Article 2 aimed at satisfying the demands of the moderates as well. It held that landowners affected by expropriation would be granted a reserve of land on their original property, providing that they farmed the land directly and earned all or most of their income from the farm. The reserve area would be at least 30 hectares in size, regardless of the quality of the land, and the productive value of the land would be equivalent to fifty thousand points, the points being related to government tax records and roughly equivalent to 50 hectares of irrigated land and 200 hectares of dry land.

The July law also aimed at satisfying moderates concerning the issue of indemnity. In addition to enjoying the right to a reserve, landowners would receive government payment for any expropriated properties. The law did not state what form the compensation would take (postponing this

[16] Personal interview, Lisbon, September 1979.

for further legislation), but it did legitimize the idea of indemnity, thereby upholding, indirectly, the argument that landowners had a "right" to the property affected and that they deserved compensation for the loss.

Despite provisions that were clearly favorable to landowners and to those who defended private property, the Law of Expropriations was nevertheless a legitimation of major transfers of farming property and in this sense a concrete attempt to meet the needs and desires of the poor farming population. As its text states clearly, the law was designed "to destroy the social and economic powers" of the "latifundiários and large agrarian capitalists" and to contribute to the "liberation and emancipation of agricultural workers and small farmers."[17]

The law also aimed at legitimating the revolutionary actions that agricultural workers and small farmers had taken independently. When asked about the rationale behind the fifty thousand points—that is, why lands exceeding this value, as opposed to any other, were deemed subject to expropriation—a minister involved in the design of the law admitted, "We wanted to protect as many of the occupations as possible."[18] The law did serve this purpose, for only 1.9 percent of the occupied properties fell below this limit.[19]

The application of the land expropriations law required the reorganization of the highly centralized Ministry of Agriculture, and this required another structural change. If the state's bureaucracy were to manage the massive responsibilities that the legal transfer of property required, it would have to be expanded on the local level. Cognizant of this requirement, the fourth provisional government drew up plans for Regional Agrarian Reform Centers (CRRAs) in late May, but the centers did not actually begin to function until much later.

As Table 3.1 indicates, only two centers existed on July 5 when the expropriations law was endorsed by the Council of Ministers, and only two more were added before the law was promulgated at the end of July.

The fact that the new state bureaucracy was slow in penetrating the latifúndia region helps to explain why the passage of the July law did not have the stabilizing effects that many hoped it might. The existence of the law did not stop the occupations. While the pace slowed in Portalegre, occupations actually increased more than 600 percent in Évora and 300 percent in Beja.

[17] The Law of Expropriations, or Decree Law 406-A/75, as it stands officially, is reprinted in Joaquim Barros Mouro and Manuel Barros Mouro, *Reforma Agrária: Legislação, Notas, Comentários* (Vila Nova de Famalicão: Centro Gráfico, 1976), pp. 167-189.

[18] Interview conducted by Michel Drain, Lisbon, March 1979.

[19] Fernando Oliveira Baptista, *Portugal 1975—Os Campos* (Porto: Edições Afrontamento, 1978), p. 53

TABLE 3.1
Regional Agrarian Reform Centers

District	Date of Founding
Beja	May 24
Setúbal	June 16
Portalegre	July 9
Évora	July 9
Santarém	September 17
Castelo Branco	September 17
Faro	September 17
Lisbon	September 23

SOURCE: Joaquim Barros Mouro and Manuel Barros Mouro, *Reforma Agrária: Legislação, Notas, Comentários* (Vila Nova de Famalicão: Centro Gráfico, 1976).

Changes Initiated Outside Government

The explanation for the continuation of the land seizures does not rest solely with the structure of the state's bureaucracy. Changes in the composition of the government and in the political leanings of the MFA also provided an impetus for the continuation if not the acceleration of the seizures of land.

The Communist party's ascendancy in the fourth government had always been precarious, but July brought successful attacks from the party's left *and* right and, in turn, a dramatic crisis in legitimacy. Between July 11 and 16, the government lost the support of a third of its cabinet, as two ministers from the PSP, two ministers from the PPD, and two independents resigned.[20] The crisis of legitimacy extended deep into civil society. Waves of antigovernment protest washed over the cities of the North and South. On July 13, ten thousand Catholics marched through the streets of the northern city of Aveiro to protest the government-sanctioned takeover of a Catholic radio station. Two days later, thousands of Socialists marched through the streets of the capital chanting "O Povo Não Está Com o MFA!"—The People Are Not With the MFA! Throughout the country, Communist and MFA party offices were burned and sacked, and individual party members were subjected to physical and verbal abuse.

Hostility to the government was not limited to attacks from the Socialist

[20] The resignations were a protest against both the government's control and censorship of the media in general and its inability or unwillingness to oust a group of far-left workers who had seized control of the Catholic radio station.

74

party and the groups to its right. Otelo and the advocates of *poder popular* became increasingly critical of government policies and, most important, increasingly influential in the MFA itself. The passage of the *Guia Povo-MFA* in the MFA Assembly of July 8 is an illustration of this. The *Guia* was an official endorsement of the system of decentralized democracy that the party had tried to discredit in the past. The assembly's endorsement suggested not only that the PCP was losing ground but that the nation might soon embark on a course that would provoke a right-wing reaction. No one could predict just how far the hostilities might go, but most observers were guessing that the days of the social revolution were numbered.

Under the conditions of these new constraints, patience was no longer a virtue. The crops could not wait while the government decided which of the nation's thousands of farms would be subject to expropriation, and the landless peasants and workers could not be certain that a new conservative government would not jettison the idea of expropriation altogether. If land were to be redistributed—i.e., if the latifúndias were to be destroyed—the rural proletariat would have to act quickly and without the backing of government officials. The law had been signed by the government, but it was up to the people to apply it.

The seizures occurring in the month of July thus had an ambiguous political nature. On the one hand, the occupations were a blatant offense to government authority, for the law stated clearly that property transfers could only be initiated by agents of the state. On the other hand, workers were seizing properties that were earmarked for transfer anyway. They were merely speeding up the transfer process by taking on a task the state itself was not equipped to assume.

THE THIRD PHASE OF THE OCCUPATIONS

The Withering Away of the Social Revolution

The dissolution of the fourth government in August 1975 suggested that the social revolution was indeed drawing to a close. The composition of the fifth government reinforced this suggestion, for though it was headed by the leftist Vasco Gonçalves, it contained a more conservative group of ministers than its predecessor. The government was nicknamed "the most provisional of the provisional governments," as Vasco Gonçalves, the Communist party, and the MDP were the targets of increasingly severe verbal and even physical attacks. Indeed, a total of three dozen Communist party offices were burned or otherwise vandalized by the month's end.

Criticism from different factions of the MFA continued unabated. Moderate Socialists produced what came to be known as the Document of the

Nine, alleging that a "revolutionary vanguard" was exercising power in a "wild and anarchic" way and demanding that the composition of the provisional government reflect the composition of the Constitutional Assembly.[21] Far leftists, led by Otelo, produced the Document of COPCON charging the Communist party with "marked authoritarianism" and arguing that PCP administrators had "proved themselves incapable of offering a solution to the principal problem they faced."[22]

Cognizant of the severity of the crisis, PCP leader Álvaro Cunhal called a press conference on August 20 and announced:

> The events of the past weeks illustrate that . . . the revolution is in danger. There is no time to lose. . . . The crisis that the Portuguese revolution faces grows more grave every day. . . . [But] the crisis might be overcome . . . through the consolidation of revolutionary measures . . . such as the nationalizations and the agrarian reform.[23]

The factors that had prevented the PCP from a wholehearted endorsement of the occupations in the past had lost their meaning in the new crisis. The harvest season was now over or close at hand (depending on the crops).[24] There was no chance that the peasantry would be attracted into an alliance with the proletariat. Most important, with only a tenuous connection with the government and dwindling influence within the armed forces, the Communist party and its allies had no possibility of overseeing an orderly, state-directed transfer of property. Indeed, it seemed that the only way that property might be transferred at all would be by the people themselves, through extralegal occupations.

The recognition that the social revolution was drawing to a close thus brought about a new phase in the chronology of land occupations. New levels of support from the PCP combined with new levels of support from farmworkers' unions. The pockets of union resistance that had existed during the second phase of the occupations disappeared. In the district of Beja, the *sindicato* began to take an active role in the organization of property occupations, seizing up to a dozen properties in a single day.

The personnel of the recently developed CRRAs, though formally discouraged from doing so, sometimes took an active role in the seizures as well. Chosen in part because of their commitment to the expropriation

---

[21] The most easily accessible translation of the document is in Jean Pierre Faye, *Portugal: The Revolution in the Labyrinth* (Nottingham: Spokesman Books, 1976), pp. 165-171.

[22] Ibid., pp. 172-179.

[23] Partido Comunista Português, *Documentos Políticos do PCP*, Speech of August 20, 1975, 3: 87, 97-98.

[24] Wheat was harvested around July; tomatoes were harvested in August, September, and October.

program, these individuals took supportive action in the belief that the government might not last long enough to put the program into effect. Their actions sometimes consisted of supplying technical assistance after lands had been seized, but they sometimes attempted, like the cultural dynamization teams before them, to establish workers' commissions that would organize occupations months later. In Portalegre, the CRRA office was particularly active.

With new levels of assistance from the Communist party, the farmworkers' unions, and occasionally the local agents of the CRRA, workers of the latifúndia area undertook an increasing number of occupations. The pace varied from district to district in the months of August and September, but by October, the districts of Beja, Évora, and Portalegre were experiencing the most massive occupations of the revolutionary period.

The change in the month of October was due to two factors. First, the frail fifth government had collapsed on September 6 and had been replaced by a government in that the Socialist party had the ascendancy. Vasco Gonçalves was removed from his position as prime minister, and the new cabinet included only one minister from the PCP and no ministers from the MDP. For many observers, the composition of the sixth provisional government was confirmation of the widespread suspicion that the social revolution was at an end. This perception no doubt contributed to the "now-or-never" attitude of would-be occupiers throughout the latifúndia region.

Ironically, the second factor that explains the acceleration of occupations was a piece of legislation sponsored by the new government—the government that so many leftists deemed reactionary. Taken as a whole, the sixth provisional government was certainly more conservative than its two immediate predecessors, but, as will be discussed at length in the third section of this study, its Ministry of Agriculture was far from a bastion of reaction. The ministry was headed by a socialist named Lopes Cardoso, who was a prominent leader of his party's left wing and a longstanding proponent of expropriation. In an effort to preserve the existing collective units, Cardoso promoted legislation that dealt with their most severe problem. The cash-flow crisis foreseen by the fourth provisional government had become chronic by August and September of 1975, and there were cases where collectives were unable to pay salaries for periods of twenty weeks.[25] Meeting a need for funds, Cardoso sponsored legislation that allowed government loans to be used for the payment of workers' salaries.[26]

[25] A journalist visiting occupied properties in August reported that "no one seems to have any money." *Expresso* (Lisbon), August 30, 1975.

[26] This was Decree Law 541-B/75, published on September 27, 1975.

The passage of the new law alleviated some financial problems but also proved to be a stimulus for more occupations. Landless workers who were unable to gain employment on private farms now knew that the state would guarantee their salaries if they became involved in collective farming. Since joining an already established collective was difficult, new occupations were initiated. In the month of October alone, a full 144,681 hectares were seized in Évora, while 186,467 hectares were seized in Beja. This represented a 60 percent increase over the previous month. As had happened throughout the social revolution, one structural change had led to another.

The difference between the third-phase occupations and the occupations that preceded them was qualitative as well as quantitative. The first-phase occupations began with farmworkers but were dominated by landless *seareiros* and *rendeiros*. The second-phase occupations were dominated by jobless dayworkers. The third-phase occupations were dominated by the latter group as well, but they included a much greater proportion of permanent workers. Though it began with the isolated actions of a small number of dayworkers, the movement for the seizure of property eventually encompassed a much broader array of political and class groups.

The End of the Occupations

The period of the massive occupations stopped abruptly in the first week of December. The end of the occupations can be attributed to four factors. First, the last harvest season had drawn to a close, and workers were less likely to seize fields that were barren than fields that were not. Second, Cardoso had begun to reorganize the regional bureaucracy. In early October he fired the CRRA leaders in Portalegre. By December he dismissed their counterparts in Évora, Beja, Castelo Branco, Setúbal, and Santarém.[27] The minister thus removed many of the bureaucrats who might have provided "independent" assistance to occupying workers in the past.

Third, small- and medium-sized farmers had joined with large landowners in dramatic protests against the agrarian reform in general and the occupations specifically. The demonstration with the greatest impact (and the highest number of participants) took place on November 24 in the town of Rio Maior, just to the north of Lisbon. Twenty-five thousand people set up a blockade and threatened to cut off Lisbon and the South from all access to the North. Spokesmen for the demonstrators urged that the occupations come to an immediate halt and that the sixth provisional government put an end to the "anarchy" in the latifúndia region. The costs

[27] Baptista, *Portugal 1975*, p. 58.

78

of allowing the occupations to continue began to rise, as public opposition turned vehement.

The final and the most important factor that explains the end of the occupations was an unsuccessful military coup that took place in Lisbon on November 25. Like its predecessors, the sixth provisional government was the focus of great public hostility. Its prime minister, Pinheiro de Azevedo, was the target of a bombing only two days after he assumed office and was later held hostage in his house for thirty-six hours by a crowd of twenty thousand supporting a civil construction strike. More important than the hostilities directed toward individual members of the government, however, were the growing hostilities within the MFA itself. The movement became so riddled with partisan divisions that even a semblance of unity was difficult to maintain. On September 25, for example, 3,500 uniformed servicemen joined an antigovernment street demonstration in Lisbon. The same day, an officer from COPCON made off with one thousand military weapons and joined an underground political party. On October 3, 70 soldiers from Beja refused transfer orders to the Azores. On October 6, hundreds of soldiers in Oporto occupied a barracks in protest of an order of transfer for their regional commander. On October 21, a far-left soldiers' organization called Soldiers United Will Win (SUV) called for all citizens to "battle against the government."

Given the magnitude of dissent within the military, it was only logical to expect an attack from the right or the left. The far left acted first and organized a coup on November 25. After less than twenty-four hours, the coup was effectively put down, and some one hundred far-left officers and enlisted men were arrested, including Otelo himself. COPCON was disbanded, and the moderate António Ramalho Eanes was made the army chief of staff.

Within less than two weeks, the occupations of farm land came to a halt. The vast majority of the region's dayworkers had already found permanent employment on worker-controlled farms. Now, they faced a radically changed environment. With new staff in the regional bureaucracy, with military units under new commands, and with the fields of the Alentejo and Ribatejo barren, the poor people of the latifúndia area ceased their incursions into the private sector and turned their attention to the defense of the properties they now controlled.

The Meaning of the Third-Phase Occupations

The third-phase occupations spanned two provisional governments, the first a remnant of a social revolution and the second a reaction to the changes that the social revolution brought about. Though there may be some doubt that the fifth provisional government sought to control the occupations, there is little doubt that the sixth government sought to do so, and both failed. This is because the seizures were not the product of orchestration "from above" but were instead the outgrowth of a complex and varied series of structural changes that allowed people to take action from below. While some of these changes originated in the period of the political revolution and some originated in the period of the social revolution, each had effects that no single clique or party or even government could control.

The only entity that could control the occupations was the coercive apparatus of the state, and it was not until this apparatus was totally transformed that the occupations came to a halt. Class organizations, unemployment, the fear of a right-wing reaction, and credits for salaries (i.e., all of the factors that had stimulated occupations in the past) continued long after November 25, but the occupations did not. The dismantling of COPCON and the purging of far-left officers marked a mending of the breach between the government and the armed forces. The consolidation of state power had taken place, and the option of autonomous mass action was eliminated. The words of a woman farmhand from Montemor describe the change succinctly. When asked why the people of her area no longer initiated occupations, she replied, "Because we fought against the land-owners and we won. Now we'd have to fight against the state and this you just don't do."[28]

FROM the first land seizures of the political revolution, through the larger land seizures of the social revolution, through the massive land seizures of the harvest season, four provisional governments proved unable to control the transfer of property in the latifúndia South. As has been discussed, much of the government's inability was due to problems within the state itself. Strictly speaking, the state, as a controlled entity, did not truly exist until after the 25th of November. The government, the bureaucracy, and the forces of coercion acted, not in concert, but as independent units with serious internal divisions of their own.

But as serious as the problems of state consolidation were, they were not the impetus behind the land seizures. They merely provided the opportunity for the rural poor to do as they wanted. The impetus for the land seizures ultimately came from below, from landless peasants and farm laborers who saw the seizure of property as the best means they had of coping with the increased insecurity that structural changes had thrust upon them.

[28] Personal interview, Montemor-o-Novo, September 1978.

80

Interviews with workers who took part in the first- and second-phase occupations illustrate that the seizures of land proceeded not because they were orchestrated by outside groups but precisely because outside groups did *not* win the confidence of the rural poor. The rural poor who seized property did so precisely because they believed that no outside group would look after their interests; no organization, no party, no government could be trusted to give the workers what they wanted when they wanted it. The workers had to initiate action alone and *then* look to outside groups for help. Support, especially from the Communist party, was indeed forthcoming but largely in a later phase of the occupation process and only after the workers themselves had led the way. As António Bento, a landless peasant who helped seize a property during the first phase of the occupations, recalled:

> The people here decided to occupy the lands and went ahead and did it. Of course others came here and criticized, trying to discourage us—people whom we wouldn't expect. . . . Those who criticize the occupations say the agrarian reform will help us more, [but] the people are leading the way.[29]

The people led the way in countless other cases as well. Another example is furnished by the occupation of Torre Bela, a property in the district of Santarém that belonged to the Duke of Lafões. The occupation was led by an elected local leader named Wilson. Wilson had been chosen by a village assembly to go to the Ministry of Labor in Lisbon and petition for some sort of relief for the chronic unemployment in the area. He traveled between Lisbon and his village for over a month, meeting with government officials in various ministries, but returned with no concrete offers of assistance. He became discouraged and, reading of successful land seizures elsewhere, decided to propose an occupation to the residents of his own village. He called a meeting and suggested a land seizure "without vandalism and without political parties." Only a third of the individuals present voted to go ahead with the plan. Needing more support, he went to Macussa, a poorer village three kilometers away, which actually adjoined the property he proposed to occupy. His idea was accepted with unanimity. The next day, approximately one hundred local residents, the vast majority of whom were unemployed farmworkers, gathered nervously at the border of the property and walked four kilometers to the main house. The owner of the property was far from the scene. Neither he nor the local armed forces nor the Institute for Agrarian Reform nor the political parties of the area were informed of the occupation before it took place.

[29] *Expresso*, April 25, 1975.

Another illustration of autonomy comes from São Miguel de Outeiro in the northern district of Viseu. This was the only occupation on record that took place outside what came to be the agrarian reform zone. It occurred in May and involved a property that technically belonged to a foundation. A local landowner had died three years earlier and had left his property to the foundation on the condition that a children's nursery and an old-age home be built for local residents. The construction was never even started, and village residents became impatient. They took their complaints to military officers when a cultural dynamization group passed through and were advised to continue to talk with the heads of the foundation. When subsequent dialogue brought no results, a local resident went through the streets with a loudspeaker suggesting that the property be occupied forthwith. Retelling the story, the leader recalled that "the whole town" followed behind.[30] No political parties, no military men, and no union leaders were involved. In fact, the district had no farmworkers' union at all.

It was precisely because the occupations were so often autonomous that they were not so easily controlled. General Pezarat Correia, the commander of the military units in southern Portugal during the occupation period, confirmed this assertion in an interview in August 1975.

> I am not in favor of the wildcat occupations, nor is the Ministry of Agriculture, nor the Institute of Agrarian Reorganization; the union leaders who have come here to speak with me are equally opposed to occupations at this time. Even the leader of the PCP, Álvaro Cunhal, . . . said he was sympathetic to the preoccupations I voiced to him concerning this subject. . . . When all is said and done, it seems that no one is in favor of the occupations. But they continue. Could it be that the workers of the Alentejo have escaped the control of the political parties?[31]

Four years later, after the general had had time to reflect on the experience, his insistence on the autonomous nature of the occupations remained unchanged. "The workers initiated the occupations. . . . Theirs was a completely spontaneous initiative. . . . It was not the MFA, nor any political party, nor the government that motivated this phenomenon."[32]

[30] *Diário de Notícias* (Lisbon), June 6, 1975.

[31] Interview with Pezarat Correia in *Expresso*; as cited in João Garin, *Reforma Agrária: Seara de Ódio* (Lisbon: Edições do Templo, 1977), pp. 127-129.

[32] Interview with Pezarat Correia, *O Jornal* (Lisbon), June 29, 1979. The views expressed here were reiterated in a personal interview in Paris in June 1981. Respected by diverse political groups, Correia is one of the few major figures in the revolutionary period to have maintained continuous communication with the entire spectrum of civilian and military actors

This chapter has pointed to the underestimated autonomy of the property seizures by illustrating how the economic and political changes associated with the social revolution brought on waves of occupations that a series of governments proved unable to control. Taking a closer look at the revolution within the revolution, the chapter that follows focuses on the occupations in a single county and illustrates the process at the microlevel.

associated with the agrarian reform. His assessments of the occupations are thus especially valuable.

FOUR

The Land to Those Who Work It: The Revolution in Portel

THUS far, we have seen the drama of the occupations in a broad panorama. Viewing the process from a distance, we have become familiar with the setting in which the drama took place, the rhythm of the action, and the names of the major actors. We know that the occupations were confined to an area of latifúndia, that they were initiated by dayworkers, and that the movement eventually included the whole spectrum of landless cultivators.

However, many questions fundamental to the drama remain unanswered. Although there were cases in which whole towns occupied properties, Portugal's land seizures usually attracted only a part of any given community and only a part of the landless laborers within it.[1] What were the social characteristics that distinguished the workers who participated in the occupations from the many who did not? What, on a more personal level, made seemingly ordinary people take such extraordinary political actions? No one can better answer these questions than the people of the Alentejo themselves, and it is on them that this chapter focuses. It illustrates, through a study of a single county, that the impression of autonomy gained in panorama holds as well in close-up.

A PORTRAIT OF A SOUTHERN COUNTY

The actors on whom we focus are the residents of the county of Portel. Situated in the south of the district of Évora, Portel stands almost in the center of the zone of the occupations—or, as it has come to be known in Portugal, the agrarian reform zone. Map 4.1 illustrates both the zone and the location of Portel.

The road leading from Évora to Portel is paved with small gray stones, uniform in size and evenly placed, side by side, one after the other, for hundreds of kilometers throughout the Alentejo. Built by hand during the dictatorship, the road is a monument to the patience of the local workers

---

[1] For one of the few land seizures on record that involved a whole town, see the story of an occupation outside the area of the agrarian reform zone in the district of Viseu in *Diário de Notícias* (Lisbon), June 6, 1975.

MAP 4.1
The Agrarian Reform Zone and the
County of Portel

Portalegre

Évora

Portel

Beja

MAP 4.2
The Parishes of Portel

Monte do Trigo

São
Bartolemeu
do
Outeiro

Oriola

Santana

Portel

Amieira

Vera Cruz

Alqueva

and a testament to the chronic unemployment that plagued them for decades.

Like so many of its people, Portel's lands are poor. Entering the county in the parish of Monte de Trigo, one sees lands of good quality, but most of the county contains soil rated as only third- or fourth-class.[2] With grossly uneven ownership patterns, poor soil, no factories, and only a handful of opportunities in the service sector, the standard of living in Portel prior to the revolution was very low. The larger parishes maintained grade schools, but there were (and are) no high schools in the county. Two of the parishes had no sewer system, and the parish of Alqueva still had no electricity in 1980. Map 4.2 illustrates the parishes of Portel.

Transportation was limited to infrequent bus service to and from the city of Évora and to horse carts, bicycles, and, for the better off, motorcycles. As late as 1980, a store clerk could name the owner of every car in the town of Portel, and even then, one gasoline pump serviced the entire county.

Prior to the revolution, money was such a scarce commodity that the county contained no banks.[3] The town of Portel contained a single dry goods store that serviced the whole area, and the little money that circulated was spent for food (often sold outdoors) and for wine, aguardiente, and coffee in small taverns. For the working man, the taverns were and remain the center for social and recreational life. Most male workers drink a quick cup of coffee there before work and then return after dinner for hours at a time. For the outsider, these all-important cafes were sometimes hard to find, for in small villages with low literacy and few strangers they were often unmarked.

Until the 1960s, escape from Portel's essentially preindustrial social system was rare. The sons of a pharmacist or a few government functionaries might go to high school in Évora, but most men associated with farming were locked into the same positions as their fathers before them. Except for the young girls who became domestic workers in urban areas, the pattern for women was the same. As an agricultural worker in Oriola explained, "If you let your daughter marry a rich[er] man [than yourself], he'll just make a fool of her and the rest of the family."

When economic change in Lisbon and abroad offered emigration opportunities in the early sixties, the county's rigid social structure began to change. The son of an aging farmworker would find a job in the shipyards

---

[2] Small farmers, cooperative members, teachers, and even shoemakers talked about soil quality with some assurance. All shared the opinion that the local land was generally third- or fourth-class; all agreed that there was no first-class soil in the county; and all suggested that the soil around Alqueva was the worst in the area.

[3] The first and only bank in the county was established in 1976 in the town of Portel.

TABLE 4.1
Employment in the Primary Sector
Southern Portugal, 1970

			Farmworkers			
Region	Employers	Farmers	All	Dayworkers	Permanent Workers	Others
Beja	1.6%	17.0%	77.7%	65.8%	8.6%	3.3%
Évora	1.0	10.6	87.6	76.0	9.9	1.7
Portalegre	1.6	14.1	83.2	67.9	13.3	2.0
Portel[a]	0.2	8.0	91.4	87.0	3.4	1.0

SOURCE: Instituto Nacional de Estatística, *Estatísticas Agrícolas Distrito de Beja, 1960-1974; Estatísticas Agrícolas Distrito de Évora, 1960-1974; Estatísticas Agrícolas Distrito de Portalegre, 1960-1974* (Évora: INE, 1976).
NOTE: These figures differ slightly (less than 1 percent) from the figures published in the *Recenseamento Geral da População de 1970*.
[a] These figures are for the county of Portel. The figures for Beja, Évora, and Portalegre are for whole districts.

outside Lisbon; the son of another laborer would sneak across the Spanish border and hitchhike to France; and others would emigrate legally, sometimes as far as Germany and even Switzerland. For men who could not or would not leave the area permanently, there was temporary agricultural work picking sugar beets or grapes in France.[4] All of these avenues provided some relief from the chronic unemployment of the past and an increase in the standard of living for family members who stayed behind.

Despite the new opportunities afforded by emigration, the population of Portel was heavily dependent on agricultural wage labor on the eve of the revolution. As late as 1970, 71 percent of the county's work force was engaged in farming, and a full 87 percent of these laborers had no permanent positions. The county was one of the more proletarianized of the area, as Table 4.1 illustrates.

Despite its location in the center of the agrarian reform zone, Portel was not a typical county of the Alentejo, if indeed such a county exists.[5] In addition to having a relatively large proportion of landless laborers, Portel also had a relatively large population of Communist voters. Before the

---

[4] The picking of sugar beets has now been mechanized, so fewer workers have this opportunity. On the eve of the revolution and increasingly today the harvesting of endives is replacing the harvesting of sugar beets as a source of seasonal employment abroad.

[5] For an interesting article that discusses the often unrecognized diversity within the Alentejo itself, see Manuel Villaverde Cabral, "Agrarian Structures and Recent Rural Movements in Portugal," *The Journal of Peasant Studies* (July 1978).

TABLE 4.2
Communist Vote in Constitutional
Assembly Elections, 1975

Portel	46.4%
Beja District	39.0
Évora District	37.1
Portalegre District	17.5
Agrarian Reform Zone[a]	33.4

SOURCE: C. Costa et al., *As Eleições no Portugal de Abril* (Lisbon: "Avante!" 1980).
[a] Districts of Beja, Évora, and Portalegre; counties of Almeirím, Alpiarça, Benavente, Chamusca, Coruche, Golega, and Salvaterra de Magos in Santarém; and counties of Alcáçer do Sal, Grândola, Palmela e Santiago do Caçem in Setúbal.

occupations gained momentum, Portel distinguished itself as one of the most Communist counties in Portugal. In the elections for the Constitutional Assembly in April of 1975, 46.4 percent of the county's electorate voted for the PCP, a full 13 percentage points higher than the average for the agrarian reform zone as a whole. Table 4.2 illustrates Portel's comparative position.

Portel was chosen as a site for intensive study precisely because of the characteristics described above. An "extreme case" in terms of class divisions, it was also an extreme case in terms of more explicitly partisan measures. Choosing such a case was the best way of addressing the question of autonomy. If the Communist party wanted to initiate occupations "from above," Portel was the logical place to do it—first, because it had so many workers without land and, second, because it offered an especially firm base of support. If, on the other hand, it appears that the occupations developed with a certain autonomy in Portel, one can suppose with some security that they developed with even more autonomy in other counties where the Communist party had weaker implantation.

The question of autonomy and other questions related to the characteristics, motivations, and opinions of the occupations' participants were addressed through a detailed questionnaire administered by the author in October 1980. One hundred eight men were interviewed individually and confidentially with the questionnaire reprinted in Appendix I.[6] The sample

[6] My U.S. nationality was less of a problem in 1980 than it was when I first started my research in 1977. By the time I administered the questionnaire, I was affiliated with the Centre National de la Recherche Scientifique in Marseille and thus presented myself (quite properly) as a member of a French research team. I never lied about my nationality, but it

included representatives of various classes and class fractions, including members of worker-controlled farms, permanent private farmworkers, *seareiros*, *rendeiros*, and small farmers.[7]

The Results of the Research

A close look at the history of the occupations in Portel confirms the importance of social class as a determinant of action. The overwhelming majority of the men who participated in the occupations were wage and salaried laborers—either dayworkers or permanent farmworkers. Landless farmers (i.e., *rendeiros* and *seareiros*) and small farmers played an insignificant role. Conversations with wage workers suggested why. *Rendeiros* and *seareiros* were thought by many workers "to be worse than the landowners." *Rendeiros*, as one worker put it, "were cheaper, meaner, and less generous." Where "certain cultured landowners treated one with courtesy," *rendeiros* "behaved grossly." Some, it was argued, were "even richer than the landowners." The author cannot speculate on the veracity of these impressions, but their content had political importance, for when Portel's occupations began in June, the farmworkers stood alone against the *agrários*. Table 4.3 illustrates the job categories of those who seized property and those who did not.

The high percentage of wage workers in the participants group is not surprising, given what was suggested in the previous chapter. What is surprising perhaps is the high percentage of permanent workers within the participants group. Nearly 20 percent of the participants interviewed left a permanent position to join a worker-controlled farm. This is perplexing. Divisions within the rural proletariat assumed a special importance after the 25th of April. As was mentioned previously, many permanent workers were reluctant to ally themselves with dayworkers in the new labor unions. In this case, however, the two class fractions managed to act together. In

---

remained ambiguous for many. Interviews lasted between thirty and ninety minutes and were conducted by the author and two Portuguese research assistants, both of whom had worked for the Gallup affiliate in Lisbon and were chosen from a group of six after a pretest in a neighboring district. The sample was restricted to men only, not because the author lacks appreciation for the economic and political contributions of women but because the study focuses on individuals who either were or continuously sought to be *permanently* employed. In a region of chronic underemployment with a strong emphasis on differences in gender roles, women did not fit this description.

[7] I am very conscious of the criticism of questionnaires and admit that sometimes responses in questionnaire interviews do not correspond to the truth, but the problem of veracity emerges with any source of information, be it from historical archives, government statistics, or open-ended interviews. Multiple measures were used here to counteract the disadvantages of any single measure.

TABLE 4.3
Occupational Breakdown of Participants
and Nonparticipants

	Participants	Nonparticipants
Dayworkers	70.7%	28.4%
Permanent farmworkers	19.5	25.4
Seareiros	4.9	10.4
Rendeiros	—	9.0
Small farmers	2.4	25.4
Others	2.4	1.5
	N = 41	N = 67

N = 108

TABLE 4.4
Participation Rate for Various Types of Cultivators

	Participants	Nonparticipants
Dayworkers	60.4%	39.6%
Permanent farmworkers	32.0	68.0
Seareiros	22.2	77.8
Rendeiros	—	100.0
Small farmers	5.6	94.4
Others	50.0	50.0

N = 108

fact, although permanent workers were not as likely to participate in the occupations as dayworkers, one out of three permanent workers took part in a seizure of land. Table 4.4 illustrates the rate of participation for the various types of cultivators interviewed.

What were the factors that determined if a permanent wage worker would participate or not? The previous chapter suggested that permanent workers began to take part in the occupations only in the last phase of the movement, after September 1975. The study of Portel confirms the generalization because all the permanent workers who participated in Portel participated after this date. The question of why they participated after September rather than after July or June has thus far remained unanswered, but taking a closer look at the cases enables me to suggest a reason.

The presence of permanent workers in the last phase of the occupations is not the result of a sudden ideological conversion. On the contrary, when they existed at all, explicitly political justifications assumed a secondary role. Having asked the respondents "Why did you participate in the oc-

90

TABLE 4.5
Age Breakdown of Participants and Nonparticipants

	20-29	30-39	40-49	Over 50	Total
Participants	17.0%	22.0%	48.8%	12.2%	100.0%
Nonparticipants	4.5	23.9	34.3	37.3	100.0

N = 108

cupations?'' 100 percent of the permanent salaried workers gave responses that were wholly materialistic, having to do with money rather than ideals. Twenty-five percent responded that they wanted to ''earn more,'' and nearly 62 percent responded that they ''wanted to maintain a permanent job.'' This last response is especially revealing of what transpired. With only one exception—a man who was convinced by his brother—each of the permanent workers who participated in the occupations occupied the farm on which they were working, and they did so, as a tractor driver explained, because ''if we didn't, others would.'' Faced with a take-over and conscious that the possibility of employment on another private farm was minimal, these workers participated in the occupations in large part because there was no alternative. As a shepherd explained, ''What was I going to do? Put the flock in a sack and head for France?'' He had to stay, and he stayed.

Related to these cases were the ones in which occupations were initiated by the landowners themselves. Hearing that their property was going to be occupied, or simply fearing the same, landowners were said to have telephoned from Lisbon or Évora and urged their own men to occupy first. Confronted with a group of permanent workers who claimed a property was ''already occupied,'' dayworkers, in some cases, went elsewhere.[8]

Whereas place of employment helps to explain the participation of permanent workers, age helps to explain the participation of farmworkers as a whole. Generational differences have political implications in most societies, and Portugal's rural South is no exception. There is a complex but strong relationship between age and participation in the land seizures. With what has often been written concerning the positive correlation between age and conservatism, one might expect a predominance of younger men among the participants in Portel. In fact this is not the case. Table 4.5 illustrates the ages of men who did and did not seize property.

[8] I do not know of cases of ''owner occupations'' in Portel but heard stories of these in the county of Évora and in the district of Portalegre.

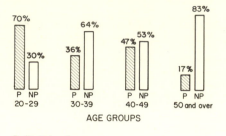

AGE GROUPS

P: Participants
NP: Nonparticipants

FIGURE 4.1
Participation in Land Seizures
among Four Age Groups

Almost half of the occupiers were between 40 and 49 years old, and the great majority of the men (61 percent) were over 40. The generational breakdown of the group that did not participate in the occupations shows relatively fewer men in the age 40-49 category and fewer younger men as well. How can this be explained? First, it is probable that the relatively low frequency of men in the 20-29 category is a reflection of the effects of conscription and urban migration: there were simply fewer young men in the area. Figure 4.1 shows that the *rate* of participation for the youngest age group is indeed very high. A full 70 percent of the youngest men in the sample participated. Within the set of younger dayworkers interviewed, almost all had participated in the occupations. In fact, the only younger dayworkers interviewed who did not participate were away on military duty.

The high proportion of participants between 40 and 49 years of age also has an explanation. These are the men who began their work lives before emigration, during the period known as "the years of hunger." It is possible that their especially difficult experience in the past reinforced their class consciousness and made them more susceptible to radicalization after 1974.

The link between radicalization and form of employment is often discussed in rural sociology. Experience in urban settings in construction or factory work is thought to contribute to radicalization and class consciousness.[9] Following this line of reasoning, one would expect that a high percentage of the men with industrial and service experience would have taken part in the land occupations, but this is not the case. In fact, as Table 4.6 illustrates, only 40 percent of all the men who worked in industry or

TABLE 4.6
Employment History and Participation in the Occupations

	Participants	Nonparticipants
Worked in industry or service sector	40%	60%
Worked abroad	15	85

N = 108

the service sector seized land. Even fewer of the men with work experience abroad took part in the seizures.

Most of those who *did* work outside agriculture or abroad but did *not* take part in the seizures were either smallholders, renters, or permanent workers with small plots. Thus, we might conclude that neither of these two forms of work experience overrides "relation to property" as a determinant of behavior, but this is not the whole explanation. If we analyze the group of farmworkers who participated in the seizures we find that just under one in four had work experience outside agriculture or outside Portugal. This is a significant minority, but still a minority. Why is the group not larger?

Part of the explanation relates to the location of Portel. Men from the interior of the Alentejo had fewer ties in urban Lisbon or abroad. But the low percentage is best explained by the nature of the sample itself, for the pool contains no men who were serving as directors of worker-controlled farms and is thus restricted to the rank-and-file of the occupation movements. With few exceptions, cooperative farm *leaders* had all spent time outside of their home parishes, either in France or in the industrial belt around Lisbon. The largest cooperative in the county was directed by a laborer in his late fifties who had spent years working in France. Other cooperatives were led by men who had worked in civil construction in Lisbon; another was led by a man who had worked on a public construction job at a nearby dam. During and after the occupations, these men played an important mobilizational role. The quarter of the "rank-and-file" participants who shared similar work experience contributed greatly to the movement, too. Thus, some relationship between work experience and radicalization probably exists, but it is neither direct nor universal and deserves more investigation.

[9] See Caroline B. Brettel, "Emigration and Its Implications for the Revolution in Northern Portugal," in Lawrence S. Graham and Harry M. Makler, eds., *Contemporary Portugal: The Revolution and Its Antecedents* (Austin: University of Texas, 1979), for a discussion of the political effects of emigration.

TABLE 4.7
Knowledge of Repression among Participants
and Nonparticipants

	Knowledge	No Knowledge
Participants	43.9%	56.1%
Nonparticipants	11.9	88.1

N = 108

Political experience has a much more direct relationship to participation than work experience. There is, for example, a strong positive association between participation in occupations and what might be called knowledge of repression. When asked if they knew anyone in their village who had been punished for criticizing figures of authority during the dictatorship, fewer than one in four of those interviewed said yes. The low percentage of people who had personal knowledge of repression is not surprising. Shoemakers, store owners, small farmers, and dozens of farmworkers informed the author that there had been little open conflict in the county before the 25th of April. As a pharmacist in Portel explained:

The workers of this zone suffered greatly, but they suffered silently. The men of the Alentejo have a certain dignity. . . . There was no trouble here before the revolution. There was no point in making a spectacle and getting nothing in return.

Landless laborers echoed his assessment. When asked why there was so little conflict before the revolution, farmworkers always mentioned the futility of revolt. A middle-aged man on the Cooperativa dos Gregos explained: "Resistance? Only for a few. For me, the father of children, there was no use. I'd go to prison or go underground, and my family would go hungry. It would have been foolish."

Despite the generally low level of overt criticism and repression in the area, there were marked differences within the community concerning knowledge of dissent. Dividing the survey sample between participants and nonparticipants, significant differences in political awareness emerge. Table 4.7 illustrates the contrast. Occupiers had greater knowledge of repression than nonoccupiers. Comparing the two groups, one sees that knowledge of repression is four times as frequent for men who seized land as for men who did not. Knowledge of repression can be related to two factors. It might derive from more personal contact or personal involvement with the underground opposition, or it might indicate no more than a better

TABLE 4.8
Willingness to Talk Politics among Participants
and Nonparticipants

	Talked Politics	Did Not Talk Politics
Participants	19.5%	80.5%
Nonparticipants	7.5	91.5

N = 108

TABLE 4.9
Nature of Interaction
with Wealthier Members of the Community
among Participants and Nonparticipants

	Friendly	Purely Professional	Hostile
Participants	70.6%	17.6%	11.8%
Nonparticipants	93.0	7.0	—

N = 108

knowledge of local history. In any case, occupiers seemed to have a clearer vision of a repressive past than nonoccupiers.

Just as the participants in the occupations were more aware of political repression, so were they more likely to have "talked politics" in the prerevolutionary period. Asked if they were "accustomed to talking politics with friends before the 25th of April," only 12 percent of the entire sample said yes. This is not surprising, given the presence of secret police and casual informers. What is surprising is the high percentage of occupiers who risked political conversation in the prerevolutionary period. Table 4.8 illustrates that nearly one in five of the men who participated in land seizures discussed politics before the revolution. Thus, the survey indicates that politicization before the 25th of April contributed to the probability of occupations after.

Prerevolutionary forms of social interaction seem to have affected the likelihood of participation as well. Speaking of the period before the 25th of April, 84 percent of the men interviewed said that they "were accustomed to speaking with people who earned much more than themselves." Asked to characterize these conversations, the sample gave the responses illustrated in Table 4.9.

95

TABLE 4.10
April 1975 Party Choice among Participants
and Nonparticipants

	Socialist Party	Communist Party	Other	No Response
Participants	31.7%	58.5%	—	9.8%
Nonparticipants	49.3	22.4	19.3%	9.0

N = 108

Given what was stated in Chapter One concerning the social structure of the rural South before the 25th of April, it is not surprising to find that nearly one in six of the men who participated in occupations had overtly hostile relations with the dominant classes. Indeed, it is surprising that nearly two-thirds had friendly relations with members of a superior class. The very high percentage of nonparticipants in the same category suggests yet another factor that might have affected the probability of participation. It is likely that for many the empathy engendered by friendly cross-class interaction tended to mitigate the hostility that differences in wealth so often produce.

A final factor affecting the likelihood of participation in the occupations was "party preference." Many individuals inside and outside the scholarly community assume that most of the participants in the occupations were Communists. Indeed, with the high level of party support in Portel, this is not an unreasonable assumption. However, reality is not so simple. Measuring party preference by vote in the April elections immediately preceding the occupations, one finds the pattern illustrated in Table 4.10.

The proportion of men voting Communist is evidently rather high, but *voting* for a party and having one's actions determined by that party are quite different. The debate about autonomy relates to this latter point, but the data are interesting in highlighting the mixed partisan preferences of the occupying group.

The frequency of Communist voters is higher for the participants group than for the nonparticipants, but the frequency of Socialist voters within the occupying group is also notable. Even if one supposes that none of the occupiers who refused to respond to the question voted Socialist, Socialist voters comprised one-third of the occupying group. Essentially, one can generalize and say that the occupations attracted men of the left, or "progressives," as the Portuguese would say, but one cannot conclude that the occupations attracted individuals from only one party.

96

TABLE 4.11

Community's Assessment of Where the Idea
of the Occupations Originated

From the workers themselves	34.1%
From the unions	17.1
From the Armed Forces' Revolution	29.3
From political parties	17.1
No response	2.4
	100.0

N = 108

THIS brief investigation of the social characteristics of the participants enables one to draw at least a profile of the typical man who took part in a seizure of property. He was likely to be a temporary worker, approximately forty-five years old, with some knowledge of repression, a certain politicization before the revolution, and little friendly contact with the dominant classes. He was also (as a result of these characteristics) likely to be a man of the left. He would probably vote Communist but had at least a one-in-three chance of voting Socialist.

Why did these men decide to take part in the occupations? From where did the idea of the occupations emerge? Table 4.11 provides the responses furnished by the participants themselves.

It is important to note that a relative majority of the participants believed that the idea for the occupations came from "the workers themselves." No other group had an equivalent influence. This suggests that even at the level of inspiration rather than action, the participants acted with a certain autonomy.

It is true that, taken together, other sources of inspiration have a greater importance, but it would be erroneous to conclude from this that the occupiers were manipulated by outside groups. Inspiration and manipulation are very different. The participants were inspired by the actions of other workers in other counties, and they were certainly helped by the assistance or neutrality of exterior forces, but they were not coerced or even "tutored" by outsiders. To understand the complex origins of the occupations, it is useful to examine the motives of the participants themselves. Asked "Which phrase best explains the reason you took part in the occupations?" the participants gave the responses recorded in Table 4.12.

It is difficult, perhaps impossible, to separate the economic from the political, but the responses suggest that economic reasons had a certain

TABLE 4.12
Reasons for Occupying Land

	% of Total Reasons	Type of Reason	
Wanted a permanent job	46.3 ⎫		
Expected to earn more money	4.9 ⎭	51.2	Economic
Believed land should belong to those who work it	31.7 ⎫		
Wanted to help destroy the latifúndias	7.3 ⎬	41.5	Ideological
Believed the owner did not deserve it	2.5 ⎭		
Was convinced by others	7.3	7.3	Social Pressure
	100.0	100.0	

N = 108

salience in the minds of at least half of the men who occupied land. Those who participated in the occupations were neither simple ideologues nor victims of outside coercion. Only 7.3 percent said they were "convinced by others," and no one, not even a permanent worker, suggested that he was forced to participate. The majority of the men who occupied the farms of Portel did so because they perceived benefits and justice in the action. For some, the occupations represented the only escape from a situation of underemployment. For others, they represented an opportunity to mete out justice after years of exploitation.

SUMMARY

REVIEWING what has been illustrated in the preceding chapters, we see that the land seizures were not orchestrated by political forces outside the rural proletariat. They did not begin as machinations of the Communist party. In fact, they were not the result of any single force.

We see instead that the land occupations and the experiment with workers' control that grew out of them emerged from a complex set of forces: some rooted deep in Portuguese history, others rooted in the twentieth-century sociology of the South, and still others resulting from the disequilibrium brought on by first a political and then a social revolution.

Historically, the Alentejo had always been plagued with problems related to land tenure, land use, and employment. Monarchs, Republican politicians, and the technocrats associated with the dictatorship had been unable to solve the region's ills, despite their national implications. Salazar's Wheat Campaign proved to be a temporary solution to the problem of land use, but it eventually caused a significant swelling in the ranks of the landless laborers. These rural proletarians were not seduced by Salazar's attempts to inject the ailing body politic of the South with corporatist institutions. Workers participated out of necessity in the modest social welfare programs of the *Casas do Povo* but were never persuaded that the *Casas* were a substitute for autonomous labor unions.

The whole sociology of the South enhanced radicalization rather than cooptation. Living together in villages, working together on the latifúndia, and suffering together in the dark days when no one would pay them to work, the landless laborers of the South did not need to be tutored in class consciousness. Their perceptions were not obscured by powerful religious figures or potent patron-client relations. On the contrary, seasonal migration to metropolitan Lisbon, forced participation in the colonial wars, and witness to the degradation and abuse of power that were part of daily life in the dictatorship enhanced the likelihood of radicalization.

When the political revolution (April 1974 to March 1975) precipitated the founding of hundreds of new organizations, the potential for radical social revolutionary action in the South was realized. Landowners balked at the demands presented by organizing workers. Laborers panicked as frightened landowners decapitalized their estates. But as the sharply divided military, the weakened state bureaucracy, and the leaders of the inchoate party system proved unable to right the disequilibrium, the people of the

99

South took matters into their own hands: if work could be secured only by seizing land, then land would be seized. When the first occupations met with no resistance, the precedent was set. Thus, a regional social revolution emerged within the national political revolution.

The regional revolution expanded after March 1975 when the Communist party gained the ascendancy in the national government, but the party did not control the seizures. In fact, the seizures continued because no one seemed to control the South. Farmworkers had the opportunity to do as they pleased because the state apparatus did not function as a single unit. With the Communists maintaining a precarious hold on the cabinet, the Socialists clinging to a small majority in the Constitutional Assembly, and the ultraleft commanding key sectors of the coercive apparatus, "the state" was immobilized. All the politicians of the left were surprised and threatened by the autonomous actions of the southern workers, but no one would move against them. Just as important, no one—no party, no institution, no leader—seemed capable of solving the structural problems that gave rise to the occupations in the first place.

The farmworkers of the South started a social revolution of their own and on their own. Their consciousness came from their history. Their justification came from the sociology of the South. Their immediate incentives came from the disequilibrium brought on by political revolution, and their opportunities came from the weakness of the revolutionary state.

The seizure of the southern latifúndia was dramatic in itself. But just as dramatic as the transfer of property was the organization of that property after it changed hands. The landless workers of the South did not parcel out the land and thereby transform themselves into small holders. They acted collectively and organized collective worker-controlled farms. The consequences of this action are analyzed in the section that follows.

II

The Consequences of Workers' Control
in Agriculture

INTRODUCTION

THE land occupations proved to be only the first phase of a continuing drama. As 1975 drew to a close, the social revolution withered away, and the occupations ceased, but the fruits of the occupations remained behind. The land seizures had given rise to more than five hundred new production units—each organized collectively and controlled by workers. The units were concentrated exclusively in the southern half of Portugal in the area outlined in Map 5.1.

At their peak, the new farms occupied a total of 2,920,000 acres and provided employment for approximately 71,900 men and women.[1] In some counties, as much as 78 percent of all farmland and 95 percent of all farmworkers were integrated into the new production units.[2] How would these massive changes in property relations affect the lives of the citizens involved?

Social scientists and political activists have written a great deal about the consequences of workers' control. Using past research as a basis for prediction, one would expect the consequences of the new production units to be both broad and positive. As one of its more realistic advocates concedes, workers' control has become "a term of almost mystic connotation expected to open gates to treasures of social and human experience."[3] Indeed, as the Dutch sociologist Mauk Mulder suggests, participation in general has become a "sort of holy cow," approached "more often with respect than practicality."[4] Unfortunately, reverence and objective empiricism are rarely found in tandem, and predictive hypotheses have suffered accordingly.

---

[1] Comissão Organizadora, *5ª Conferência da Reforma Agrária* (Évora, 1981), mimeographed.

[2] Centro Regional da Reforma Agrária de Évora, "Novas Unidades de Produção: Distrito de Évora" (Évora, 1976), mimeographed. See also, Eduardo de Freitas, "Alguns Dados Referentes à Reforma Agrária no Distrito de Évora," *Análise Social* (April-June 1977), pp. 492-493.

[3] Ichak Adizes, "On Conflict Resolution and an Organizational Definition of Self-Management," in Eugen Pusic, ed., *Participation and Self-Management*, vols. 1-6 (Zagreb: Institute for Social Research, 1972), 5: 33. Here and throughout the discussion that follows I have used *workers' control* as a synonym for worker participation and self-management, taking into account the precise meanings that individual authors intend. In the literature cited, these terms are synonomous, and I have used the term *workers' control* only for stylistic uniformity.

[4] Mauk Mulder, "The Learning of Participation," in ibid., 4: 219.

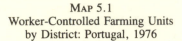

MAP 5.1
Worker-Controlled Farming Units
by District: Portugal, 1976

SOURCE: Ministério de Agricultura e Pescas. Instituto da Reorganização Agrária. Unpublished records.

Many of the most interesting and far-reaching predictions are presented by theorists with little or no reference to empirical studies. Other hypotheses are indeed based on empirical work, but the vast majority of these focus on the unique cases of Yugoslavia and Israel. Thus, despite a voluminous and ever-growing literature, social scientists are still unable to make even the most cautious predictions. Optimistic hypotheses abound—and they may not in fact be untenable—but they remain untested.

Four of the most widely accepted predictive hypotheses are discussed in the following chapters, first at a theoretical level and then within the real-world context of workers' control in Portugal. Chapter Five deals with the effects of workers' control on the enterprise itself. It begins with the question of how the formal institution of workers' control affects management and concludes with a discussion of the effects of workers' control on productivity. Chapter Six discusses the effects of workers' control on workers, assessing first how participation in a worker-controlled enterprise affects workers' political participation in general and then examining the connection between workers' control and radicalization. Focusing again on the county of Portel, this section will suggest that the institution of workers' control has affected the lives of rural workers in dramatic, though not always predictable, ways.

FIVE

Workers' Control and Its Effects
on the Workplace

The Participatory Management Hypothesis

Advocates of workers' control typically argue that changing the structure of enterprise decision making changes the behavior of enterprise workers. If workers are given control of and access to managerial roles, they will behave differently. Management will no longer be the task of an elite but of all the producers in an enterprise system. One of the consequences of the institution of workers' control is thus "participatory management," a situation in which fixed enterprise hierarchies are reduced and even eliminated by workers' active participation in decision making.

The participatory management hypothesis has a long history. It is rooted in the work of eighteenth-century visionaries such as Owen, Blanc, and Proudhon, but it has extended well beyond the Utopian Socialists. John Stuart Mill's plea for a system of industrial democracy whereby workers associated "on terms of equality" with "managers elected and removable by themselves" was based on the two-part notion that workers would participate if given the opportunity and that management would thereby be changed.[1]

G.D.H. Cole made similar assumptions in his call for guild socialism. He predicted that if workers were given the opportunity to organize freely, they would soon assume "all the functions of industrial management" themselves.[2]

Modern theorists repeat these ideas in a variety of forms. At one extreme are scholars such as André Gorz who argue that workers will easily assume the function of management because they realize that existing differences are "senseless," "irrational," and "artificial."[3] From another, more cau-

---

[1] John Stuart Mill, *Principles of Political Economy* (London: Longmans, Green and Co., 1926), p. 773.

[2] G.D.H. Cole, *Chaos and Order in Industry* (New York: Frederick A. Stokes Co., 1920), p. 46.

[3] See André Gorz, "Workers' Control is More than Just That," in Gerry Hunnius, G. David Garson, and John Case, eds., *Workers' Control: A Reader on Labor and Social Change* (New York: Random House, 1973), p. 339. Gorz argues in fact that "every one of us [workers and others alike] knows from experience that this hierarchic division is irrational

tious, perspective, Paul Blumberg writes that workers' control has the potential to transform laborers from "unwilling subordinates" to "equal partners."[4]

Despite differences in both the blueprints and the optimism of these authors, the participatory management hypothesis remains a recurrent theme: the formal establishment of workers' control can eliminate the hierarchy of "managers and . . . men" and produce "one group of equal decision-makers" instead.[5]

Like all hypotheses, the participatory management hypothesis needs testing and refining. As most of its proponents would likely admit, many questions remain unanswered. Some of the more interesting questions regard whether the hypothesis would be borne out as easily in some societies as others. For example, is the longing for participation in management universal or does it vary across cultures and levels of development? And if the desire for participation does vary, might the capacity for participation vary as well?

The participatory management hypothesis implies, at minimum, that workers can *evaluate* managerial skills (and thereby choose good managers). At maximum, it implies that workers can assume managerial roles themselves. In both of these cases, one presumes that a knowledge of management skills can be easily transferred. Here, too, questions regarding differences in culture and level of development emerge. In states at lower and middle levels of development, managerial skills (and even literacy) are closely concentrated at the top of the occupational hierarchy. Will individuals with management skills invest—or even have—the time to school workers in the intricacies of accounting, marketing, and production? Will workers invest—or even have—the time to learn? The answers to these questions are not yet clear, but empirical evidence from outside the advanced industrial societies suggests that, in certain states at least, the barriers to participatory management are higher than certain advocates might wish.

It is ironic but significant that much of the evidence on this point comes from Yugoslavia, where the state has an official commitment to workers' self-management. In this seemingly congenial environment, analysts con-

---

and senseless . . . and that education serves much less to increase a man's competence . . . than it serves to breed . . . conformity to the values and ideology of capitalist society."

[4] Blumberg's work is widely read in North America. See Paul Blumberg, *Industrial Democracy: The Sociology of Participation* (New York: Schocken Books, 1973), p. 130.

[5] Carol Pateman, *Participation and Democratic Theory* (Cambridge: Cambridge University Press, 1970), p. 39. These words are taken from Pateman's interpretation of G.D.H. Cole, but they represent the ideas of several theorists whom she describes as advocates of "participatory democracy." See pp. 22-44.

tinually report only a modest level of participatory behavior. The desire for participation does not manifest itself in the manner predicted. Analysts find that workers are reluctant to participate in factory affairs[6] and that instrumental norms consistently take primacy over participatory norms. As a factory controller put it, workers "are always interested when they think that their pay packets are directly involved, otherwise not."[7]

When we turn from evidence on interest to evidence on actual behavior, the participatory management hypothesis still appears problematic. Once again, most data on this point come from Yugoslavia. They suggest very strongly that workers and professional managers do not behave as equals. A three-year study of twenty self-managed firms concluded: "Participation of rank and file employees in the most important policy making areas is almost nil."[8] Another study compared United States and Yugoslavian firms and found "no difference in executive power."[9] Systematic content analyses of workers' council meetings suggest that technocrats dominate these bodies as well,[10] and analysts go so far as to say that "all surveys dealing with power show that top management is the most influential group."[11] What is most interesting in the context of the participatory management hypothesis is that those elected to workers' councils are not representative of plant personnel in general. After decades of self-management, council managers are consistently from the more skilled and better educated strata of society.[12] Information and interest in participation remain closely concentrated at the top of the hierarchy, and behavior is not radically altered. The participatory management hypothesis is both appealing and widely popular, but we still do not know its limitations.

[6] See Josip Zupanov, "Employees' Participation and Social Power in Industry," in Eugen Pusic, ed., *Participation and Self-Management*, vols. 1-6 (Zagreb: Institute for Social Research, 1972), 1: 37; Jiri Kolaja, *Workers' Councils: The Yugoslav Experience* (London: Tavistock Publications, 1965), p. 53; and Ichak Adizes, *Industrial Democracy Yugoslav Style* (New York: Free Press, 1971), p. 223.

[7] Kolaja, *Workers' Councils*, p. 60.

[8] Zupanov, "Employees' Participation," p. 38.

[9] Ibid., p. 38.

[10] See Mauk Mulder, "Power Equalization Through Participation?" *Administrative Science Quarterly* (March 1971), p. 33; Kolaja, *Workers' Councils*, pp. 21 and 50; and Josip Obradovic et al., "Workers' Councils in Yugoslavia: Effects on Perceived Participation and Satisfaction of Workers," *Human Relations* (October 1970), p. 470; and Veljko Rus, "The Limits of Organized Participation," in Eugen Pusic, ed., *Participation and Self-Management*, vols. 1-6 (Zagreb: Institute for Social Research, 1972), 2: 172.

[11] Rus, "The Limits to Organized Participation," p. 172.

[12] See Sidney Verba and Goldie Shabad, "Workers' Councils and Political Stratification," *American Political Science Review* (March 1978), p. 94. They argue that workers' control does not "ensure a more equitable dispersion of decision making." Similar findings emerge in Thomas Olesczuk, "Convergence and Counteraction: Yugoslavia's Anti-technocratic Campaign," *Comparative Political Studies* (July, 1980), pp. 224-225.

An alternative and much more pessimistic hypothesis might be proposed in view of the empirical findings just discussed. Given conditions that are common in middle- and less-developed economies—i.e., a work force with low participatory experience and enterprises with radically skewed distributions of technical information—the establishment of worker participation may lead not to participatory management but to manipulative management.

Participatory enterprise structures have been established and manipulated in the interest of existing elites since at least 1848, when the French government set up fraudulent national workshops merely to keep dissidents off the streets.[13] Though many widely read proponents of the participatory management hypothesis neglect this issue, lesser known writers are beginning to make reference to it. Participation may actually increase differences between certain groups and thus reinforce rather than destroy hierarchy.[14]

The possibilities of manipulative versus participatory management cannot be assessed without many more case studies, and the negative data from Yugoslavia allow us merely to question rather than dismiss the participatory management hypothesis. It is possible that the problems encountered in this single case are peculiar to workers' control in single party states or due to some other factor related to Yugoslavia itself.

Though comparable studies from other states at middle and lower levels of development are relatively infrequent, the evidence they present is somewhat more positive. For example, studies of worker-controlled enterprises in Chile and Peru report that workers were eager to participate in the management of factories and farms. A quantitative study of Chilean *autogestión* suggests that workers valued participation in management twice as much as participation in ownership.[15] Cynthia McClintock's very thorough study of agricultural cooperatives in Peru revealed fairly high levels of participation and, contrary to the manipulation hypothesis, "no co-optation or conciliation between technocrats and peasants." Peruvian workers quickly developed the "new political will" and "new political

---

[13] When Marx and Engels described the early communal associations as "mystifying," they no doubt recognized this. Evelyne Huber Stephens discusses the problem of manipulation in *The Politics of Workers' Participation: The Peruvian Approach in Comparative Perspective* (New York: Academic Press, 1980), pp. 169-212.

[14] Rus, "The Limits to Organized Participation," p. 171, cautions: "When differences among participants are small, they tend to be diminished by participation, but when they are great, they are only increased." Mulder, "Power Equalization," p. 34, argues: "When there are relatively large differences in the expert power of members of a system, an increase in participation will increase the power differences between members."

[15] Teresa Jeanneret, Leopoldo Moraga, and Lorraine Ruffing, *Las Experiencias Autogestionarias Chilenas* (Santiago: Universidad de Chile, 1976), p. 99.

capacity'' to avoid the dangers of manipulative management[16] and revealed a profound suspicion of the "well trained and well educated."[17]

This said, though, the evidence on the likelihood of fully participatory management remains mixed. In the Peruvian sugar cooperatives, we have reports that "at least *some* sharing of executive authority emerged,"[18] but there and in Chile as well, self-managing workers continued to participate unevenly[19] and "continued to choose leaders from high socio-economic strata."[20] On at least one cooperative in Peru, participation was viewed as "a dead letter" involving only issues of "a trivial nature."[21] More discouraging than these reports (which might have changed with time) are the observations that workers' control is simply incompatible with certain cultures. A major study of workers' control in Algeria concludes that workers' attitudes toward participation were "radically circumscribed" by a "life situation and belief system" that was "inimical to . . . the consciousness implied by self-management."[22] Viewed against the backdrop of this mixed evidence, the Portuguese case seems especially useful.

Participatory Management in Portugal

An in-depth analysis of the management of Portugal's worker-controlled farms helps us to understand the association between structural change and egalitarianism and illustrates that the consequences of workers' control are neither as positive nor as negative as certain bodies of literature would have us believe. In the following discussion three points will be made: first, that workers' control in Portugal is indeed associated with increased egalitarianism; second, that a fairly stable management hierarchy remains the norm anyway; and, third, that interior and exterior constraints generally prevent the individuals at the top of the hierarchy from manipulating those below. Management is thus neither egalitarian nor manipulative but gen-

[16] Cynthia McClintock, *Peasant Cooperatives and Political Change in Peru* (Princeton, New Jersey: Princeton University Press, 1981), p. 168.

[17] Ibid., p. 176.

[18] Ibid., p. 202. Emphasis mine.

[19] Ibid., pp. 164-166, and Juan Espinosa and Andrew Zimbalist, *Economic Democracy: Workers' Participation in Chilean Industry* (New York: Academic Press, 1978), pp. 68, 95.

[20] McClintock, *Peasant Cooperatives*, p. 332.

[21] These are Sean Conlin's observations of a cooperative in Cuzco. He argues that the government's experts dominated all decision making and that the institution of formal participation created only "a more subtle form of dependence." See Sean Conlin, "Participation versus Expertise," *International Journal of Comparative Sociology* (September-October 1974), pp. 151, 153, 155.

[22] Ian Clegg, *Workers' Self-Management in Algeria* (New York: Monthly Review Press, 1971), p. 172.

erally democratic. Despite substantial impediments, at least the minimal version of participatory management has been achieved.

Egalitarian Structures and Symbols. Workers' control in agriculture took two forms in the aftermath of the occupations.[23] Some of the new production units called themselves *Cooperativas de Produção*, or cooperatives, while others called themselves *Unidades Collectivas de Produção* (UCPs), or collectives. The nominal distinction between the two types of enterprise was originally based on size and schemes of payment. The early cooperatives were generally smaller in acreage and number of workers and based compensation exclusively on the surplus that each unit produced. The collectives based compensation on a fixed salary, geared, in theory, to union wages in the private sector. By the beginning of 1976, the differences in designation lost their original meaning as UCPs began to call themselves cooperatives and cooperatives began to pay fixed salaries. Virtually all of the new production units were paying fixed salaries by 1976, though these varied somewhat from unit to unit.

The managerial systems of both sorts of enterprises were similar in their formal emphasis on egalitarianism and democracy. The written statutes for each type of organization established that enterprises would be run by an elected board of directors and an elected fiscal council, typically serving for renewable three-year terms. All enterprise workers would meet regularly in a general assembly that represented the supreme decision-making body of the enterprise. Within the assembly, the one-man, one-vote principle was the rule. Shares in the production unit were purchased for under three dollars, and no member was entitled to more than one share. If a member left the production unit, his share reverted back to the unit itself. Membership was thus controlled entirely by the general assembly itself: new members were voted in, and existing members—when necessary—were voted out.

Compensation schemes generally served to reinforce the formal egalitarianism just described. Compensation differentials were determined by the workers themselves, and (for men, at least) were usually minimal, if existent at all. Schemes varied from one unit to another, but generally only three types of workers were given higher wages: accountants, shepherds, and, when present, mechanics. In most cases, the special treatment accorded these workers emerged without controversy. Accountants and mechanics were given special treatment because they had to be lured in from

---

[23] The use of the past tense in this and the following chapter reflects only the timing of my research and implies nothing about the contemporary applicability of the generalizations made.

"outside" the original occupation group, sometimes from another town, often from a better-paying position with the civil service or, in rare cases, with a private company. Shepherds were accorded special treatment because of the peculiar nature of their work. Having to graze their flocks all night in the summer and all day in the winter, they could not confine themselves to a steady forty- or forty-five-hour week. Thus they received slightly more payment in cash. They also had the right to own a small number of their cooperative's animals (just as they had when the farms were individually owned).

Greater responsibility was not thought to be justification for greater pay. Contrary to the official policy of the farmworkers' union, even tractor drivers usually received the same compensation as unskilled workers. The rationale explained to the author was that the drivers "*did* have more responsibility and more training" but that their work was less demanding physically. So "everyone's effort is more or less equal." The same principle was applied to the individuals at the top of the firm hierarchy. Members of the board of directors and fiscal council usually received the same compensation as unskilled workers, despite the fact that they typically worked longer hours and had to cope with complex decisions. On one of the production units I visited, the board member who gave out the daily work assignments worked at least two hours longer than the average laborer, arriving at the office an hour before the work day began to arrange transportation and assignments and then staying behind after the official work day was over, making certain that workers and equipment had returned, recording what they had done, and drawing up plans for the following day. With hundreds of laborers working on properties that were sometimes not even contiguous, these tasks were complex. They became more complex during planting and harvest times when temporary workers were hired and had to be distributed in the same way. Though some of the men in this position bemoaned their long schedule, none suggested publicly that he deserved higher compensation.

The egalitarian norms just described did not extend to women workers, who were paid approximately 30 percent less than men and, with few exceptions, were absent from boards of directors and fiscal councils. This was not because women did not participate in land occupations. In fact, many occupation groups included women, and one or two were reportedly led by women. The rationale behind differences in treatment related to different positions in the work force.

The revolution did little to change women's work opportunities. As was the case before the 25th of April, women were generally confined to temporary work involving weeding and picking tomatoes, olives, or grapes. They were paid less, allegedly, because they did different work, but tradition and economic necessity certainly helped to perpetuate the inequities. Women were restricted to temporary work in part because they were charged with the responsibilities of cooking, cleaning, and child-rearing. But they were also confined to temporary labor because they were convinced that there simply were not enough permanent positions to go around. When asked why she did not join her husband as a permanent member of the local cooperative, a woman of fifty explained to the author, "Because my husband and I would have two jobs, and the couple next door would have none. That would be pretty, wouldn't it?" On at least ten other occasions, the response to this question, though less colorful, was always the same. Women recognized that they were being treated differently but had a ready economic rationale to explain their situation. Inequality between sexes was justified as a means of promoting equality among families.

Egalitarian norms were not confined to formal statutes and pay schemes. They were also embodied in a whole range of symbolic behavior. The professional titles that are so prominent in daily communication throughout Portugal were totally absent within cooperatives and collectives. Instead of being called "doctor" or "engineer," as is the rule in other parts of Portugal, the trusted outsider with post-secondary education was called "friend," or under some circumstances, "comrade." Within the cooperative, men used nicknames, family names, or first names, but never the formal *Senhor*. Once again, women were the occasional exception to the rule. Older women were sometimes accorded the title *Dona* (in combination with their first name), but this was not always the case and was rare with younger women.

Elections, egalitarian pay schemes, and a pervasive sense of camaraderie made the new production units radically different from the latifúndias that preceded them. At a formal and at a personal, interactive level, inequality of treatment (among men, at least) was certainly the exception rather than the rule. Thus, the institution of workers' control both reflects and reinforces deep-seated egalitarian drives.

Although the institution of workers' control has meant major strides toward participatory management, fully participatory, egalitarian management is, at this point, impossible. The members of the new collective units differ greatly in both their ability and their willingness to assume managerial tasks, and as a consequence decision-making power often remains concentrated in the hands of a stable enterprise subgroup. This is not the result of machiavellianism or opportunism within the firm but simply a legacy of social inequities that predate the revolutionary period.

Structural Constraints. The most important constraint on participatory management was a high level of illiteracy. This was one of the most

TABLE 5.1
Level of Education in District
of Évora Cooperatives

	Men and Women	Men
Illiterate	50.4%	52.5%
Three years or less	15.9	13.5
Four years	28.9	29.0
Other	2.8	2.5
Unknown	1.9	2.2

SOURCE: Centro Regional da Reforma Agrária: Évora. As recorded in Eduardo de Freitas, "Alguns Dados Referentes à Reforma Agrária no Distrito de Évora," *Análise Social* (April-June 1977).

damaging legacies of the Salazar period. The dictator feared the political ramifications of public education and actually discouraged literacy among the lower classes. The effects in the agrarian reform zone were far-reaching. As Table 5.1 illustrates, over half of the workers on the new production units in Évora were completely illiterate. The situation in the poorer sections of Beja and Portalegre was even worse. These workers obviously were not able to assume normal managerial responsibilities. There were probably no written rules stating that illiterates could not run for office, but they rarely, if ever, chose to do so. The same observation held to some degree for workers with three years or less of schooling. Many of these individuals had forgotten the few reading skills they were able to acquire and had become functionally illiterate, capable of signing and reading their names but unable to cope with correspondence or even maps. Thus, in real terms, the actual ability to assume the demanding tasks of management was confined to less than a third of the average cooperative's membership— certainly a serious barrier to truly egalitarian management.

Even if a farmworker were able to read and calculate, there were other subtle factors that sometimes prevented him from doing so comfortably. The author recalls observing three members of a directive council working in the main office of a collective in Évora. Night was falling and the men sat huddled around the single office lamp, poring over a technical brochure and passing a single pair of reading glasses among them. The glasses belonged to one of their wives, and the lamp had been purchased by the collective's accountant. Both objects had become communal property, but neither was adequate to the needs of the group. From lighting to eyeglasses to illiteracy, the legacy of regional poverty extended deep into daily life.

Educational skills were not the only factors that hampered access to management positions. Organizational skills were a problem as well. Most cooperative members had little, if any, organizational experience preceding the 25th of April. As was stated previously, farmworkers' unions were illegal during the Salazar-Caetano regime, as were independent political parties or any other sort of workers' organization. The southern Catholic Church was unable and unwilling to provide the organizational alternatives it provided in other authoritarian states.

Thus, workers who did not participate actively in the dictatorship's corporate organizations or in underground political parties had no organizational experience at all. Workers in the first category were rare, and many were considered politically "suspect" when the dictatorship fell. Workers in the second category—i.e., with experience in an underground party—were also rare. The exceptions to these generalizations were the men who gained some sort of union experience outside their local community, either in Portugal or abroad. These workers usually constituted the core of any cooperative's management group, as was mentioned previously.

A third barrier to fully participatory management derived from prerevolutionary patterns of land tenure. Since the vast majority of cooperative members were landless before the 25th of April they had little or no opportunity to organize even a small-scale production process from beginning to end—as any manager must do. Workers knew a great deal about certain steps in the farming process but were obviously excluded from many of the most important, such as purchasing, financing, and marketing. Small farmers, *seareiros*, and a few permanent workers did have an overview of the management process, but they were less likely to join the cooperatives in the first place. Those who did were in great demand.

There were thus at least three ways in which truly egalitarian management was made impossible by the legacies of past inequality. Differences in schooling, in access to organizations, and in land tenure inevitably gave rise to inequalities of ability within the new production units. Since reading skills, organizational experience, and managerial expertise were limited to a small proportion of cooperative members, the management experience could not be universally shared.

No one was more aware of these differences in ability than the cooperative members themselves, and this awareness affected participation. My interviews suggest that many of the cooperatives' elections involved uncontested lists of candidates. This was partly the result of the differences in abilities just outlined, but it was also the result of the fact that many workers simply did not wish to assume the extra hours and headaches that management tasks involved. Managing hundreds of workers and thousands of acres of property was not an easy task under any circumstances, but it was especially difficult under the political conditions existing in the agrarian reform zone today.

As will be explained in detail later in the text, the new production units had many conflicts with both the private farming community and the Portuguese state, and cooperative managers dedicated a great deal of energy to the essentially political problems that these conflicts involved. This aspect of management was decidedly unappealing. As an older worker who refused a second term on a board of directors in Portel explained, "It's not just land and work, you know, it's trips to Évora and discussions, discussions, discussions. I have enough of these with my wife."

While some workers shunned managerial responsibilities because of lack of interest, others avoided responsibilities because of lack of confidence. Many capable workers preferred to leave management to someone else out of deference. A young worker in the county of Beja illustrated this in an interview: "I could be [on the board of directors]—I'm no dope and I get along well with everyone, but why take the risk? I'm no better than the guys [who are on the board], and I could be worse."

Other forms of participation were also affected by a certain sense of deference. General assemblies were often forums for a one-way flow of information rather than forums for debate. If a board of directors decided that a cooperative would benefit from the purchase of a tractor or the digging of a well or a new planting of sunflowers, the arguments were presented to the workers in open meetings, but they rarely provoked resistance or even discussion. This was not because workers were uninterested in the future of the cooperative but because they seemed to trust the judgment of their directing boards. The sense of camaraderie previously discussed involved a sense of trust, and with this came a reluctance to challenge most board decisions. Attending meetings on several different cooperatives, I sometimes observed an embarrassed silence when cooperative leaders asked repeatedly for comments from the floor.

An emphasis on solidarity also contributed to the reluctance to challenge board decisions. Hostility from outside the new production units created a sort of "seige mentality" within them. The need for "solidarity" was underscored time and again in conversations and in meetings. This was a normal, if not inevitable, reaction to exterior threats, but it reinforced uniformity of opinion, or at least uniformity of expression. A worker explained the effects with the following phrase: "We have no debates among ourselves—our fights are with the Ministry of Agriculture and with the fascists."

The speaker was exaggerating somewhat, for there were conflicts within the farms. The silence one observed in formal settings should not be mistaken for either a lack of interest in managerial decisions or a lack of concrete challenges from below. There were plenty of these.

Most of the issues that provoked these disputes were related to compensation. The challenges themselves were quite complex. Formal group complaints about low wages were rarely made in the general assembly, or anywhere else. There were discussions of wage levels in 1975 when the new units were being formed, but the financial situation of most cooperatives eventually became so difficult that any sort of mobilization for an increase in wages was thought of as unrealistic. As an older worker responded when asked why there were no demands for higher wages, "you don't get wine from an empty bottle."

Though public group challenges to management wage policies were rare, management councils labored under a steady barrage of petitions and challenges of another sort. I witnessed three examples of this type of participation in a typical week on a cooperative in southern Évora. The first involved the wife of a worker who claimed that she never got to buy the cooperative's low-cost beans. A second involved a young man who claimed that his wife had been passed over in temporary work assignments. A third involved another young man who said his wife was having a baby and he'd soon be forced to look for work on a private farm because the cooperative paid him a "wage of hunger." Each of these complaints involved an explicit attack on management policies. The woman argued that the cooperative should offer its members more beans; the first young man argued that work should be assigned in a different fashion; and the second man argued that the cooperative should pay more. These critiques would have been unthinkable before the institution of workers' control, and they attest to the essentially democratic nature of the new organization.

Issues related to equal treatment provided challenges as well, and these also exemplified the democratic nature of the cooperative farms. A good example of such a challenge came from a cooperative in a remote part of northern Beja. Shepherds there, like shepherds in other cooperatives, were allowed the use of livestock that technically belonged to the cooperative. Years after the cooperative's establishment, some shepherds complained that they had less livestock than others. The inequity was partially the result of individual initiative and partially a legacy of what the shepherds had been given by landlords before the occupations, but the issue became a politically difficult one for the cooperative membership as a whole.

Times were hard. Wages were low. No one argued that the shepherds with the larger flocks were living a life of luxury at the cooperative's expense, but the shepherds with fewer animals were clearly disadvantaged and complained accordingly.

The membership had several options. It could ignore the inequality. It

117

could force the advantaged shepherds to give up their excess, or it could give more livestock to the disadvantaged. Ignoring the petitions of the disadvantaged shepherds was dismissed immediately. Forcibly taking the other shepherds' animals was extremely distasteful and yet acquiring more animals for the disadvantaged would merely exacerbate the differences between the shepherds and the rest of the membership. After a great deal of debate, it was decided that the advantaged shepherds buy their animals from the cooperative in small installments at cost.

The story is significant not merely in its egalitarian resolution but also for what it illustrates about the nature of participation, for the issue was not discussed at the general assembly until it was resolved. To discuss the inequality in a formal, public gathering would have been embarrassing to both the shepherds who were better off and the shepherds who raised the complaint. Much of the town discussed the issue in cafes, in doorways, and at mealtime, but the issue was finally resolved through a series of personal negotiations involving groups of three or four. Interested parties made their preferences known in private conversations with the board. The board weighed the alternatives in light of public opinion and then presented what turned out to be an unchallenged proposal. The shepherds' original challenge to elected management was real, and participation was remarkably broadly based, but none of the process was manifest in formal meetings.

It is important to note that none of the other three challenges just described emerged in an official meeting either. Each was delivered in a private conversation: two over the counter in the main office of the cooperative and one in a local cafe. Observers who looked for ''participation'' only in large assemblies and official forums were likely to underestimate the more personal manifestations of workers' control. This was especially true in an enterprise in which workers and managers had fraternal and even familial bonds. Discussions in formal settings were limited because people were unaccustomed to public speaking but mostly because the issues had often been raised (and resolved) beforehand, in an office, in a field, in a cafe, or at a dinner table.

While personal contacts enabled cooperative members to participate in management in informal ways, they also functioned as a barrier to manipulative management. No individual was simply a member of a management board—everyone was a member of a larger community as well. Community communication channels carried details about cooperative life to everyone within the working class. The salaries paid, the prices obtained, the livestock slaughtered were all discussed openly by everyone even peripherally associated with an enterprise. If an enterprise was being badly managed, people heard about it, and the managers had to bear the burden. Certain problems could be attributed to harassment from the government or sabotage from landowners, but these explanations were of limited utility. This was especially true in the larger communities that contained more than one cooperative. There, comparisons were easily made, and the less efficient, less dedicated management teams were well known. Knowledge was not limited to the people most affected. Even local landowners seemed cognizant of who was doing well and who was not. A young and dynamic landowner in Redondo ranked the cooperatives in his area exactly as a union official in Évora did weeks later.

News of inefficiency and dishonesty spread quickly, not only within a single town, but often throughout a whole region. This was illustrated during a casual conversation I had with a bus driver in a small town in western Beja. The town is quite literally the end of the line for the public bus service, and drivers are forced to stay overnight there on the last run from Évora. Like many of his counterparts in other countries, this particular bus driver was talkative and full of news. On a night in mid-September, he brought word of a cooperative several hours away that was being "destroyed" by a "thief" of a manager. The driver had gotten the news from his father (who was a member) and had apparently discussed it with several people on his way south. His information spread throughout the town the next day—so quickly in fact that I heard it from two other sources before the following sundown.

The incident with the bus driver suggests two things. First, that dishonest managers were sometimes found out. But second, and more importantly perhaps, that dishonesty was rare enough to be shocking. Corruption might in fact exist, but it was not taken for granted, as it is so often in the private sector. Certainly news of a dishonest landowner would not have spread as fast in the days before workers' control.

Why is this the case? Surely cooperative managers were not chosen from a community of saints, but they were subject to constraints that private managers generally avoid. First, there were social constraints that emanated from the fact that the manager was probably related to many of the cooperative members: if he was being dishonest, he was being so to the detriment of his own family. Second, the costs of mismanagement were high. A dishonest manager could not, as he could in Lisbon, for example, disappear into anonymity and find another means of supporting himself. There was little anonymity in even the district capitals of the agrarian reform zone, and no anonymity at all in the smaller towns that typify the area. A disgraced manager, especially an older individual, could not easily pick up and move to Lisbon, for he was not likely to find work there. Nor could he emigrate easily to another part of Europe, for immigration has been virtually halted in the more advanced industrial societies. For many managers, a position in the cooperative was the only position available.

Awareness of this enhanced dedication. A manager in the district of Portel made this patently clear in an interview:

> This [cooperative] is ours. It's the only thing we have, the only chance we have after so many years of misery. I work like a mule here. . . . There is no other life for me. Not for me and not for the others.

Social constraints could of course be ignored, but they were not the only constraints on management's behavior. More concrete constraints had their impact as well. For example, new production units had to allow their members free access to farm records. Managers therefore operated under the real or potential scrutiny of their fellow members; they also operated under the scrutiny of district federations. More than 90 percent of the new production units were members of these groups. Federations served to provide legal and technical assistance to affiliated cooperatives, but they also served as informal data banks for information on production, marketing, and management for each farm. The federation's existence depended on the efficiency of the cooperatives that comprised it, and there was a concerted effort to monitor cooperative activities and to intervene when necessary.

Intervention could have dramatic consequences. A cooperative north of Lisbon was having difficulties that political factors alone failed to explain, and a middle-aged manager, who had returned to Portugal after years of exile in France, was burdened with the blame. Under pressure from workers and the district federation, he was removed from his position and forced out of the cooperative. A short while later, he was expelled from his political party and then eased out of a temporary government job. Having failed at his "only chance" to make a life for himself in Portugal, he eventually returned to France, where he was supported by his French wife. The manager was never actually charged with a crime, but suspicion alone was sufficient to drive him from his homeland and ruin his professional and political life.

THE preceding discussion illustrates that fully participatory egalitarian management has not yet been achieved in Portugal. The management of Portugal's worker-controlled farms remains a mixture of democracy and benign hierarchy. The cooperative members are aware of this but by and large seem satisfied with the arrangement. When the members of Portel's cooperatives were asked if the task of management fell to the more educated, the response was overwhelmingly yes: 65 percent of cooperative members agreed. But when asked if there were issues on which they would *like* to be consulted but were not, only 2 percent said yes. The workers in Portel, at least, view their cooperatives as wholly democratic. A good percentage

TABLE 5.2
Workers' Perceptions of Who
Runs Cooperatives

Possibilities	Responses
Labor unions	—
Elected officers	55.0%
All the members	45.0
No one	—
Other	—

N = 108

even view them as structures of direct democracy. These points are illustrated in Table 5.2.

Empirical evidence illustrates that the members of the new production units felt that they were "in control." For them, workers' control was a reality. No members argued that their workplace was controlled by anyone outside the cooperative, and though a majority argued that cooperatives were controlled by elected officials, a full 45 percent believed that control lay directly with the workers themselves. This is not fully participatory management, but it is not undemocratic management either.

Despite the constraints emerging from differences in education and experience, it was not unusual for directive councils to change from election to election and even for councils to call for new elections prior to the completion of their three-year terms; elections on the cooperative with the shepherds' conflict were frequent enough that thirty-seven members served in elected office in less than nine years. This was approximately one-third of the cooperative's existing membership and a dramatic illustration of the potential of participatory management.

The institution of workers' control did not lead to the dramatic behavioral change necessary for fully participatory management, but it did lead to a degree of democratization that seemed to satisfy the vast majority of workers. Though worker-members often deferred to the judgment of elected leaders in a formal setting, there was no fear-based deference between individuals. There was, instead, a camaraderie and solidarity that contrasted markedly with the organization of work in the past.

THE PRODUCTIVITY HYPOTHESIS

A close corollary of the egalitarian management hypothesis is a chain of assertions that I call the productivity hypothesis. Workers' control has long been associated with increases in productivity. Briefly stated, the argument runs like this. Wage laborers recognize that they are alienated from both the ownership and the control of the means of production. They react to their alienation in two ways. Often, they do as little work as possible, minimizing exploitation by minimizing effort expended. Other times, they engage in outright revolt, with work slowdowns, work-to-rule periods, or actual strikes. Both forms of reaction take their toll on production. If workers were given their share in the planning and ownership of the production process, counterproductive behavior would be eliminated and productivity would rise.

Karl Marx and Friedrich Engels laid the foundation for this line of argument in the last century with their writings on alienated labor. In postwar America, the argument was restated by industrial organization specialists whose motives were radically different from those of Marx and Engels. Beginning with the Mayo experiments at General Electric,[24] and duplicated again by Strauss in a toy factory[25] and Lawrence and Smith in a garment factory,[26] a long stream of empirical studies began to confirm the connection between participation and productivity. When workers were allowed to control even a small part of their job situation, productivity rose. If control were taken away, productivity dropped off again.

Studies of other nations suggested that the findings were generalizable to a broad range of societies. Whether the subject was a Volvo plant in Sweden, a kibbutz in Israel,[27] a home appliance factory in Spain,[28] or an entire economy in Yugoslavia, researchers discovered a positive correlation between participation and productivity. After decades of comparative research, Jaroslav Vanek goes as far as to say that "the labor managed system seems to be superior by far, judged on strictly economic criteria, to any other economic system in existence."[29] Self-management, or work-

---

[24] Elton Mayo, *The Human Problems of an Industrial Civilization* (New York: Macmillan Co., 1933).

[25] This and similar experiments are discussed in Blumberg, *Industrial Democracy*, esp. pp. 96-99.

[26] L. C. Lawrence and P. C. Smith, "Group Decision and Employee Participation," *Journal of Applied Psychology* (October 1955).

[27] Blumberg, *Industrial Democracy*, p. 153.

[28] For information on productivity in Spain's cooperative community in Mondragón, see Ana Gutierrez Johnson and William Foote Whyte, "The Mondragón System of Worker Production Cooperatives," *Industrial and Labor Relations Review* (October 1977), and J. Eaton, "The Relevance of Mondragón to Britain," *Political Quarterly* (October 1978).

[29] Jaroslav Vanek, *Self-Management: The Economic Liberation of Man* (Baltimore: Penguin Books, 1975), p. 364.

TABLE 5.3
Job Satisfaction by Form of Labor
Would you like to do different work?

	Yes	No
Cooperative members	22.5%	77.5%
Farmworkers	46.4	53.6
Small farmers	10.0	90.0

N = 108

ers' control, as we call it in this context, is to Vanek's mind "a very efficient *modus operandi* for firms and economies."[30]

There exists, of course, a school of thought that runs counter to the productivity hypothesis. Indeed, it is so popular here in the United States that it hardly needs elaboration. Many scholars and businessmen argue that workers lack the technical and personal skills that efficient management requires. Democracy takes time and is thus a luxury that a busy enterprise cannot afford. And the fruits of democracy are likely to be meager anyway. Workers will inevitably have a tendency to endorse policies that increase their short-term income, neglecting capital investment and thus the future of the firm.

Productivity in Portuguese Cooperatives

How has workers' control affected productivity in Portugal? The complex set of factors that contribute to an increase in productivity cannot be fully discussed here, but there is evidence to suggest that the basic elements of the productivity hypothesis are correct. Workers on the new production units do appear more satisfied than their counterparts in the private sector, and they do in fact feel that they produce more.

Worker Satisfaction. Worker satisfaction was assessed through a variety of questions in my survey research, and each question supported the same conclusion. The most direct question asked whether an individual would like to do "different work." Responses from the three occupation groups are presented in Table 5.3.

Small farmers are by far the most contented group, but there are marked differences between the two groups of wage workers. Less than one-fourth of all cooperative members would like to switch jobs, while nearly one-

[30] Ibid., p. 29.

123

half of all farmworkers would like to do so. This marked difference is surprising, given the wage differentials between the two groups. Farmworkers in the private sector earn substantially more than workers in the cooperative sector. In the county of Portel, for example, workers on cooperatives earned a monthly average of 6,666 escudos, while workers in the private sector earned 7,585 escudos, or 13.8 percent more.[31] That cooperative workers would be more content in their relatively low-paid positions suggests that the qualities of the cooperative experience itself have a strong effect on worker satisfaction.

Most, though not all, cooperative members view work on a cooperative as fundamentally different from work in the private sector. In the Portel study, a full 65 percent of cooperative workers denied that "work on a cooperative and work on a private farm are essentially the same," and a full 85 percent said that they would seize land and start a cooperative again if they had the opportunity.

For most, the desirability of cooperative work is not based on the conception that cooperative members have to work less. Only 25 percent of cooperative members believed that private farmworkers "worked harder," and a full 85 percent were convinced that "cooperatives produced more." Eighty-five percent of cooperative members even went as far as asserting that "poverty would be eliminated if all land were cooperativized."

Those who contend that workers' control enhances job satisfaction would not be surprised by the previous findings. But the relative contentment of cooperative workers is indeed surprising, given the severe political and economic difficulties they faced at the time of the survey. That the members of the new production units managed to sustain a strongly positive view of their work life in the face of low wages, land devolutions, and credit denials is a clear illustration that cooperatives have special and profound effects on their members' world views.

Increased Productivity. Whether higher levels of work satisfaction are transferred into higher levels of productivity is not so easy to resolve. We know that the vast majority of cooperative workers *feel* that cooperatives are more productive, but the components of increased production are many and intertwined. There is no doubt that the new production units have at least attempted to produce more than the latifúndia before them. Even the harshest critics of agrarian reform concede that more land was seeded than ever before. The hunting preserves that once occupied the greater part of whole parishes were replaced by fields of wheat or rye. Lands that were covered with stones and brush for decades have now been cleared and

---

[31] This was the wage in October of 1980. Wages have changed since then and the differential has grown greater over time.

TABLE 5.4
Cultivated Land in the Agrarian Reform Zone

	Cultivated Area	Cultivated Area as % of Arable Land (in hectares)	Variation in Relation to 1974
Before the Occupations	94,500	8%	—
1975-76	271,000	23	176,500
1976-77	265,000	23	170,500
1977-78	312,000	28	217,500
1978-79	279,000	30	184,500
1979-80	315,000	36	220,500

SOURCE: Comissão Organizadora, *5ª Conferência da Reforma Agrária* (Évora, 1981), mimeographed.

planted with grains or sunflowers. Table 5.4 illustrates how the use of land has been increased since the time of the occupations. By 1979, the amount of cultivated land had more than tripled.

Faced with supporting four times as many workers as their wealthy predecessors, it was only natural that the managers of worker-controlled farms would attempt to increase the amount of land under cultivation. The table suggests that the amount of land planted with crops increased nearly 200 percent in the first year of workers' control. Members of cooperatives performed tasks that the previous landlords had either neglected or deemed insufficiently profitable. Stones were cleared, brush was burned, and sometimes crops were planted up to the very base of cork and olive trees.

As worker-managers expanded the amount of land under cultivation, they expanded the investment in farm equipment and livestock. As was discussed in Chapter One, Portugal's agricultural sector was notoriously undercapitalized. With fewer than 9 tractors per thousand hectares, Portugal had the least mechanized farming sector in Europe,[32] far behind Greece and even Spain (which had respectively 17 and 15 tractors per thousand hectares). Only 9 percent of all farms used mechanical rather than animal or human energy for cultivation, and only 25 percent used credit for either current accounts or investment.[33] Recognizing that increased productivity was closely associated with increased mechanization, many worker-managers invested heavily in farm machinery. Table 5.5 records the amount

[32] António Lopes Cardoso, *Luta Pela Reforma Agrária* (Lisbon: Diabril, 1977), p. 69.
[33] Henrique de Barros, *A Estrutura Agrária Portuguesa* (Lisbon: Editorial República, 1972), pp. 45-46.

TABLE 5.5
Increase in Mechanization on Worker-Controlled Farms

	Tractors	Harvesters	Cultivators	Trucks	Motors	Plows and Other Machinery
1975-76	1,520	760	700	70	570	4,010
1976-77	410	340	610	130	1,250	4,190

SOURCE: Comissão Organizadora, *5ª Conferência da Reforma Agrária* (Évora, 1981), mimeographed.

of new machinery purchased by worker-controlled farms during the first two years of the agrarian reform.

Investment in livestock was no less ambitious than investment in machinery. The number of head of livestock on worker-controlled farms increased some 60 percent during the first year of the agrarian reform, and an additional 100 percent in the second year.[34]

The changes in cultivation and investment just described led to increases in production. Grain production in the agrarian reform zone in 1975/1976 exceeded the previous ten-year average by a full 26 percent. Wheat production stood at 13 percent above average, barley at 20 percent above average, and oats stood at 10 percent above average.[35]

There is great controversy over the extent to which this early increase in production was due to workers' control per se. Critics of the agrarian reform argue that increases in production were the result of the sudden availability and expenditure of government credit. For a period, the new production units did indeed receive more government credit than the private farming units they replaced. Between the summer of 1975 and February of 1977, loans to the new production units exceeded $100 million.[36] It is logical to predict that this relatively great infusion of capital would be responsible for part of the production increase. But what part? Does credit explain the increase better than the establishment of workers' control itself?

[34] Comissão Organizadora, *5ª Conferência da Reforma Agrária* (Évora, 1981), mimeographed, p. 13.

[35] Cardoso, *Luta*, p. 58. It should be noted that productivity has decreased on many farms since 1977. Bad weather contributed to the decline, but the 1977 passage of legislation allowing landlords to resume possession of large portions of occupied land disrupted production significantly. The legislation is discussed in Chapters Seven and Eight.

[36] Ministério de Agricultura e Pescas, unpublished collection of agricultural credit expenses (Lisbon, 1977), mimeographed, p. 1. The official figure, given to me in October 1980, was 4,380,892,000 escudos.

FIGURE 5.1
Percentage Increase in Wheat Production by Percentage
of Land under Workers' Control, 1975-1976

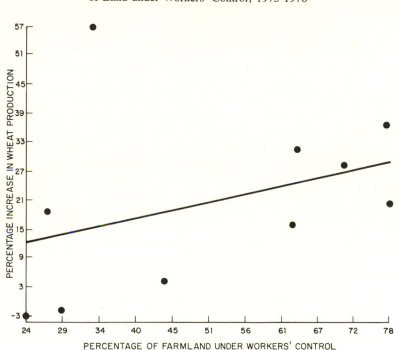

SOURCES: Centro Regional da Reforma Agrária do Distrito de Évora, unpublished records; Eduardo de Freitas, "Alguns Dados Referentes à Reforma Agrária no Distrito de Évora," *Análise Social* (April-June 1977); Instituto Nacional de Estatística, *Boletim Mensal das Estatísticas Agrícolas* (Lisbon: INE, 1976); and Instituto dos Cereais, unpublished records.

A close look at official statistics on production, credit, and cooperative land suggests that the increases in production were probably due to workers' control and not to increases in credit. The scatterplot pictured in Figure 5.1 depicts the relationship between percentage increase in wheat production and percentage of land under workers' control. The data are from ten counties in the district of Évora where the author could verify both production and occupation figures. The amount of land under workers' control varied from just under 25 percent to nearly 80 percent. The data indicate that grain production rose around 28 percent in those counties where the most land was seized and about 12 percent in those counties where the least land was seized.

In general, the greater the amount of property under workers' control, the greater the increase in productivity. The only case in which we observe a relatively great increase in productivity and only a modest-sized cooperative sector is in the county of Alandroal. (The outlier in the upper-left-hand corner of the figure.) This county was unusual in having the least mechanized agricultural sector in the district. The last prerevolutionary census of machinery (carried out in 1968) reports only 57 tractors in the entire county—a ratio of 1 per 770 hectares versus 1 per 330 hectares for the district as a whole. Yields on what had been grossly underutilized property increased quickly with a minimal investment in machinery. This investment was possible because the county's cooperatives maintained an extremely favorable land-to-labor ratio. With a relatively high ratio of 39 hectares per worker (as opposed to around 24 hectares per worker for the Évora district average), these cooperatives had relatively low wage bills and could more easily channel funds toward innovation and mechanization.

Excluding the unique case of Alandroal, these data suggest that workers' control is positively associated with increases in productivity. They indicate that for every 10 percent of land under workers' control, there was a 3 percent increase in production. The relationship between increases in output and increases in credit was stochastic, i.e., there was no association at all between the two.[37]

Although one must be extremely cautious in generalizing from aggregate data, we have here suggestive evidence that the cooperatives were more productive than the private farms that they replaced. They were more productive not because they received more credit but because of qualities intrinsic to the cooperative experience itself.[38] Very few cooperatives have

---

[37] There is some question as to whether significance tests have much meaning with this size sample, but for those who are interested the relationship described in Figure 5.1 approaches statistical significance despite both the small number of cases and the outlier in the upper-left-hand corner (p≈.16). The relationship between percentage of land under workers' control and absolute increase in production is significant at the .03 level. Relating wheat production to credit extended, R = .048, with a significance level of .44. More important, the scatterplot of the two variables reveals a completely random relationship. The lack of a relationship between credit and production is troublesome in terms of public policy and is largely reflective of the use of credit to pay wage bills.

[38] This is probably due to an increase in land use as well as an increase in simple hard work. Both are reflected in higher productivity. The Portuguese case is not the first in which production rose after the institution of workers' control. Malefakis describes "a considerable rise in Aragonese wheat production" during collectivization in Spain. McClintock discovered that cooperatives performed as well as or "slightly better" than haciendas in Peru, and Espinosa and Zimbalist discovered an increase in productivity in worker-managed industrial firms in Chile. See Edward Malefakis, "Peasants, Politics, and Civil War in Spain, 1931-1939," in Robert Bezucha, ed., *Modern European Social History* (Lexington, Massachusetts: Heath, 1972), p. 223; McClintock, *Peasant Cooperatives*, p. 246; and Espinosa and Zimbalist, *Economic Democracy*, p. 187.

had the opportunity to experiment with new crops or techniques, but the units do possess a relatively enthusiastic labor force. The members of the new productive units are not alienated workers. The possessive *nossa* (ours) enters into any description of cooperative life. Even the names of the new production units reflect a sense of communal ownership. In the parish of Odemira one will find a cooperative named "The Victory Is Ours"; in the parish of Loura, a cooperative named "It's Difficult But Ours."

Cooperative members have the sense that they are working for themselves and their community rather than for a boss (or *patrão*), and this reduces a great deal of counterproductive behavior. Gone are the days of the silent strike when laborers worked as slowly as possible in an effort to engage in some form of resistance during the years when real strikes were illegal. Gone are the days when workers would steal farm produce without fear of peer group sanction—when even for the police, as a policeman recalled, "the issue was never if one stole, but whether one stole in quantities above an acceptable limit." Lethargy and stealing have probably not been eliminated, but they are at least not sanctioned by the working community as they were in the past.

Stronger social controls are not the only advantage that cooperatives have over private farms. Unlike their private competitors, worker-controlled farms make seasonal use of volunteer labor. Busloads of men and women travel from urban areas for day-long *jornadas de trabalho* (volunteer work trips) during the harvest season, picking tons of grapes or tomatoes at no cost to the producers. Cooperative produce often reaches the marketplace faster, cheaper, and in better condition as a result.

Thus both informal observation and statistical analysis suggest that the cooperative workers of Portel were in fact correct: cooperatives do appear to produce more. Of course, this is a generalization that does not apply to each of the new production units. Cooperatives and collectives, like private farms, vary markedly from one case to the next. Some are more efficient than others, and some are wholly inefficient. But at a general level, the cooperatives and collectives of the agrarian reform zone appear to confirm what the productivity hypothesis predicts.

IN summary, the emergence of workers' control in agriculture appears to have had quite significant effects on the working lives of the men and women of the rural South. In the past, employer-employee relations were marked by hierarchy and bitterness. With workers' control, the employer-employee relationship has disappeared. One might argue that a hierarchy based on education and experience has emerged instead, but differences in power are now based on the outcome of free elections. Workers rightfully feel that they can control who the people at the top of the hierarchy *are*— and this is the most important control of all. The camaraderie within the cooperatives and the overwhelming sense that the land really *does* belong to the workers themselves contribute to increased productivity and thereby serve the interests of the larger community as well.

SIX

Workers' Control and the Lives
of Workers

THE PARTICIPATORY SOCIETY HYPOTHESIS

Social scientists' predictions concerning the consequences of workers' control extend beyond the workplace and into the public lives of the workers involved. Proponents of what might be called the participatory society hypothesis argue, first, that the democratization of enterprise structures stimulates workers to participate in politics outside the firm and, second, that this increase in participation serves the interests of democracy, social consensus, and good government in the society as a whole.

John Stuart Mill was one of the first to connect the management of industry, the behavior of workers, and the strength of democracy in a single argument. In 1848, in what was probably the first widely publicized "review" of worker participation literature, Mill discussed collective experiments in a variety of European countries and pointed out how each experiment had favorable effects on the behavior of the workers involved. Mill believed that self-management would provide workers with "a school of the social sympathies and the practical intelligence."[1] These newly transformed workers would, in turn, create "a moral revolution,"[2] elevating political life in general. Mill insisted, in fact, that society would not "improve" unless self-management became the principal means of enterprise governance. He wrote:

> The form of association which, if mankind continues to improve, must be expected in the end to predominate, is the association of the labourers themselves on terms of equality, collectively owning the capital, . . . and working under management elected and removable by themselves.[3]

In 1920, when the debate about industrial management and political democracy was much more lively than it had been in Mill's day, G.D.H.

---

[1] J. S. Mill, *Principles of Political Economy* (London: Longmans, Green and Co., 1921), p. 790. See also p. 765.

[2] Ibid., p. 787.

[3] Ibid., pp. 772-773.

Cole presented a more graphic version of the participatory society hypothesis. In *Guild Socialism Restated*, he argued explicity that social structures determine both the behavior of individuals and the health of political democracy. To get "structural mechanisms right," he stated, "is the surest way not only to the . . . happiness and well-directed achievement of individuals but to the well-being of the body politic."[4] The well-being of the body politic demanded democracy, and, as Cole saw it, democracy demanded a wholly active citizenry.[5] An active citizenry could, however, never be produced under the existing system of industrial employment, for "a servile system of industry inevitably produced political servility."[6] If democracy were to prevail, all social structures, especially industrial structures, had to be democratized.

There is much of Cole's theory in contemporary arguments for worker participation. Rodney Barker asserts, for example, that today's workers' control movement in Britain has its roots in Cole's plan for guild socialism,[7] and, in fact, statements of the participatory society hypothesis are frequent in today's literature. We read that "self-management and influence over small areas . . . creates a more highly developed demand for participation" in other spheres[8] and that "individuals who work in a self-managing mode will, over time, become more . . . participatory in other parts of their life, especially politics."[9]

Many argue, as Cole did, that democracy will not succeed unless worker participation does. Pateman states: "Participation in non-governmental authority structures is necessary to foster and develop the psychological qualities required for participation at the national level."[10]

The benefits of increased participation at the national level seem obvious to the proponents of the participatory society hypothesis. Full participation would "contribute to creating authentic creative resourcefulness among the masses."[11] It would "encourage the search for objective truth"[12] and

[4] G.D.H. Cole, *Guild Socialism Restated* (London: L. Parsons, 1920), p. 26.

[5] Ibid., p. 18.

[6] G.D.H. Cole, *Labour in the Commonwealth* (London: Headly Bros., 1918), p. 35.

[7] Rodney Barker, "Guild Socialism Revisited?" *Political Quarterly* (July 1975).

[8] David Jenkins, *Job Power* (Baltimore: Penguin Books, 1974), p. 291.

[9] M. J. Elden, "Organizational Self-Management," in Eugen Pusic, ed., *Participation and Self-Management*, vols. 1-6 (Zagreb: Institute for Social Research, 1972), 5: 77.

[10] Carole Pateman, *Participation and Democratic Theory* (Cambridge: Cambridge University Press, 1970), p. 50.

[11] Alexander Matejko, "The Sociotechnical Principles of Workers' Control," in Eugen Pusic, ed., *Participation and Self-Management*, vols. 1-6 (Zagreb: Institute for Social Research, 1972), 3: 46.

[12] Ichak Adizes, "On Conflict Resolution," in ibid., 5: 33.

"offer a maximum of efficiency, maneuverability, and flexibility, with a minimum of complexity."[13]

Would the beneficial effects of worker participation be confined only to developed countries? Apparently not. These analysts add no such caveats to their arguments, and several, such as Vanek, assert that their theories are especially applicable in the modernizing world.

The participatory society hypothesis is both appealing and enduring, but its proponents may be basing their arguments on assumptions that do not hold outside the advanced industrial societies. To begin with, the projected increases in participatory behavior, if they exist at all, may not easily find institutional outlets. Many major worker participation experiments in the industrializing world have been established under military dictatorships or one-party regimes.[14] Workers who are exposed to a participatory enterprise structure in these nations might indeed be stimulated to participate more in politics, but their opportunities for participation will be sharply restricted.

And what effect does high participation have in modernizing societies in the first place? Can we assume that high participation does, in fact, serve the interests of democracy in the poorer nations? Studies outside the worker participation literature suggest that we should not make this assumption,[15] and the proponents of the participatory society hypothesis have thus far marshalled little evidence to the contrary. Carole Pateman is one of the few theorists who has attempted to substantiate her arguments with empirical data. Though she views recent empirical investigations as proof that the theorists of participatory democracy are on "firm ground" and that the individual "generalises from his experience" in industrial authority structures "to the wider, national political sphere,"[16] a closer look at her evidence illustrates that this is not necessarily true.

In citing findings from the *Civic Culture* as illustration of her argument, Pateman neglects to mention (or to heed) the caveats that the authors themselves attach to their findings. Almond and Verba acknowledge a causality problem that Pateman ignores. They do agree that there is "a

[13] Jaroslav Vanek, *The Participatory Economy* (Ithaca, New York: Cornell University Press, 1971), p. 162.

[14] Some examples of this are the Mondragón cooperatives under Franco in Spain, the self-managed units of the Yugoslav economy, and the agricultural cooperatives established after the Peruvian revolution of 1968.

[15] See, for example, Myron Weiner, "Political Participation: Crisis of the Political Process," in Leonard Binder et al., *Crises and Sequences of Political Development* (Princeton, New Jersey: Princeton University Press, 1971); David Apter, *Choice and the Politics of Allocation* (New Haven: Yale University Press, 1971); and Naomi Caiden and Aaron Wildavsky, *Planning and Budgeting in Poor Countries* (New York: Wiley, 1974), p. 221.

[16] Pateman, *Participation and Democratic Theory*, p. 47.

tendency toward homogeneity between job and political authority patterns" but quickly add that it is difficult to tell "whether job participation leads to democratic political orientations, or vice versa."[17] The authors also view workplace participation as a much less potent force than Pateman leads us to believe. Their data indicate that "work-place participation does not have as broad an effect upon one's sense of political competence as educational attainment does" and that "job participation, though it can reinforce that which is learned in the family and the school, *cannot* replace it."[18]

Another problem with the evidence used to justify the participatory society hypothesis derives from the reliance on studies of "sense of efficacy." Blumberg, Pateman, and most other analysts who have attempted to integrate "participatory society" arguments with empirical data have relied heavily on surveys of efficacy. This is inappropriate, for sense of efficacy is not a behavioral measure but a psychological orientation. Workers' *feelings* about their abilities to influence politics are certainly less relevant than their actual *attempts*, for participation is not an attitude but a form of behavior.

Unfortunately, there are remarkably few studies that associate changes in political behavior with changes in job authority patterns. The works that are available contradict each other. A study conducted in the United States found a positive association between participation at work and participation outside.[19] Another, more extensive work, compared different rates of participation in four countries and concluded that self-management was *not* associated with increased participation in community life.[20] Scattered evidence from other studies suggests the same conclusion.[21] Worker participation might indeed be a stimulus to political participation, but advocates have not yet illustrated that this is the case in either the developed or the developing worlds.

With even this basic evidence unavailable, the second premise of the hypothesis is, of course, unsubstantiated (i.e., one cannot illustrate that an increase in participation is good unless one illustrates that the increase

[17] Gabriel Almond and Sidney Verba, *The Civic Culture* (Boston: Little, Brown, 1965), p. 297.

[18] Almond and Verba, *Civic Culture*, pp. 301-302. Emphasis mine.

[19] Elden, "Organizational Self-Management," 5: 85.

[20] Miroslav Disman, "The Values and Participation: Comparison" [*sic*] in Eugen Pusic, ed., *Participation and Self-Management*, vols. 1-6 (Zagreb: Institute for Social Research, 1972), 2: 64. Emphasis mine. The countries were Yugoslavia, the United States, the Soviet Union, and Canada.

[21] Ichak Adizes, *Industrial Democracy Yugoslav Style* (New York: Free Press, 1971), p. 219, draws a correlation between worker participation and *decreased* party involvement, and Jiri Kolaja, *Workers' Councils: The Yugoslav Experience* (London: Tavistock Publications, 1965), p. 31, draws a correlation between self-management and decreased union involvement.

exists in the first place). Case studies that associate the institution of workers' participation with a strengthening of democratic structures at the national level are rare (if, indeed, they exist at all), and the histories of various worker participation experiences suggest an opposite effect. The institution of worker participation in Algeria, Chile, Czechoslovakia, and Poland was followed not by a strengthening of democratic structures but by the institution of more coercion.

As with the other hypotheses analyzed here, these generalizations lack empirical justification. Workers' control has rarely been implemented on a major scale in any sort of society, but historical experience suggests an unappealing counterpart to the participatory society hypothesis. In nations with scarce resources and weak steering mechanisms, the increased activism associated with workers' participation may trigger drives for the coercive maintenance of order rather than drives for democratization. Studies outside the worker participation literature make frequent reference to the connection between high participation and disorder. Dennis Thompson reminds us:

> There is no particular reason why participation should lead necessarily to more cooperation and better communal relations. Political activity may just as easily create social antagonisms as facilitate social relations.[22]

Seymour Lipset argues similarly in discussing the democratization of workers' organizations: ''Institutionalized democracy within private governments . . . may in fact . . . weaken the democratic processes of civil society.''[23]

In the context of developing societies, high participation has a special meaning. Political participation involves, intrinsically, the making of demands. In a system with limited material resources, demands are likely to exceed the rewards available. Frustration and disorder may result and, in turn, provoke alterations of the system. As Jürgen Habermas states:

> When more problems are posed in a given environment than the system's steering capacity can solve, logically derivable contradictions appear that require, on pain of ruin, an alteration of system structures.[24]

Even if industrial democracy does stimulate greater political participation, we cannot (with the evidence available) assume that increased participation will have the systemic impact that proponents of the participatory

---

[22] Dennis Thompson, *The Democratic Citizen* (Cambridge: Cambridge University Press, 1970), p. 66.

[23] S. M. Lipset, *Political Man* (Boston: Anchor Books, 1965), p. 431.

[24] Jürgen Habermas, *Legitimation Crisis* (Boston: Beacon Press, 1973), p. 27.

society hypothesis suggest. There are historical materials and scholarly arguments that lead to a more pessimistic forecast. Here, as with the other hypotheses, we can make no predictions until more cases are studied.

Participation in Portugal

In the Portuguese case, the connection between workers' control and political participation is, in some respects, exactly as the participatory society hypothesis suggests. Cooperative workers do appear to be considerably more active politically than either farmers (small holders, *rendeiros*, or *seareiros*) or private farmworkers. The reason for this association is not at all clear and may be due to factors that previous scholars failed to anticipate. The second half of the participatory society hypothesis is also only partially confirmed by the Portuguese case. The high levels of political participation associated with cooperatives have some positive ramifications on the local level but provoke reaction and hostility at the national level.

Macrolevel evidence bearing on the association between workers' control and participation is difficult to find. Voting statistics provide one of the few sources available, but conclusions drawn from these are merely suggestive. Nevertheless, if workers' control does indeed stimulate higher levels of participation, one would expect that voting rates would, first, be higher in the agrarian reform zone than in other parts of the country and, second, increase over time as workers' control became institutionalized.

Figure 6.1 demonstrates that rates of electoral participation are in fact consistently higher in the agrarian reform zone than in the nation as a whole. The voters of Portalegre, Évora, and to a lesser extent, Beja, have voted in greater proportions than the national average since the first post-revolutionary election. But contrary to what the participatory society hypothesis might lead us to expect, electoral participation rates have not risen over time. At the district level at least, voters are even less inclined to participate in national elections than they were four years ago—before workers' control had actually begun.

Of course, this evidence is merely suggestive, for it aggregates voters who are involved with workers' control with voters who are not, but the same pattern seems to hold at a more refined level of analysis. In the six counties where more than 50 percent of the labor force works on cooperative farms, participation in national elections takes on the pattern shown in Figure 6.2. Once again electoral participation rates exceed those of the nation as a whole but do not increase over time. The rate of increase from 1976 to 1979 is no greater inside these counties than in the nation as a whole.

The relationships described do not disprove the participatory society

136

FIGURE 6.1
Electoral Participation: Three Counties of the
Agrarian Reform Zone and Mainland Portugal

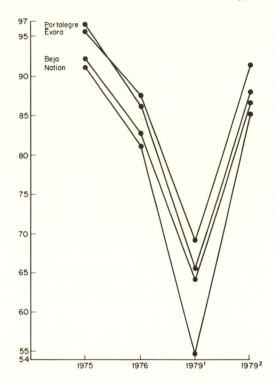

SOURCES: Ministério da Administração Interna, *Eleição para a Assembleia Constituente-1975*
(Lisbon: Imprensa Nacional, 1975); Ministério da Administração Interna, *Eleição para a
Assembleia da República-1976* (Lisbon: Imprensa Nacional, 1976); Ministério da Admin-
istração Interna, *Eleição Intercalar para a Assembleia da República-1979* (Lisbon: Imprensa
Nacional, 1979).

NOTES: [1] Local elections.   [2] National assembly elections.

hypothesis. Voting is merely one of many forms of participation, and it is
possible that these other forms do increase over time. It is also possible
that individuals who are not connected with cooperatives or collectives
distort the patterns observed—perhaps the proportion of voting cooperative
members has risen to 100 percent, while the proportion of voting outsiders
has dropped off considerably. Whatever the case, the data suggest at least
some limitations to the participatory society hypothesis: first, that increases
in participation might be limited to certain forms of political activity and,

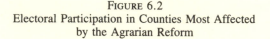

FIGURE 6.2
Electoral Participation in Counties Most Affected
by the Agrarian Reform

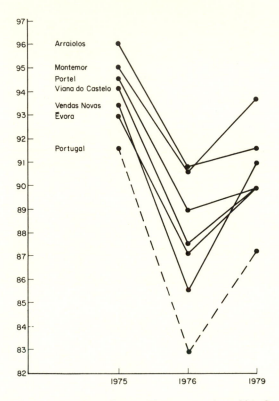

SOURCES: Ministério da Administração Interna, *Eleição para a Assembleia Constituente-1975* (Lisbon: Imprensa Nacional, 1975); Ministério da Administração Interna, *Eleição para a Assembleia da República-1976* (Lisbon: Imprensa Nacional, 1976); Ministério da Administração Interna, *Eleição Intercalar para a Assembleia da República-1979* (Lisbon: Imprensa Nacional, 1979).

second, that they may be no greater in scope than the worker-controlled sector itself.

At the microlevel, the relationship between workers' control and political participation appears more robust. My questionnaire research assessed several forms of participation. By all but one of the measures used, cooperative members appeared considerably more active than either farmers or private farmworkers.

An important but relatively passive form of political participation is the

TABLE 6.1
Exposure to Political Information in the Media
by Form of Labor
*Do you read, hear, or watch the political
news in the media?*

	No	Yes	Don't Know/ No Response
Cooperative members	17.5%	82.5%	—
Private farmworkers	25.0	71.4	3.6%
Farmers	12.5	82.5	5.0

NOTES: N = 108
Unless otherwise specified, references to cultivators in the
postrevolutionary period are made according to the following scheme: cooperative members are worker-managers on
collectives or cooperatives; private farmworkers are wage
or salaried farmhands on traditional, privately owned farms;
farmers are small farmers, *seareiros*, and *rendeiros*.

TABLE 6.2
Individuals Who Discuss Politics with Friends
by Form of Labor

Cooperative members	60.0%
Private farmworkers	28.6
Farmers	20.0

N = 108

willingness to receive political information through the print and broadcast
media. Table 6.1 illustrates that there is little difference between sectors
on the issue of exposure to information. Exposure is high for each category,
involving well over two-thirds of each sector. Cooperative workers seem
more interested in media news than private farmworkers, but they are not,
by this measure, the most active group in the community. Farmers are just
as likely to become involved in this most passive form of participation.

Measures of other forms of political participation reveal significant differences between cooperative members, private farmworkers, and farmers.
Workers in the cooperative sector discuss politics more frequently than
either of the other two groups. When asked, "Do you discuss politics with
your friends?" survey respondents offered the answers recorded in Table
6.2. Cooperative members are three times as likely to have political dis-

TABLE 6.3

Increases in Political Discussion
by Form of Labor

	Point Increase Pre- and Postrevolution
Cooperative members	37.5%
Private farmworkers	25.0
Farmers	12.5

N = 108

TABLE 6.4

Frequency of Political Discussion by Form of Labor

	Daily	Several Times a Week	Occasionally	Rarely or Never	No Response
Cooperative members	5.0%	20.0%	35.0%	40.0%	—
Private farmworkers	—	3.6	25.0	67.9	3.6
Farmers	5.0	2.5	12.5	72.5	7.5

N = 108

cussions as farmers and approximately twice as likely to have discussions as private farmworkers.

As was mentioned in the preceding discussion of land occupations, differences in participation levels predate the institutionalization of workers' control. When asked if they were accustomed to discussing politics with their friends *before* the 25th of April, 22 percent of the cooperative members said yes, 3.6 percent of the private farmworkers said yes, and 7.5 percent of the small farmers said yes. Does this predisposition to political discussion account for the difference in participation observed today? Table 6.3 suggests that it does not. Comparing prerevolutionary figures with postrevolutionary figures, the proportion of individuals who became more active is much greater for cooperative members than for either of the other groups: More than one-third of all cooperative members became more active, while only one-fourth of all private farmworkers and one-eighth of all farmers did the same

Looking at frequency of political discussion in the postrevolutionary period alone, one again sees marked differences between the three types of cultivators. Table 6.4 illustrates these differences. Forty percent of all cooperative members report that they discuss politics rarely, if at all. This is a substantial minority, but an overwhelming *majority* of private farmworkers and farmers fall into the same category. Cooperative members are

TABLE 6.5
Types of Political Activity by Form of Labor

	Cooperative Members	Private Farmworkers	Farmers	National Sample[a]
Party leader	10.0%	—	—	3.0%
Party member	30.0	—	2.5%	5.0
Distributor of propaganda	5.0	—	5.0	4.0
Participant in demonstrations	52.5	—	22.5	14.0

NOTES: N = 108

[a] These figures are taken from an excellent survey conducted by Thomas Bruneau and Mário Bacalhau. See Mário Bacalhau, *Os Portugueses e a Política Quatro Anos Depois do 25 de Abril* (Lisbon: Editorial Meseta, 1978), p. 70.

much more likely to engage in political discussion than other groups. Within the subset of people who do discuss politics, cooperative members do so most frequently. The table illustrates that one-quarter of the members of worker-controlled farms discuss politics at least several times a week. This is more than six times the rate for private farmworkers and more than three times the rate for farmers. It is clear that cooperative membership and political discussion are positively related.

A positive association also exists between cooperative membership and other, more partisan forms of political activity. Asked to record the partisan activities in which they had participated since the revolution, respondents offered the information illustrated in Table 6.5. These measures of the more direct forms of participation point to the most marked contrast between the three forms of labor. The most striking responses are those of the private farmworkers who appear to be especially passive, engaging in none of the activities listed. Farmers are more active; over one-fifth have participated in demonstrations, but their participation in other forms of political activity is negligible.

Cooperative members, in marked contrast, appear to be active in all areas of political life, from the most to the least demanding. A full 10 percent held or had held some party office, nearly one-third were party members, and over half had participated in demonstrations. The only activity that did not attract a substantial proportion of cooperative members was the distribution of party literature, which, given the high rate of illiteracy in the region, is highly predictable.

The cooperative members' rates of participation are remarkably high, not only relative to rates in the surrounding community, but relative to the nation as a whole. The fourth column of Table 6.5 illustrates the proportion of the national population that participates in these particular activities.

TABLE 6.6
Sense of Political Efficacy by Form of Labor

	Positive	Negative	No Response
Cooperative members	42.5%	47.5%	10.0%
Private farmworkers	14.3	71.4	14.3
Farmers	25.0	67.5	7.5

N = 108

Once again, cooperative members are more active by each measure. The relationship between political participation and workers' control seems strong indeed.

Table 6.6 suggests that sense of political efficacy may be related to workers' control as well. Despite the political problems that the cooperatives have experienced since their founding, cooperative members have a higher sense of political efficacy than either of the other groups surveyed. When asked, "Do you believe that you can help resolve the national and regional problems that affect you?" more than 40 percent of the cooperative members said yes. Comparing responses across employment groups, one notes that cooperative members are significantly more confident than farmers and three times more confident than private farmworkers.

The data presented in this section illustrate that cooperative members are more inclined toward political participation than either of the other farming groups. Only in a rather passive form of participation—i.e., the receipt of media news—are they even equalled. Taken as a whole, however, the questionnaire evidence supports the participatory society hypothesis but does not decisively confirm it, for the question of causality has not been resolved. Causality might have been illustrated with a series of questions assessing participation before and after the establishment of workers' control, but this was impossible in the context of Portugal, because the Salazar-Caetano regime restricted political participation to such a degree that very few of the survey respondents could have had any prerevolutionary participation experience at all. Thus, contextual factors limit the degree to which one can generalize from the findings.[25]

Contextual factors also suggest that the causal link between workers' control and increased political participation might be forged of materials that scholars writing at the purely theoretical level failed to anticipate.

[25] The one study available that does succeed with "before and after" measurements is Cynthia McClintock's study of Peruvian cooperatives. She began with a survey conducted by scholars from Cornell in 1969 and then did comparative work in 1974. See *Peasant Cooperatives and Political Change in Peru* (Princeton, New Jersey: Princeton University Press, 1981).

Much of the cooperative members' political activity is directed toward the defense of the cooperative per se. The political discussions in which the workers took part were discussions of policies related to the agrarian reform. The demonstrations so widely attended were, by and large, demonstrations in support of the agrarian reform. The political party that attracted such high rates of membership was the Communist party—the party most closely associated with the agrarian reform. These sorts of political activities are precisely what proponents of the participatory society hypothesis had in mind, and they are no doubt associated with the existence of workers' control, but one cannot assess the extent to which these activities would continue if the cooperatives were not under siege. The cooperative members' high sense of political efficacy (which endures despite the siege situation) suggests that workers' control is indeed associated with qualities that are not related to a temporary position of self-defense, but these ambiguities can only be resolved with more research.

While the Portuguese case supports the first part of the participatory society hypothesis by offering strong limited evidence of a positive association between workers' control and participation, it does not support the second part of the hypothesis. Workers' control and the high rates of political participation related to it are not necessarily associated with social consensus.

The societal effects of workers' control depend on the content that political participation assumes. Throughout the agrarian reform zone, increases in political participation have meant increases in protest activity and, with few exceptions, increases in support for the Communist party. This has a neutral or positive effect on consensus and stability in some regions and a very negative effect in others. In counties like Portel where the local government is Communist and the vast majority of citizens have little or no private farmland, social consensus seems to have been enhanced by increased participation. In counties with a greater proportion of peasant holders and, relatedly, a local government controlled by the PSP or a party to its right, the increased participation associated with the cooperatives is a source of polarization.

The contrasting attitudes of two southern merchants illustrate the point. One, whom I'll call Dona Regina, ran a dry goods store in an area where most of the community were farmworkers or cooperative members. The other, whom I'll call Senhor Portas, ran a store in a region with a sizeable middle and small peasantry. Judging from their homes and visible stock, Sr. Portas was only slightly better off, but the two merchants had vastly different views of the cooperatives and the agrarian reform. Dona Regina had a generally positive view. She spoke sympathetically of a modest *rendeiro* who had lost land during the occupations, but she also told stories

143

of how a local landlord had denied food to begging workers and fed his pheasants well instead. She argued that he and many others had no use for their land and that the workers were justified in seizing it. She worried about "where everyone would work if all the cooperatives disappeared." Though she doubted that workers' protests in defense of the agrarian reform would be successful, she argued that "they, like everyone else, have *the right* to speak and protest." Her feelings about the increases in participation were thus guarded but positive.

A few counties away, her counterpart argued differently. For him, the men who occupied the estates were "thieves." The cooperative members had been transformed from "honest men" to "criminals" who were now paid not for work but for "going to demonstrations." The whole agrarian reform had "destroyed the town and its tranquility." His feelings about the increases in participation were extremely hostile.

These two radically different perspectives are not easily explained by early socialization. (In fact, Dona Regina took pride in the fact that her father had held local office during the dictatorship.) The differences were explained instead by the nature of each merchant's community and clientele. Dona Regina lived from the purchases of the cooperatave members who now had a steady income for the first time in their lives. While she sold more fabric, more underwear, more socks, etc., Sr. Portas lived with a sense of relative deprivation. He depended on the purchases of the small and medium peasantry, whose disposable income had decreased over time. He had dreamt, before the revolution, of selling to tourists and had purchased copper pots and painted plates for a market that never materialized. He believed that "the Communists, with all their noise and trouble, kept everyone away."

When we analyze the "noise and trouble" of participation in the context of an actual community, we see that social consensus is not the necessary outcome. One needs only to watch the faces in a village square as a truckload of protesting workers rolls by to recognize how increased participation can provoke polarization. In all but the most homogeneous communities, the political activities of the cooperative members is seen as divisive. The increased activity *is* divisive, in a certain respect, for it highlights any communal differences that exist. Since the polarization that emerged from these differences affected the state's reaction to workers' control, it is discussed further in the third and final section of this study.

THE RADICALIZATION HYPOTHESIS

Closely related to the participatory society hypothesis is another conception about the effects of workers' control that I will call the radicalization hypothesis. This hypothesis holds that the democratization of enterprises promotes workers' class consciousness and fosters the growth of egalitarian, radical activism in the larger political sphere.

Like the other hypotheses discussed here, this one has a long history. Antonio Gramsci is one of its early proponents. Gramsci viewed the establishment of Italy's workers councils in the 1920s as the first phase of communist revolution. To Gramsci, the birth of the councils represented "a major historical event heralding a new era in the history of mankind." It was the revolution "burst forth,"[26] the force that would drive "the working class unwaveringly onward toward the conquest of industrial power."[27] The impetus for the conquest came from the council structures themselves. "Meetings and propaganda" would "bring about a radical transformation of the workers' psychology," and "all [would] eventually acquire a communist consciousness."[28]

Though Gramsci's predictions were not borne out in the context of Italy, his basic argument is still widely popular, especially with members of the European left. André Gorz, for example, argues that the struggle for workers' control creates possibilities that "point beyond capitalism and . . . render the status quo all the more intolerable."[29] According to Gorz, workers' control "will place the workers in an offensive . . . position; it will elevate their level of consciousness," have a "militant and mobilizing" effect, and "stimulate a continually resurging struggle with more and more advanced goals, at a higher and higher level."[30] Like Gramsci, Gorz sees a structural change causing a behavioral change in a "natural" and predictable manner: he states that "the demand for and the exercise of workers' power . . . *quite naturally* lead to a challenge of the priorities and purposes of the capitalist model."[31]

In reasoning that radical behavior is the "natural" result of a particular structural change, proponents of the radicalization hypothesis are forced to make weighty assumptions about the norms of the workers involved. Scholars must assume either that a) the workers were normatively committed to radicalization before the structures changed or that b) the operation of the structures themselves will encourage the workers to adopt new normative positions. How reasonable are these assumptions in the context of a nation such as Portugal?

Case studies from nations at a middle level of development suggest that

[26] Antonio Gramsci, "Selected Writings from *L'Ordine Nuovo*," in Branko Horvat et al., eds., *Self-Governing Socialism* (White Plains, New York: International Arts and Sciences Press, 1975), 1: 232.

[27] Ibid., p. 228

[28] Ibid., pp. 223 and 226.

[29] André Gorz, *Strategy for Labor* (Boston: Beacon Press, 1964), p. 60.

[30] Ibid., p. 53.

[31] Ibid., p. 54; emphasis mine.

worker participation does not necessarily produce class-conscious radicalization. In Yugoslavia, for example, where egalitarian, communal norms are the essence of the national ideology, self-managed enterprises allegedly sacrifice jobs for the sake of higher profits[32] and then, according to one analyst, show no "great willingness to contribute to communal, welfare, or social improvement."[33] Despite decades of self-management and national resocialization programs, "all empirical research" has shown "that in the hierarchy of [Yugoslavian workers'] motivational factors, personal income ranks first."[34]

Even on Israeli kibbutzim, where the normative climate would seem most conducive to collective consciousness, materialistic motivations have eroded even the most fundamental radical values. Though the kibbutzim were founded on the "self-labor" principle, economic incentives have forced virtually every industrial kibbutz to hire labor. These hired laborers are, by and large, not included in the facilities of the commune. Though the "exploitation" of the hired labor provokes great controversy and has accordingly diminished over time, the proportion of wage labor on industrial kibbutzim still constitutes a minimum of 19 percent and a maximum of 85 percent of the movement's work force.[35]

Since the radicalization hypothesis is not borne out in seemingly conducive environments, it is not surprising that evidence from other social contexts is also negative. Algeria's brief experiment with *autogestion* was aborted in part because worker-owners were not behaving according to radical principles. Class consciousness and egalitarian principles were conspicuously absent when the Algerian agricultural proletariat seized major agribusinesses in the aftermath of the revolution. They refused to share property with any outsiders, regardless of class. Army excombatants, local peasants, and seasonal workers were often driven forcibly from the seized properties, though each group had contributed to the revolutionary effort, and some had contributed more than the worker-owners themselves.[36] The Algerian workers' control experience was not Gramsci's "revolution burst

[32] Paul Blumberg, *Industrial Democracy: The Sociology of Participation* (New York: Schocken Books, 1973), p. 213.

[33] Kolaja, *Workers' Councils*, p. 27.

[34] Veljko Rus, "The Limits of Organized Participation," in Eugen Pusic, ed., *Participation and Self-Management*, vols. 1-6 (Zagreb: Institute for Social Research, 1972), 2: 184.

[35] Figures are from a 1978 survey. The use of hired labor varies from one kibbutz movement to another. See Uri Leviatan, "Hired Labor on the Kibbutz: Ideology, History and Social Psychological Effects," in Uri Leviatan and Menachem Rosner, eds., *Work and Organization in Kibbutz Industry* (Norwood, Pennsylvania: Norwood Editions, 1980), p. 68.

[36] See Ian Clegg, *Workers' Self-Management in Algeria* (New York: Monthly Review Press, 1971), pp. 48-61.

forth'' but rather a bold ''attempt to preserve jobs and increase income at the expense of any outsider, whether capitalist or peasant.''[37]

Peru's recent experience with worker-owned sugar plantations suggests a pattern similar to the Algerian case. The Peruvian workers who control this agribusiness have been consistently unwilling to share profits or decision-making powers with workers and peasants outside the self-managed community. Furthermore, membership in the community itself is being whittled down by worker-leaders who seek to maximize profits per worker and accordingly prefer capital-intensive investment to labor intensification. The *egoismo*, or selfishness, of these and other worker-owners became an important national issue during the recent years of military rule.[38]

Self-interested behavior among ''third world'' worker-owners has not been confined to the Peruvian and the Algerian experiences. When Bolivia's mines were under worker control, the workers sometimes restricted employment, hoarded enterprise profits, and alienated the Bolivian peasantry with coercive acts. Similarly, workers involved in the establishment of *autogestión* in socialist Chile found that the workers' own ''proprietary attitude'' led to exploitation of fellow workers and the evolution of a second-class citizenry within firms.[39]

Historical experience suggests that the democratization of enterprise structures does not lead ''naturally'' to ''a radical transformation of the workers' psychology,'' as Gramsci hoped it might. In the cases reviewed here, at least, workers did not evince the class-conscious and egalitarian behavior predicted.

Radicalization in Portuguese Cooperatives

Do the members of the agricultural cooperatives in Portugal behave as Gramsci would predict, or as many of their counterparts in other countries have done in the past? Workers' control in Portugal appears to be associated with radicalization rather than embourgeoisement. Evidence related to both ideology and behavior supports the same conclusion.

[37] Ibid., p. 48. Algeria's most recent attempts to reinstitute self-management have met with some success, but these new experiments have not attracted much attention from Western academics.

[38] See McClintock, *Peasant Cooperatives*, pp. 19, 236, 262, and 278; Alfred Stepan, *State and Society: Peru in Comparative Perspective* (Princeton, New Jersey: Princeton University Press, 1978); and Peter Knight, ''New Forms of Economic Organization in Peru: Toward Workers' Self-Management'' in Abraham Lowenthal, ed., *The Peruvian Experiment* (Princeton, New Jersey: Princeton University Press, 1975).

[39] Victor Arroyo, ''Experiences of the Federation of Workers' Brigades and Enterprises,'' in Branko Horvat et al., eds., *Self-Governing Socialism* (New York: International Arts and Sciences Press, 1975), 1: 284.

TABLE 6.7
Votes for Portuguese Communist Parties in the Agrarian Reform Zone:
National Elections, 1975-1979

	Votes	%	% Change
Constitutional Assembly 1975	159,874	33.5	—
National Assembly 1976	175,321	37.6	9.7
National Assembly 1979	214,795	44.2	22.5

SOURCE: C. Costa et al., *As Eleições no Portugal de Abril* (Lisbon: "Avante!" 1980).

TABLE 6.8
Votes for Portuguese Communist Parties in the Agrarian Reform Zone:
Local Elections, 1976-1979

1976		1979		% Increase	
Votes	%	Votes	%	Votes	%
155,729	41.8	208,240	48.8	52,511	33.7

SOURCE: C. Costa et al., *As Eleições no Portugal de Abril* (Lisbon: "Avante!" 1980).

Radical Beliefs. Voting patterns in the agrarian reform zone suggest that radicalization has increased steadily since the first election for the National Assembly in 1976. Table 6.7 illustrates the trends in the Communist party's popularity. The 22 percent vote increase between the first and second National Assembly elections reflects a genuine and impressive increase in radical party support.

Voters were apparently turning to the parties of the left at both the national and the local level. Table 6.8 illustrates the proportion of local election votes garnered by the PCP-MDP coalition in the agrarian reform zone. The proportion of voters supporting Communist parties rose from 42 percent in 1976 to nearly 50 percent in 1979. The number of citizens supporting these parties rose a full 33.7 percent in just three years.[40]

These macrolevel trends in voting correspond closely to the individual ideological positions of cooperative members. The author's questionnaire research revealed that cooperative members are highly class conscious and are very little inclined toward the sort of embourgeoisement evident in other cases of workers' control. On a broad array of ideological measures, the contrast between cooperative members and other elements of the farm-

[40] It is interesting to note that in Portel the proportion of cooperative workers who switched from voting Socialist to voting Communist is approximately one-third, too.

TABLE 6.9
Community Members' Categorization of Village Social Groups

	Cooperative Members	Private Farmworkers	Farmers
All workers	25.0%	7.1%	35.0%
Rich and poor	7.5	—	2.5
Farmers and farmworkers	7.5	21.4	5.0
3 classes: all in agriculture	37.5	32.1	12.5
3 classes: in all sectors	10.0	7.1	10.0

NOTES: N = 108
The proportion of respondents listing social groups that fell outside the categories listed was 10.0 percent for cooperative members, 17.9 percent for private farmworkers, and 10.0 percent for farmers.

ing community is sharp and consistent, with private farmworkers and farmers thinking in individualistic ways and cooperative members thinking along group lines.

The tendency to perceive division in society varies considerably within the farming community. Cooperative members are most likely to think in class terms and farmers are least likely to do so. The percentage of respondents who stated that they simply did not know what social classes were was 25 percent for farmers, 14.3 percent for private farmworkers, and only 2.5 percent for cooperative members. Of the individuals who were familiar with the term *class*, cooperative members were most likely to think in terms of class divisions. When asked in an open-ended question to list the social classes in their town or village, survey respondents gave the answers recorded in Table 6.9.

More than 47 percent of all cooperative members saw three or more separate social groups in their communities. Private farmworkers were slightly less likely to perceive or to discuss the complexities of rural society, and farmers were the least likely to do so. More than one-third of the farmers interviewed insisted that there were no real social divisions and that society was comprised of "workers only." When respondents listed social divisions, they typically listed occupational groups: private farmworkers, *seareiros, rendeiros*, and small farmers. Few respondents mentioned large landowners or *agrários*, though several took pains to mention that there were landowners in the area *before* the 25th of April, and others suggested that the landowners "would soon be back."

The fact that most respondents' notion of social class corresponds to what many outsiders would perceive as merely different groups of peasants

149

TABLE 6.10
Explanations for Poverty before the 25th of April by Form of Labor

	Cooperative Members	Private Farmworkers	Farmers
Poor soil	—	10.7%	12.5%
Lack of technical expertise	5.0%	3.6	12.5
Lands badly divided	17.5	42.9	20.0
Lands belonged to people who did not want to farm them	40.0	14.3	40.0
Landowners had huge profits but did not want to pay well	37.5	25.0	12.5
Other	—	3.5	2.5

N = 108

indicates the social importance of sometimes subtle differences in property relations. The vast majority of the men interviewed did not view society in terms of a dichotomous division between rich and poor or landed and landless. They noted instead the difference between men who owned land, men who rented land, and men who worked for wages. Absent from all responses was any Marxist terminology. Not a single individual used the terms proletariat or bourgeoisie. Thus the recognition of social division was probably not an imported concept brought to the countryside by an urban intelligentsia but a realization that emerged quite naturally in a society with scarce resources. Cooperative members were more aware of these divisions than any other group.

Cooperative members were also more likely to view a connection between social divisions and material well-being. When asked to explain why there was such poverty in rural areas before the 25th of April, respondents offered the answers shown in Table 6.10. A full 77.5 percent of all cooperative members chose answers that placed blame directly on landowners. Farmers used this sort of reasoning in more than 50 percent of all cases, but farmworkers were much less likely to do so.

Though cooperative members were most negative in their views of upper-class landowners, they were most positive about the feasibility of eliminating class differences. This too is in keeping with a radical perspective. Asked "Do you think it would be possible to eliminate class differences?" 80 percent of all cooperative members responded affirmatively. Table 6.11 illustrates the contrast with other social groups. Farmers and private farmworkers are much more pessimistic in their views. This is in keeping with the contrasting feelings of political efficacy discussed previously, and it

TABLE 6.11
Assessment of the Possibility of Eliminating
Class Differences by Form of Labor

	Possible	Impossible
Cooperative members	80.0%	20.0%
Private farmworkers	32.1	67.9
Farmers	37.5	62.5

N = 108

TABLE 6.12
Sector Solidarity by Form of Labor
*Percentage Responding That Their Interests
Were Identical to the Interests
of Others in Their Sector*

Cooperative members	97.5%
Private farmworkers	64.3
Farmers	60.8

N = 108

is also in keeping with what is known about the link between optimism and radical behavior. In order for an individual to become politically mobilized, he or she must be optimistic about the feasibility of radical social change. Cooperative members are in fact extremely optimistic.

Cooperative members are also the most cohesive group in the farming community. Their "solidarity" is another indication of the sort of radicalization that Gramsci had in mind. Individual cooperative members feel nearly total solidarity with the other individuals in their sector (see Table 6.12). By this measure, cooperative members are the most class conscious group.

The class consciousness of cooperative members extends to private farmworkers in general. Table 6.13 suggests that less than one-third of all cooperative members fail to identify their interests with those of farmworkers in the private sector.

Just as cooperative members show themselves to be radical in their views of class and class interests, so are they radical in their views of political parties and party leaders. According to self-reports, the cooperative members are, once again, the most radical members of the farming community. Table 6.14 illustrates how cooperative members, private farmworkers, and farmers rank themselves on a left-right political spectrum.

TABLE 6.13
Identification with Farmworkers' Interests
by Form of Labor

	Cooperative Members	Private Farmworkers	Farmers
Identical	17.5%	64.3%	10.0%
Very similar	10.0	17.9	5.0
Similar	40.0	10.7	45.0
Different	30.0	7.1	32.5
Very different	2.5	—	7.5

N = 108

Nearly 90 percent of all cooperative members describe their views as left of center, and more than 42 percent state that they are as radical as possible. As is the case with other measures, private farmworkers are much more conservative. Only 35.7 percent of this group see themselves as left of center, and nearly one-third see themselves as moderate. Small farmers, not surprisingly, are the most conservative members of the community.

The radical positions of cooperative members are reflected in an affinity for radical political leaders. Álvaro Cunhal, the secretary-general of the Portuguese Communist party, is the most popular political figure. Table 6.15 illustrates that 65 percent of all cooperative workers strongly agree with Cunhal.

Attitudes toward the late leader of the moderate Popular Democratic party take an opposite turn. Asked if they generally agreed or disagreed with the politics of Francisco Sá Carneiro, the men of Portel gave the responses shown in Table 6.16. He was clearly most popular with small farmers and least popular with cooperative members.

The differences in solidarity, optimism, and political judgment that distinguish cooperative members from other members of the farming community are underscored by their opinions on the objectives of good government. Here too the cooperative workers show little interest in embourgeoisement. Table 6.17 illustrates responses given to the question "What should be the purpose of good government?" A full 65 percent of all cooperative members believe that the primary objective of government should be either the promotion of equality or the promotion of socialism. This is consistent with the radical perspective illustrated by other measures and sharply inconsistent with both local and national sentiments.[41] In Portel,

---

[41] In 1977, Mário Bacalhau and Thomas Bruneau carried out a national survey in which this and many other interesting questions were asked. See Mário Bacalhau, *Os Portugueses e a Política Quatro Anos Depois do 25 de Abril* (Lisbon: Editorial Meseta, 1978).

TABLE 6.14
Self-Described Political Orientation by Form of Labor

	Left 1	2	3	4	5	6	7	8	9	Right 10	No Answer
Cooperative members	42.5%	5.0%	35.0%	5.0%	10.0%	—	—	2.5%	—	—	—
Private farmworkers	14.3	10.7	7.1	3.6	32.1	10.7%	—	10.7	3.6%	—	7.1%
Farmers	2.5	—	10.0	10.0	37.5	5.0	5.0%	10.0	10.0	2.5%	7.5

N = 108

TABLE 6.15
Agreement with Leader of the PCP by Form of Labor

	Totally Agree	Agree	Neither Agree Nor Disagree	Disagree	Completely Disagree	No Answer
Cooperative members	65.0%	15.0%	10.0%	5.0%	5.0%	—
Private farmworkers	17.9	14.3	10.7	35.7	14.3	7.1%
Farmers	2.5	5.0	22.5	20.0	42.5	7.5

N = 108

TABLE 6.16
Agreement with Leader of the PPD by Form of Labor

	Totally Agree	Agree	Neither Agree Nor Disagree	Disagree	Completely Disagree	No Answer
Cooperative members	—	7.5%	2.5%	10.0%	80.0%	—
Private farmworkers	14.3%	17.9	17.9	10.7	28.6	10.7%
Farmers	20.0	17.5	22.5	17.5	15.0	7.5

N = 108

153

TABLE 6.17
The Objective of Good Government by Form of Labor

	Cooperative Members	Private Farmworkers	Farmers	Nation
Equality	32.5%	28.6%	2.5%	14.0%
Order/stability	2.5	7.1	10.0	11.0
Socialism	32.5	17.9	15.0	10.0
Peace	12.5	14.3	22.5	45.0
Liberty	20.0	25.0	47.5	4.0
Development	—	3.6	2.5	10.0
No answer	—	3.6	—	6.0

N = 108

SOURCES: For nation: Mário Bacalhau, *Os Portugueses e a Política Quatro Anos Depois do 25 de Abril* (Lisbon: Editorial Meseta, 1978), p. 62. Other columns are from the Portel study.

only 29 percent of those outside the cooperative sector share this view, and on the national level only 24 percent agree.

The responses that would be consistent with a tendency toward embourgeoisement receive relatively little support within the cooperative sector. Only 20 percent of cooperative workers believe that government should concentrate most on the promotion of liberty or development, while exactly half of all small farmers share this view.

Reviewing the broad range of attitudinal measures just summarized, we get an image of a cooperative worker that corresponds quite closely to Gramsci's ideal—at the attitudinal level. However, since radicalization involves behavioral *and* attitudinal factors, we must assess the behavior of the cooperative members as well.

Radical Behavior. In general, the behavior of cooperative members within their workplace confirms the Gramscian image. The new production units' organizational schemes and employment practices suggest an orientation that is basically class-centered rather than individualistic.

In the previous discussion of land occupations, I mentioned that labor leaders, political parties, and unaffiliated workers and intellectuals were fearful that spontaneous occupations would lead to inequities of wealth and employment. A certain tendency to hoard land and even prevent the entrance of other occupiers did in fact occur in the early phase of the occupation period. Some of the machine-renters who seized land early in March had no intention of sharing their new property with landless laborers, and there were several incidents in which permanent workers turned other jobless workers away.

Local political leaders saw these events in a comparative context. I spoke with a young Communist party leader from Beja who made reference to both the "kulacks" in Russia and the sugar workers in Peru and said that there had been a fear of a new rural elite emerging in Portugal.[42] Workers were also aware of the danger. A tractor driver in Redondo explained that "there were workers who didn't feel linked with us at all and just occupied land for themselves. If there had been many, we'd all be unemployed today." Self-interested seizures did in fact occur, but they were the exception rather than the rule as the revolutionary period wore on.

As more and more workers began to view the establishment of cooperatives as the solution to their employment problems, the new production units grew in size. More farms were seized simultaneously, and cooperatives that had been formed with a small number of occupied properties began to group together to form larger units. The rationale behind the organization of larger farming units was based on a desire for homogeneity among units. The *Unidades Colectivas de Produção* were large for administrative purposes, but they were also large because they were designed to encompass bad land and good in proportions that would give workers on one unit access to more or less the same resources as workers on another. The idea that cooperatives should have equal or similar resources is a clear reflection of class consciousness.

Labor policies also reflected a high degree of class consciousness. For most of the people involved, the organization of cooperatives was a means of securing permanent employment and not a means to quick money. Employment was provided not to a select few but to as many people as possible. The words of the founders of what had once been a small cooperative outside Beja illustrate the connection between increased employment and increased size:

> Although we possessed a farming unit with good potential, we did not think only of ourselves. We saw our jobless comrades, fathers of children just like us, and we saw our comrades on the other farms in the area. . . . Our cooperative, Monte Outeiro, died, and a UCP called Vanguard of the Alentejo was born.[43]

The original production unit grew from 776 hectares accommodating 20 workers to 5,575 hectares accommodating 80 workers.

---

[42] It should be emphasized that knowledge of comparative experiences was exhibited only occasionally and by *party* leaders, not cooperative leaders. The particular individual described here was a high school teacher who had spent years in exile in Switzerland. In educational terms he was unlike typical cooperative leadership.

[43] *Apontamentos sobre o Outeiro: Do Senhor da Terra à Reforma Agrária* (SAFIL, 1976),

The drive to provide employment to as many men as possible produced dramatic changes in the employment structure of the agrarian reform zone. Whereas in 1968 the ratio of hectares to permanent workers was approximately 62 to 1, the new production units brought the ratio down to 28 to 1.[44] A 1976 survey of 436 new production units revealed an almost fourfold increase in the number of permanent employees. The number of permanent workers in the agrarian reform zone rose from approximately 11,000 in 1973 to approximately 44,000 in 1976, an increase of 33,000 positions.[45]

Though critics of the agrarian reform have claimed that positions on the new production units were reserved for Communist workers only, the author has found no evidence that this was the case. On the contrary, even in Portel, a strongly Communist county, fully one-third of the original occupying group claims to have voted socialist in the election immediately preceding the occupations. In most cases, employment policies reflected neither embourgeoisement nor partisan politics but rather a class-conscious desire to share newly acquired resources with anyone who needed them. Had this not been the case, the new production units would not be associated with "the virtual disappearance of unemployment," as scholars from a variety of perspectives suggest they are.[46] Had workers organized the cooperatives on the basis of self-centered criteria, many of their fellows would have been left jobless. Instead, the new production units accommodated most, if not all, of the labor available and even absorbed demobilized soldiers as they returned from the colonial wars. Their class consciousness was so great that even sympathetic observers believe that they took on an "excess of labor."[47]

Commitment to class interests continued long after the occupations subsided. Until 1980 at least, cooperatives and collectives had generally refused to dismiss "members," despite the fact that many units have had to relinquish much of their land to former owners.

As Table 6.18 illustrates, the new production units do not provide an income for as many people as they did in the past. Many workers have left the new enterprises to look for more lucrative work on private farms, while others have been eased into an early retirement. No new members

p. 6. The original is written in the third person in some sections. I have used the first-person plural for stylistic reasons.

[44] Afonso de Barros, *A Reforma Agrária em Portugal: Das Ocupações de Terras à Formação das Novas Unidades de Produção* (Oeiras: Instituto Gulbenkian, 1979), p. 122.

[45] Eugénio Rosa, *O Fracasso da Política da Direita* (Lisbon: Seara Nova, 1978), p. 52.

[46] Ana de Vale Estrela, "A Reforma Agrária Portuguesa e os Movimentos Camponeses: Uma Revisão Crítica," *Análise Social* (April-June 1978), p. 247.

[47] Pezarat Correia, "Interview," *Cadernos de O Jornal* (August 1976), p. 66.

TABLE 6.18
Positions of Employment Provided by New Production Units
in the Agrarian Reform Zone, 1974-1980

	Permanent Workers	Temporary Workers	Total
Before the Occupations	11,100	10,600	21,700
1975-76	44,100	27,800	71,900
1976-77	45,200	19,000	64,200
1977-78	43,000	16,000	59,000
1978-79	34,000	9,900	43,900
1979-80	31,000	5,000	36,000

SOURCE: Comissão Organizadora, *5ª Conferência da Reforma Agrária* (Évora, 1981), mimeographed, p. 13.

are taken on, though a cooperative with a severe financial crisis sometimes succeeds in transferring its workers to other cooperatives with fewer difficulties. Since virtually all of the new production units will eventually be forced to relinquish much, if not all, of their best land to former owners (under the government-sponsored devolution program), it is difficult to imagine how these generous but costly employment policies can continue. But they have endured at least until the early 1980s despite the most adverse circumstances and remain a source of pride for cooperative managers.

The only aspect of cooperative management that seems not to conform to radical principles is the use of lower-paid, usually female, temporary labor. Cooperatives vary considerably in their reliance on seasonal labor, but all use it to some degree, and almost all exclude these laborers from formal decision making.[48] Given the crisis brought on by the devolution of property, this is not likely to change.

[48] The policy is a source of embarrassment for cooperative managers but is rationalized as the only alternative given the administrative difficulties inherent in including temporary workers in a permanent political structure.

SUMMARY

THE consequences of workers' control in Portugal are many and diverse. Some correspond fully to what the advocacy literature would have us predict, some correspond to a limited degree, and others correspond not at all.

The formal institution of workers' control has not produced fully egalitarian participatory management. Sharp educational differences remain insurmountable and perpetuate a hierarchy that could only be dismantled at a great cost to production. There is no evidence that workers seek to dismantle the existing system anyway. The democratic nature of interpersonal relations within the farms gives workers the sense that they can exert control if a need arises but that daily decisions are best left to better educated leaders. Informal networks seem to provide adequate channels for challenges to authority.

Workers' control does appear to be associated with both high levels of participation and high levels of radicalization. There is no doubt that cooperative workers are more radical and more active politically than any of the other groups in the southern farm community, but it is difficult to assess the extent to which these characteristics were actually caused by the workers' control experience. The single before-and-after measure that makes sense in the context of Portugal's recent history is a measure of political discussion, and this does indeed suggest that workers' control causes people to become more active politically, but more research at a later period is needed for confirmation. On the question of radicalization, there is strong evidence that participants in a workers' control experiment do become more radical over time. Communist party vote support has increased steadily since 1976, and support for the Socialist party, on the moderate left, has dwindled.

Of all the hypotheses discussed, the productivity hypothesis receives the strongest confirmation at both a micro- and a macrolevel. Microlevel research illustrates that cooperative workers are in fact much more satisfied than their counterparts in the private sector. Macrolevel analysis suggests that this satisfaction was transformed into higher levels of productivity just as Vanek and other proponents of the productivity hypothesis would predict.[49]

---

[49] To be certain that this was the case it would have been useful to trace a relationship

The diverse consequences discussed here are not the necessary outcome of workers' control but the outcome of workers' control in a particular political and cultural context. As even our cursory review of other workers' control experiments makes clear, outcomes vary markedly from one state to another. The existing literature on workers' control fails to predict these variations, just as it fails to predict the consequences of workers' control in a single case like Portugal because our experience with workers' control has been limited and too often analyzed in a political vacuum. Reasoning directly from a structural change at the enterprise level to a behavioral change on the individual level, previous analysts have often failed to recognize that state structures serve as powerful intervening variables.[50]

The peculiar qualities of the Portuguese state explain much about the outcomes analyzed thus far. Fully egalitarian participatory management proved impossible in Portugal because the prerevolutionary state failed to educate a large proportion of the rural proletariat. Increased participation proved possible because a new state allowed new participation structures to emerge. Radicalization emerged because an old state had tolerated gross inequalities in property and because a new state provided, paradoxically, both the institutions through which radical behavior could be made manifest and enough of a counterrevolution to serve as a stimulus to further radicalization.

The relationship between Portugal's worker-controlled farms and Portugal's postrevolutionary state was essentially dialectical. The worker-controlled farms had consequences that affected elements within the state, and these elements took action that affected the later consequences of workers' control. Both the new production units and the state apparatus itself underwent transformations as a result. The third and final section of this study focuses on the nature of the interaction between worker-controlled farms and the larger, more complex political structures in which they were embedded.

---

across time, but the disruption of production caused by the devolution of land made this impossible.

[50] Two studies of self-management in Peru—one by Evelyne Huber Stephens and the other by Cynthia McClintock—provide exceptions to this generalization. It is not coincidental that both authors, having carried out fieldwork, recognized that the actual outcome of the Peruvian experiment in workers' control would be strongly affected by the larger political system in which it emerged. See the concluding chapters of Stephens, *The Politics of Workers' Participation: The Peruvian Approach in Comparative Perspective* (New York: Academic Press, 1980), and McClintock, *Peasant Cooperatives and Political Change in Peru* (Princeton, New Jersey: Princeton University Press, 1981).

III

Workers' Control and the Problem
of Articulation

INTRODUCTION

How would worker-controlled farms interact with Portugal's emerging liberal democracy? As the postrevolutionary state began to take shape, the question became more and more pressing. The Constitutional Assembly (elected in April 1975) had drawn up a constitution that promised both socialism and liberal democracy. Its first articles referred to the goal of "a classless society" and to "the transition to socialism,"[1] but the document also laid the foundations of a liberal democracy which was similar to that of other Western European states. Lawmaking power in government would be shared by a directly elected president, a freely elected National Assembly, and a prime minister approved by both.[2]

The major elements of the liberal democracy were already falling into place by the 25th of April 1976, for it was then—on the second anniversary of the revolution itself—that the people of Portugal went to their polling places to elect their first representative National Assembly in more than four decades.[3] A year earlier, on the same day, they had chosen representatives for the Constitutional Assembly. Though the list of parties was almost identical, the country had undergone profound and far-reaching changes in the year between elections.[4] Two provisional governments had fallen, an ultraleft coup had been stifled, and the avenues of Lisbon, Porto, and many smaller cities had filled with millions of demonstrators.

The economy was greatly affected by a year of political change. Social revolutionaries had gained and then lost control of the state, but the social revolution itself had left a legacy. Banks and insurance firms had been nationalized, basic industries had been taken over by the state, and workers

---

[1] See Articles 1 and 2, Constitution of the Portuguese Republic, promulgated April 2, 1976.

[2] There was, additionally, a Council of the Revolution that could rule on the constitutionality of all laws.

[3] A national assembly met sporadically during the Salazar-Caetano regime, but it was not a genuine representative body. In 1973, for example, only members of the government's Popular National Action party were elected because the opposition was "so harassed that they withdrew." See Thomas C. Bruneau, "The Portuguese Coup: Causes and Probable Consequences," *World Today* (July 1974), p. 281.

[4] The only change on the ballot was the new coalition between the PCP and the MDP-CDE. The coalition was named the APU for Aliança do Povo Unido, or the Alliance of the United People.

had seized control of more than 2.9 million acres of land. Excluding farming, the public sector now embraced some 30 percent of the nation's economy.[5] What would become of the legacy of the revolution when the new representative democracy took shape—that is, when the new National Assembly and president and prime minister were finally chosen?

The question was of practical importance in Portugal, of course, but it is relevant to politics in other states as well, for it bears directly on the issue of democratic socialism and, more specifically, on the alleged necessity of combining representative democracy at the national level with workers' control at the base.

Beginning with Bernstein and the revisionists around the turn of the century, and then emerging again in the mid-fifties with the New Left critique of the Soviet Union, leftists have repeatedly underscored the alienation intrinsic to state management and the need for genuine workers' control of production. The experiment with self-management in Yugoslavia, the frustrated struggles for workers' control in other parts of Eastern Europe,[6] the LIP occupation in France, and finally the rise of Eurocommunism—emphasizing "new links between representative democracy and democracy of the base"[7]—have stimulated many scholars to view workers' control as a fundamental element of democratic socialism. As Kolakowski points out, workers' control "has come to be of *key* importance in discussions on democratic socialism" throughout the world.[8]

Though expanding at an ever-increasing pace, the existing literature on workers' control and democratic socialism is of little value for those who seek an understanding of the Portuguese case. This is not because the Portuguese experience is so unique but because the literature on workers' control and democratic socialism is so empirically naive. The discussion that follows will illustrate these points. I begin with a brief critique of the literature, pointing to conceptual errors that emerge from a neglect of empirical work. I then move on to my own empirical work, answering the

[5] See Organization for Economic Cooperation and Development, *Economic Survey: Portugal* (Paris: OECD, 1979).

[6] For a good recent study of the Yugoslavian experience, see Ellen Turkish Comisso, *Workers' Control under Plan and Market* (New Haven, Connecticut: Yale University Press, 1979). For brief discussions of ill-fated experiments in workers' control in other parts of Eastern Europe, see Karel Kovanda, "Czechoslovak Workers' Councils," *Telos* (Summer 1976), and Jiri Kolaja, *A Polish Factory* (Lexington: University of Kentucky, 1960).

[7] Christine Buci-Glucksmann, "State, Transition and Passive Revolution," in Chantal Mouffé, ed., *Gramsci and Marxist Theory* (London: Routledge and Kegan Paul, 1979), p. 211.

[8] Leszek Kolakowski, *Main Currents of Marxism*, vol. 3, *The Breakdown* (Oxford: Oxford University Press, 1978), p. 493. Emphasis added.

question posed—i.e., how *did* the worker-controlled farms fare in the new liberal democracy?—and suggesting how a major conceptual error of the past might be avoided in the future. In the concluding chapter, I discuss the more general implications of the Portuguese case.

DEMOCRATIC SOCIALISM AND WORKERS' CONTROL

An extremely broad range of scholars have described workers' control as an integral part of democratic socialism. Robert Dahl, Fernando Claudín, Fernando Henrique Cardoso, and Nicos Poulantzas are some of the most prominent scholars to make the association.[9] Since a detailed review of the literature would take us too far from Portugal itself, I have decided to focus almost exclusively on the work of the late Nicos Poulantzas, in part because he is so influential but also because his discussions of workers' control and democratic socialism are the most detailed.

Workers' control plays a prominent role in Poulantzas' vision of a democratic socialist society. At one level, the vision involves "a real permanence and continuity of the institutions of representative democracy."[10] At another level, the vision involves the "unfurling of forms of direct democracy and the mushrooming of self-management bodies."[11] Though the terminology is different (Poulantzas uses "self-management" rather than workers' control), the message is the same: true socialism requires democracy in the workplace.

But how to make the transition? How might democratic socialism be established? Here too the institution of workers' control is critical in Poulantzas' mind. Self-management is not merely one of the *ends* or goals of democratic socialism; it is a means of transition as well. Poulantzas is specific, and even didactic, on this point. He writes:

> If the popular masses wish to win the leadership of the [transition] process . . . and therefore their own bases of political power, they must organize without fail forms of popular power at the base (work-

[9] See, for example, Robert Dahl, *After the Revolution?* (New Haven, Connecticut: Yale University Press, 1968); Fernando Claudín, *Eurocommunism and Socialism* (London: New Left Books, 1978), p. 117; and Fernando Henrique Cardoso, "Regime Político e Mudança Social," *Revista de Cultura e Política* (November-January 1981), p. 25. The works of Nicos Poulantzas are cited in the text.

[10] Nicos Poulantzas, "Towards a Democratic Socialism," *New Left Review* (May-June 1978), p. 84.

[11] Ibid., p. 79.

ers' control, community and factory councils, peasants committees, etc.).[12]

Without self-management, the transition to democratic socialism is impossible. If the twin evils of reformism and statism are to be avoided, representative democracy "should be accompanied [by] the flowering of self-management networks and centres."[13] Workers' control is thus both the foundation of democratic socialism and its progenitor.

Poulantzas is surprisingly optimistic about the feasibility of the project he describes. Though he concedes that history has left us only "negative examples to avoid" and "mistakes on which to reflect,"[14] he insists that the fusion of workers' control and representative democracy is "the *only* kind of socialism possible,"[15] and that the barriers to achieving it are no longer what they used to be.[16]

Given the negative experience in the past, and the insistence that the dynamic role of workers' control is indeed viable, the reader expects an elaborate and convincing blueprint as to how the transformation might be brought about, but here Poulantzas' work proves most disappointing.[17] He cautions only that the masses must remain mobilized and that the problem of "articulation" must be solved. We must know "in what fields, concerning which decisions, and at what points in time . . . representative assemblies have precedence over the centers of direct democracy."[18]

This sounds logical, if not obvious, but Poulantzas fails to suggest how

[12] Nicos Poulantzas, *The Crisis of the Dictatorships: Portugal, Greece, Spain* (London: New Left Books, 1976), p. 151.

[13] Nicos Poulantzas, *State, Power, Socialism* (London: New Left Books, 1980), p. 261.

[14] Poulantzas, "Towards a Democratic Socialism," p. 87.

[15] Poulantzas, *State, Power, Socialism*, p. 257; emphasis added.

[16] Ibid., p. 265.

[17] Poulantzas' vagueness on the issue of socialist transition is characteristic of a wide range of scholars and activists on the European left. From Daniel and Gabriel Cohn-Bendit, who write that they "cannot produce a blueprint," to Georges Marchais, who describes "the democratic road to socialism" as simply "transition without civil war," readers must rely heavily on their own imaginations to envision how a transition might actually be brought about. Though José Maravall has recently called attention to the "weak" quality of discussions of socialist transition, and Santiago Carrillo has dedicated some effort to describing precisely how a transition might take place, the area remains one of the most neglected in politics today. See Daniel and Gabriel Cohn-Bendit, *Obsolete Communism: The Left-Wing Alternative* (New York: McGraw Hill, 1969), p. 105; Christian Guy's interview with George Marchais in Etienne Balibar, *On the Dictatorship of the Proletariat* (London: New Left Books, 1977), p. 163; José M. Maravall, "The Limits of Reformism: Parliamentary Socialism and the Marxist Theory of the State," *British Journal of Sociology* (September 1979), pp. 285-286; and Santiago Carrillo, *Eurocommunism and the State* (Westport, Connecticut: Lawrence Hill and Co., 1978), pp. 99-105.

[18] Poulantzas, "Towards a Democratic Socialism," p. 86.

decision-making powers might be distributed, or who, in essence, will be the agent of articulation. The most likely agent would be a political party, but Poulantzas pays little attention to parties.[19] Indeed, when he makes explicit reference to parties at all, it is to discourage party interference.[20]

PARTIES AND THE PROBLEM OF ARTICULATION

The problem of articulation is a real one, but Poulantzas' perspective is not realistic. The task of articulation cannot be divorced from party politics, for parties will always be important forces in both the state apparatus and in the organs of workers' control as long as the commitment to "the institutions of representative democracy" exists.

Even when states have not made a commitment to free party competition, the connection between units of workers' control and political parties is likely to be strong. Perhaps Poulantzas would not have overlooked this if he had related his own articulation problem to the one faced by Lenin in 1905. Learning, while in exile, of the spontaneous establishment of soviets in Petrograd, Lenin wrote: "The only question and a highly important one is how to divide, and how to combine, the tasks of the Soviet and those of the Russian Social Democratic Labour Party."[21]

The task of transforming the state was not yet at hand, but Lenin was already concerned with the division of political labor. In fact, he gave the soviets little support at all until he saw that they might be used as a means through which the party could gain power. After a period of ambivalence (and the outbreak of the February Revolution), he finally announced that the soviets were an acceptable form of struggle, for they provided: "An organizational form for the vanguard, . . . an apparatus by means of which the vanguard . . . can elevate, train, educate, and lead."[22]

Lenin was not the last party leader to recognize that workers' control and party control could be linked. Structures of workers' control provide

[19] One of Poulantzas' few discussions of political parties is presented in an interview published posthumously. Speaking of the longstanding conflict between socialists and communists in France, he says: "The main problem is not so much that of political alliances between political organizations. The main problem, as we know is the political alliance between the classes and class fractions which are represented by those parties." Here, as elsewhere, parties are not seen as relatively autonomous organizations but as agents of classes instead. See "Interview with Nicos Poulantzas: Political Parties and the Crisis of Marxism," *Socialist Register* (November-December, 1979), p. 59.

[20] Poulantzas, *The Crisis of the Dictatorships*, p. 151.

[21] Vladimir Lenin, "Our Tasks and the Soviet of Workers' Deputies," in *The Collected Works of Lenin* (1962), 10: 19, from Ralph Miliband, *Marxism and Politics* (Oxford: Oxford University Press, 1977), p. 137.

[22] Lenin, in ibid., p. 138.

a natural environment for party activity everywhere. Initiatives for workers' control can erupt autonomously, as they often did in the Portuguese countryside, but initial autonomy does not mean perpetual organizational independence. If the leaders of the movement are not linked to parties from the outset, they are natural targets for party recruitment. If the structures of the movement are not linked to parties from the outset, they are natural targets for party assistance. Troubled by the private sector, and troubled by forces associated with the state, the structures of workers' control are likely to accept assistance from any friendly sources, and political parties are a likely source indeed.

Historical experience illustrates these points. Experiments in workers' control are almost inevitably initiated by, or permeated by, political parties. The experiments might be linked to a single government party, as was the case with the *ujamaa* villages in Tanzania. They might be linked to ultraleft opposition parties, as was the case with the MIR and the Mapuche cooperatives in Allende's Chile. Or they might be linked to a variety of Labour and religious parties, as is the case with many kibbutzim.[23] But workers' control and political parties are likely to be linked wherever the two exist. The greater the controlled resources, the higher the stakes and the greater the likelihood of party presence. Party involvement is not inevitable, but it is certainly likely, and no discussion of articulation or workers' control and democratic socialism is complete without recognition of this fact.

Poulantzas is not alone in his neglect of party politics. Most, if not all, of the best-known Marxists make the same mistake, and for obvious reasons. If "to the Marxist a political party is [merely] the most organized and the most conscious fraction of a class"[24] or, as Gramsci puts it, "only the nomenclature for a class,"[25] it makes good sense to study classes directly and to ignore their structural artifacts. With this line of reasoning, political parties can quite properly be left to the pluralists.

The careful reader will note that I have used the term parties and not party, for Marxist scholars have obviously exerted a great deal of effort discussing the ideal relations between "the party" and the working class,

[23] The largest political party with links to kibbutzim in Israel today is MAPAM, The United Party of Workers. See Leonard Fein, *Israel: Politics and People* (Boston: Little, Brown, 1968), for information on other party-kibbutzim links.

[24] Roger Garaudy, *The Crisis in Communism: The Turning Point of Socialism* (New York: Grove Press, 1969), p. 215.

[25] Antonio Gramsci, *Selections from the Prison Notebooks*, ed. and trans. Quintin Hoare and Geoffrey Nowell Smith (White Plains, New York: International Arts and Sciences Press, 1975), p. 152.

but discussions of relations *between* parties per se are infrequent and practically nonexistent in the literature on workers' control.

The neglect of party politics obviously derives from the perception that class relations are most important. As Miliband tells us, the relation of "the two polar classes" is "the primary determinant of economic and political life."[26] This might indeed be true, but classes often act through parties, and this makes matters more complicated. To begin with, the working class, to the extent that it is singular at all, is not likely to confine its loyalty to one party alone—not even one party on the left. Sophisticated Marxist scholars like Fernando Claudín are aware that "*the* party of the working class is a myth,"[27] and Miliband himself reminds us that "more than one party is in fact the 'natural' expression of the politics of labour."[28] Though he goes on to admit that parties are the "most important means" of class expression,[29] we never learn what implications a plurality of "working-class" parties might have. This is a complication that clearly affects experiments in workers' control.

Another relevant but neglected complication is the role of working-class parties in power. Assuming (as Poulantzas and other proponents of democratic socialism do) that the road to socialism passes through the polling place, what are the constraints on the left-wing party that wins an election? What determines whether left-wing power in government will be articulated with popular power at the base? Trotsky asked the question long ago. Writing between the February and October Revolutions, he wondered "what would happen if the cogs of the wheels of formal democracy failed to mesh with the cogs of the Soviet system[?]"[30] We know precisely what happened in the Bolshevik case—both formal democracy *and* the autonomous soviets were destroyed—but this is clearly not the scenario that Poulantzas and his colleagues have in mind. Is another form of articulation possible?

Analysis of the Portuguese case and others like it has convinced me that the possibilities of articulation depend in large part on the nature of left-wing party competition. Left-wing parties are not the only structures that affect articulation, but they are the means through which these other factors make their influence felt. Moreover, left-wing party competition takes on a dynamic of its own that a bipolar model of class conflict cannot explain. Parties sometimes behave not as agents of one class or another but as

[26] Ralph Miliband, *The State in Capitalist Society* (London: Weidenfeld and Nicolson, 1969), pp. 16-17.

[27] Claudín, *Eurocommunism*, p. 124.

[28] Miliband, *Marxism and Politics*, p. 129.

[29] Ibid., p. 131.

[30] Leon Trotsky, *1905* (London: Penguin, 1971), pp. 21-22.

organizations with relative autonomy driven by organizational imperatives that make alliances with one group or another rather fluid.

In the Portuguese case specifically, the root cause of the articulation problems lay in the' fact that the Socialist party had the ascendancy in the representative government while the Communist party had the ascendancy in the new production units. What might have been a feasible articulation of democratic structures at the level of state and base became, instead, the impossible articulation of two highly competitive parties. Both parties were threatened by the respective spheres of influence of the other, and the threats seemed to escalate over time. Eventually the units of direct democracy were assaulted by the state.

The chapter that immediately follows illustrates the specific problem of articulation in Portugal. The final chapter presents comparative material, summarizes the study's conclusions, and presents generalizations that might apply to other experiments in workers' control.

SEVEN

Party Politics and the Problem
of Articulation in Portugal

THE problem of articulation in Portugal began with the formation of the sixth provisional government in September 1975. Though the institutions of representative democracy were not yet in place, this was when the Socialist party gained de facto control of the government and thus when the problems of party competition and structural articulation began to crystallize. Both the Communists and the Socialists had reasons for misgivings as the sixth provisional government began.

THE COMMUNIST PARTY

The future looked bleak for the PCP in the fall of 1975. When nine leading members of the MFA successfully released a document that decried the "excesses" of the social revolution, it became clear that party allies had lost their influence within the MFA. The Document of the Nine illustrated that the coercive apparatus of the state was in the hands of antiparty forces who would ensure that the transition to socialism would take place within the parameters of formal, liberal democracy—if at all.

Recognizing that electoral strength was the only means by which government power might be obtained, the party began an extensive analysis of its voting base. The only measures available were the results of the elections for the Constitutional Assembly in April 1975. The elections suggested that the party had narrow but highly concentrated bases of support. Nationwide, it had gathered only 12.5 percent of the vote, or the support of approximately 710,000 electors, and the party's electoral showing varied greatly from one district to another. Map 7.1 shows the geographic distribution of party support.

The PCP's strongest base of support was in Beja, but even there it won less than 40 percent of the vote. In Setúbal, a district that was both part of the agrarian reform zone and the site of a major industrial center, the party had done almost as well, but there were areas where its share of the vote was extremely meager. The party received less than 3 percent of the vote in the rural districts of the North and less than 7 percent even in the

Map 7.1
Geographic Distribution of PCP Votes
by District, April 1975

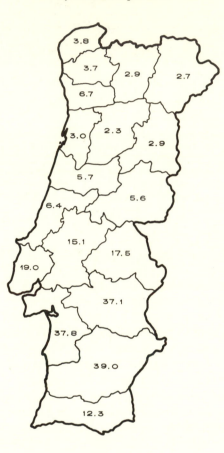

SOURCE: Colectivo das Edições Avante, *"Dossier" Eleições: Em que Sentido se Desloca o Eleitorado Português?* (Lisbon: "Avante!" 1977).

northern districts with a sizeable urban proletariat.[1] Having no hope of winning votes from the centrist PPD, the Communists could only expand at the expense of the Socialists.

It was clear that the South was the area in which the party might realistically hope to build support. But how to do it? The new production units

[1] The northern rural districts in which the party received less than 3 percent of the vote

of the rural South provided a ready answer. Encompassing large concentrations of rural wage workers, and being geographical entities themselves, the new production units provided the ideal vehicle for localized party expansion. Since gaining power through a military coup or through a national election was not feasible, the building of solid bases of localized support was the party's best alternative. The land occupations, which had started and gained momentum autonomously, could easily be given more direct support. Once the land had changed hands (and the worker-controlled section was thus expanded), the party could assist the new production units through the indirect provision of technical advice, legal defense, organizational skills, and funding.

Though the PCP's links with the worker-controlled units were deemed Machiavellian by party critics, its position was perfectly in keeping with its program and philosophy. Indeed, its open support for the workers' movement was more consistent with party philosophy than the restraints and reservations it had shown during the summer.

Consistency was not without its disadvantages, however, for the party's newly aggressive action brought mixed results. On the one hand, it increased the rhythm of the occupations. On the other, it provoked a strong, right-wing reaction. The hostility that had focused on the party in government during the summer focused more intensely on the PCP in the Alentejo in the fall.

Aware that the pace of the occupations was increasing daily, and that the coercive apparatus of the state was allowing the workers' movement to proceed unchecked, property owners throughout the nation were seized with panic and outrage. Rumors of violence and even rape spread northward, feeding on illiteracy and isolation. Simple people who had been apolitical all their lives became convinced that they should prepare for an armed invasion from the South. For months, the small- and medium-sized farmers in the Alentejo itself were relatively inactive, in part because their proximity to the seizures gave them a more realistic picture of what really went on but largely because they were so clearly outnumbered by salaried workers. In the North, the opposite was true, and the atmosphere was reminiscent of the Great Fear. The words of a landowner illustrate the tenor of the times:

In the autumn that followed the Hot Summer of 1975, the national crisis grew worse. Communist aggression increased to a frightening level. They were preparing for the *vitória final* [the last, victorious

---

were Bragança, Guarda, and Vila Real; the northern districts with major cities in which the party fared badly were Braga, Coimbra, and Porto, where the PCP won 3.7 percent, 5.7 percent, and 6.7 percent of the vote respectively.

battle of the revolution]. . . . Originating from the most diverse sources, . . . professional revolutionaries fomented subversion. [But] the patience of the farmers was running out. From day to day their indignities increased, generating a very strong class consciousness.[2]

By October, it became clear that the private farmers were going to take action, not just in the North but in the South as well. On October 24, more than one thousand farmers gathered in Beja to denounce the Communist party and to demand new "democratic" elections in the local peasant leagues.[3] Several hundred kilometers to the north on the same day a bomb went off in Alcaçer do Sal, destroying a section of the government's agrarian reform center. The left blamed the right and the right blamed the left. The result was increased hostility and uncertainty on both sides. November 6 brought more violence. This time the scene was Santarém, where several hundred farmers gathered in another anti-PCP rally. A young demonstrator was stabbed, and his attacker was killed on the spot by the crowd. The demonstrators had been called together with a handbill that read:

> The occupations and the stealing of properties are jeopardizing next year's production. If the situation continues, the anarchy in the countryside will lead the Portuguese people down the road to misery. . . .
> It is imperative that farmers take concrete measures to prevent partisan minorities from destroying what remains.[4]

The concrete measures took the form of more anti-Communist demonstrations, each one larger and better organized than the previous. The scene in Rio Maior on November 24 was the most dramatic. Church bells tolled the carol reserved for "the defense of the nation," as hundreds of farmers streamed into town in trucks, buses, and even tractors. One group erected barricades across the road routes to Lisbon. Another group blocked the north-south railroad tracks. Signs pointing southward to Moscow and northward to Portugal were erected at "the border."

A young agricultural agent named Manuel Casqueiro seemed to be in charge. He presented thirteen demands to the sixth provisional government in a fiery speech to a crowd of several thousand. Each met with delirious support. He called for the immediate change of the land expropriations law, the prohibition of future occupations on cultivated land, guaranteed indemnities, a purge of all the professionals in the local CRRA, and the

---

[2] João Garin, *Reforma Agrária: Seara de Ódio* (Lisbon: Edições do Templo, 1977), pp. 163, 178.

[3] Ibid., p. 185.

[4] Ibid., p. 212.

removal of a young, Communist undersecretary of agriculture named António Bica.

The central purpose of the meeting was not the presentation of demands,
however. As Casqueiro told me in an interview years later, the demonstration was really planned to provoke a reaction from the left.

> We weren't planning a coup or any sort of attack, but we wanted
> them to think we were. We wanted them to think we were capable
> of anything so that they would be forced to act first, and fail, of
> course.[5]

The ruse worked perfectly. The far left launched their own coup on November 25 and failed miserably. As a consequence, moderate officers
tightened their control on the MFA.

The PCP was clearly disadvantaged by the change. The party's hopes
of gaining the support of the small peasantry looked less and less realistic,
and now even the prospect of continued occupations looked bleak, for the
passivity of the armed forces could no longer be guaranteed. What had
appeared a feasible program for the expansion of the cooperatives would
now of necessity become a program for their defense. The "Defense of
the Agrarian Reform" was to be the party's slogan for years to come.
Protecting the reform, it protected its constituents and ultimately itself.

THE SOCIALIST PARTY

Compared to the position of the Communists, the position of the Socialists
looked relatively good in the fall of 1975. The party could count on the
support of the MFA and could be almost certain that the elections which
it had so desired would be held as planned.

The party's electoral prospects were mixed. The elections for the Constitutional Assembly in 1975 illustrated that the PSP was the most popular
party in the nation, but they also reflected a rather precarious base of
support. The party attracted nearly 40 percent of all votes nationwide and,
unlike the PCP, managed to establish a truly national constituency. There
was not in fact a single district on the continent in which the PSP failed
to gain more than 20 percent of the vote.

Ironically, it was the very breadth of the party's constituency that made
the PSP seem vulnerable. In the northern districts, the party was outdis-
tanced by the right, while in the southern districts, it was threatened by
the left. Though the PSP was the number one party nationwide, it was the
number two party in most of the nation. Map 7.2 depicts the problem.

[5] Personal interview, Portalegre, October 1980.

MAP 7.2
Socialist Party Electoral Majority Versus Majorities
of Parties to Right and Left

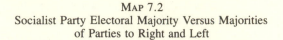

	Socialist
	Communist } Majority
	PPD / CDS
	Geographic } District
	Electoral } Borders

SOURCE: Jorge Gaspar and Nuno Vitorino, *As Eleições de 25 de Abril: Geografia e Imagem dos Partidos* (Lisbon: Livros Horizontes, 1976), p. 35.

The PSP obtained an absolute majority of the votes in three sorts of areas: the southern coastal counties in the district of Faro, the eastern urbanized counties of Porto, Coimbra, and Lisbon, and a band of agricultural counties in the center of the nation.

These agricultural counties were located in the districts of Santarém, Castelo Branco, and Portalegre in a transitional region where latifúndia and small peasant holdings stood side by side. These were precisely the sorts of areas where the increased participation associated with workers'

TABLE 7.1
Socialist and Communist Votes
in the Alentejo, 1975

District	PSP	PCP
Beja	35.5%	39.0%
Évora	37.8	37.1
Portalegre	52.4	17.5
Setúbal	38.1	37.8

control was likely to lead to polarization. Santarém was the most important of these districts, for it was the most populous and offered the greatest number of Constitutional Assembly seats. Santarém was also the site of the famous demonstrations at Rio Maior and a center of political mobilization. In Rio Maior itself, the Socialists and the moderate Popular Democratic Party fought a close battle for support. In 1975, the Socialists managed to beat the PPD but only by less than 4 percentage points. There was no guarantee that this slim lead could continue. It was necessary, however, to defend the party's position in Rio Maior and elsewhere if the victory of April 1975 were to be repeated.

In the heart of the Alentejo, the Socialist party's task appeared especially difficult. As Table 7.1 illustrates, the PSP had a comfortable lead in only one of the southern districts. In Beja, the party was behind the PCP, and in Évora and Setúbal, it led by less than 1 percentage point. Of course, Portugal's system of proportional representation meant that minor differences in voter support would not have the impact they would have in a winner-take-all election, but there was a sense that every vote counted. The party had won 116 of the 243 seats in the Constitutional Assembly. If it managed to maintain its past support and attract approximately 125,000 new votes, it would win an absolute majority in the new legislature. If the PSP failed to expand its constituency, or even lost votes, it would have to depend on either the right or the left for the passage of legislation and thus be forced to compromise its program.

Ironically, the party's leading role in the sixth provisional government was in many ways a liability in the battle for more votes. While other parties could avoid committing themselves to concrete policies, the PSP was forced to take action, assuming center stage and thus becoming more susceptible to criticism. A strong move rightward would lose votes on the left, while a strong move leftward would lose votes on the right. The party's policy toward the new production units was particularly problematic in electoral terms, for the agrarian reform involved the salient groups in both of the party's more vulnerable regions. The mobilization of the small and medium peasantry in the central zones pushed the PSP in one direction, while the party's platform and desire for expansion in the South pushed it in another. The problem of articulation was clear, but the solution was not. How would the Socialist party react?

If the party had really been no more than the left arm of the bourgeoisie, we might have witnessed a rapid reversal of the previous government's policies. Agricultural credits would have been cut, expropriations would have ended, occupations would have been prevented by force, and the expropriations law itself might have been revoked. What emerged instead were two contrasting policies. The first involved a concrete commitment to articulation. The second included a reversal of past policies and an open confrontation with the rural structures of workers' control.

A FAILED ATTEMPT AT ARTICULATION

The Socialist party's attempt to articulate the new production units with the emerging institutions of representative democracy corresponded with the tenure of Lopes Cardoso as minister of agriculture from September 1975 to November 1976. Cardoso was committed both to the concept of workers' control and to the protection of small- and medium-sized farmers. Ironically, his policies won him the enmity of farmworkers and farmers alike.

Cardoso's commitment to the expansion of the new production units was obvious, even during his first days in office. Shortly after being sworn in, he journeyed to the agrarian reform zone and announced that landowners were "fooling themselves" if they believed that the sixth provisional government would not continue the expropriation of latifúndia. As if to underscore his point, he chose a prominent Communist party militant (António Bica) as his secretary for the "restructuring of agriculture." Bica had held the same post during the radical fourth and fifth provisional governments and had played a major role in the formulation of the expropriations law. His position in the ministry suggested a continuity of policy that relieved some and panicked others.

There were objective reasons for fear on the part of those who opposed the agrarian reform. First, Cardoso continued to expropriate properties in accord with requests from the regional CRRAs.[6] Second, he established a costly program through which the new production units could pay workers'

---

[6] Before the end of his first month in office, Cardoso expropriated 170 occupied properties in Évora and Setúbal alone. See Garin, *Reforma Agrária*, p. 152.

wages with government loans. Most importantly, he and his government colleagues allowed the occupations to continue at an unprecedented pace.

Taken as a whole, these policies were viewed as incontrovertible proof that Cardoso and the PSP sought the continuation and even the expansion of workers' control in agriculture. But there were other PSP policies that were seen as assaults on the agrarian reform, and these were the source of Cardoso's troubles on the left. The most controversial of such policies was embodied in a set of laws restricting the scope of the existing expropriations legislation. These held that the existing legislation would a) not apply outside a certain section of the country, and b) not apply to any property under thirty hectares, regardless of its value. Both of these policies were intended to placate the fears of small- and medium-sized farmers. The law limiting the zone of expropriations was directed at farmers in the North, while the law protecting properties under thirty hectares was directed at farmers in the South.

Cardoso's concern for the interests of the peasantry is not to be confused with a concern for the interests of landowners in general. He modified past policy precisely because he wanted the expropriation of large properties to continue. As he explained in an interview:

> If we seek to move ahead with the agrarian reform and this is an objective that the sixth provisional government . . . and I . . . will not discard, . . . if we seek to defend the agrarian reform we have two options: either we gain support for the reform from the small- and medium-sized farmers or we attempt to impose the reform through the force of repression. Neither the sixth government nor I myself could accept the second alternative.[7]

Choosing to gain the support of the small- and medium-sized farmers, Cardoso went beyond the policies just outlined and made structural changes in the Ministry of Agriculture itself, replacing the controversial professionals in the agrarian reform centers and founding a special department to evaluate disputes deriving from the occupations. Most important, Cardoso initiated a program of *desocupações* wherein occupied lands that did not meet the criteria for expropriation would be returned to their original owners.

Why did Cardoso's policy assume the form it did? Part of the reason was ideological. The PSP program of December 1974 had advocated "the expropriation of large properties." It had endorsed the founding of "cooperatives for rural workers" and had stated explicitly that "in the area

---

[7] António Lopes Cardoso, *Luta Pela Reforma Agrária* (Lisbon: Diabril, 1977), pp. 139-140.

of the latifúndia," the "fundamental objective of the agrarian reform [should be] the transfer of the land to those who work it."[8]

In addition to being consistent with the party's public ideology, Cardoso's policies also seemed consistent with its needs in the upcoming election. Moving forward with expropriations, allowing the continuation of occupations, and granting government funds for wages would, in theory at least, protect the party's support within the new production units. Correcting past excesses, placing limits on expropriations, and restricting the area of the agrarian reform would, in theory, protect the party's support with the small and medium peasantry. This latter group was of critical importance to the party's future. The small peasantry was the very foundation of the PSP support in the zone of the latifúndia.[9] Cardoso himself owed his seat in the Constitutional Assembly to the peasantry in his home district of Beja. It was to be expected that the interests of the peasants in the South would not be ignored.

It was also to be expected that the peasantry in the North would be the focus of attention. The Socialists had already captured the loyalty of a large proportion of northern industrial workers and would now have to concentrate on developing a larger rural constituency if the party were to expand. If Cardoso could convince the small peasantry that "the agrarian reform would not jeopardize their property rights,"[10] the party's interests would be served, the forces of reaction would be stymied, and a major stumbling block on the path to democratic socialism would be overcome— or so it was hoped.

Unfortunately for the PSP, events did not proceed as expected. Cardoso's plans for articulation went awry almost immediately. Within a few months, the minister was being vehemently criticized by the leadership of the new production units *and* by leaders of the small and medium peasantry. By January, thousands of farmers were clamoring publicly for Cardoso's dismissal.

Hostility toward Cardoso was quickly transformed into hostility toward the PSP itself, with negative electoral consequences. Instead of attracting more votes and winning an absolute majority, the Socialist party lost votes in sixteen out of eighteen districts. Though the Socialists did not lose the election, they did lose approximately 260,000 votes. Three months after the party took control of the first constitutional government, Cardoso was

---

[8] Partido Socialista, *Declaração de Princípios: Programa e Estatutos do Partido Socialista-Aprovado em Dezembro do 1974* (Lisbon: Partido Socialista, 1975), p. 11.

[9] John L. Hammond, "Electoral Behavior and Political Militancy," in Lawrence S. Graham and Harry M. Makler, eds., *Contemporary Portugal: The Revolution and Its Antecedents* (Austin: University of Texas Press, 1979), pp. 266-267.

[10] Cardoso, *Luta*, p. 133.

forced to resign in frustration. His resignation marked a major change in party policy and the abandonment of articulation.

Why did Cardoso's attempts at articulation fail? The answer had little to do with workers' control per se. It also had little to do with direct pressure from the few hundred *agrários* who had lost land. It had something to do with the bureaucratic apparatus of the Portuguese state; it had something to do with Portugal's position in the world economic community; and it had a great deal to do with party politics. Failed articulation in Portugal was largely the result of the fact that one party had the ascendancy in government while another party had the ascendancy in the structures of workers' control. The "cogs of representative democracy" *could not* "mesh with the cogs" of workers' control as long as the competition between the parties continued. In other words, the problems of workers' control derived as much from the struggle between Socialists and Communists as from the struggle between the "two polar classes." Problems related to Portugal's bureaucracy and level of economic growth served to exacerbate the problem of articulation as time went on. Bureaucratic problems were critical for the Cardoso ministry, while larger economic pressures were critical for his successor.

Bureaucratic Problems

Many of Cardoso's problems with articulation emerged from discordant elements within the Ministry of Agriculture itself. The problems began during the fourth provisional government, when *pessoas de confiança*, or "trusted people" were put in charge of the ministry's most sensitive departments.[11] This was a perfectly rational and predictable step for the social revolutionaries to take, but it had consequences that Cardoso could not easily manage.

The "trusted people" who were injected into the old bureaucracy were often classmates and colleagues of Fernando Oliveira Baptista, then minister of agriculture. Like Baptista himself, most were in their late twenties or early thirties. All were on the left; most were noncommunist, many had studied in France, and many had studied rural sociology rather than the more technical subjects associated with farming per se. Outside of Lisbon, this new group of functionaries staffed the CRRAs in fairly autonomous islands of the bureaucracy. Inside Lisbon, the young functionaries headed departments that were staffed with men in their late forties and fifties. These older functionaries represented another, very different group. They

[11] The Portuguese term *pessoas de confiança*, often means people who are politically trustworthy. There is no equivalent in English.

had studied exclusively in Portugal and were trained as agronomists, economists, or agricultural engineers. They were not defenders of the old regime, but they were not revolutionaries either. Occasionally they supported the Socialist party, but usually they voted for the moderate PPD. More often than not, they had entered agricultural studies because they had some link with farming themselves—coming from families with small- or medium-sized properties. The older functionaries thus had both practical experience with farming and decades of experience in the bureaucracy itself. Often, and through no fault of their own, the younger group of leftists lacked both. A mutual resentment emerged.

Cardoso inherited a bureaucracy that was thus divided horizontally and vertically. Generational differences combined with political differences, producing confusion and hampering the pace of change. As a result, policy modifications that might have enhanced articulation were slow to emerge and difficult to implement. Working with an awkward apparatus that was the amalgam of two very different regimes, Cardoso changed too little too late. The new production units accused him of foot dragging with the pace of expropriations, while the farmers accused him of foot dragging with the *desocupações*. The new production units accused him of withholding technical and financial support, while farmers' groups accused him of providing services only to cooperatives and collectives.

Policy seemed to emerge in the aftermath of crisis rather than in its anticipation. The commission to investigate illegal seizures was not established until January 1976, after farmers were already clamoring for Cardoso's resignation. The ministerial information campaign was not established until the summer of 1976, after rumor and confusion had caused havoc in nearly every district and brought about antigovernment rallies. The law that limited expropriations to a certain part of the country and to properties over thirty hectares emerged only in April 1976, after hundreds of thousands of farmers had already been panicked by the prospect of losing land.

Cardoso recognized that his ministry would be the target of attacks from the right, but he seemed unable to avoid them. He believed that his ministry would be criticized by "all the forces which are interested in stopping the revolutionary process." And he recognized that "the agrarian reform [would] become the battle horse of the most reactionary forces in [the] country,"[12] but he was unable to curb the reaction.

The ministry appeared compromised when it was really simply impotent. Cardoso complained that the devolution of land was hampered by "a certain

[12] Cardoso, *Luta*, p. 138.

inertia.''[13] He complained that the ''state lacked control over the whole process of agrarian reform.''[14] He complained that people were ''not even minimally interested in collaborating'' in a public information campaign. Moderate technocrats complained that the ministry lacked the professionals necessary for the execution of existing legislation.[15] The Socialist newspaper complained that the whole ministry was being sabotaged from within.[16]

The occasions when Cardoso's ministry actually managed to make alterations in policy were often ill-timed. The concessions on credits for wages came during Cardoso's first weeks in office—just in time to fuel rumors that the ministry was ''still controlled by Communists,'' but too far from the elections to assure the support of the new production units themselves.

While the credit law came too early, the modification of the expropriations law came too late. Legislation restricting the scope of expropriations emerged less than three weeks before the national elections—just in time to be dismissed by farmers as a ruse for getting farmers' votes,[17] and just in time to counteract the favorable effects of the credit concessions months earlier.

Party Politics and Partisan Image

The subject of the elections brings us back to the issue of party politics and to its importance in the failure of the articulation process. No factor impaired the process more than the perceived association between the Communist party and the worker-controlled farms. The partisan image of the new production units made them especially vulnerable to attack, for it panicked the leadership of the Socialist party and strengthened the cause of private farmers' opposition groups.[18] Facing strong resistance

[13] António Lopes Cardoso, ''A Defesa Intransigente com a Correcção dos Erros (Inevitáveis?) Cometidos,'' *Cadernos de O Jornal* (August 1976), p. 54.

[14] Press Conference, *Diário de Notícias* (Lisbon), September 2, 1976.

[15] *Expresso* (Lisbon), October 31, 1975.

[16] *Portugal Socialista* (Lisbon), November 19, 1975.

[17] The connection between policy formation and political campaigning was obvious to the peasant farmers who were the focus of attention. For example, after criticizing Cardoso, a January farmers' rally in Braga criticized the PSP itself, saying the leadership ''was only interested in the votes of the North.''

[18] The competition between the Socialists and Communists had started in 1969 when exiles under the tutelage of the Socialist International established a new organization to replace the original Socialist party crushed by Salazar. The new Socialist party immediately presented itself as an alternative to the Communist left. Mário Soares, one of the party's principal founders, wrote at the time: ''We ask no one's permission to exist. Not the [dictatorial]

within his own party and a highly mobilized opposition, Cardoso's attempts at articulating liberal democracy and workplace democracy were doomed.

There is no systematic research on the actual connections between the Communist party and the worker-controlled farms. What does exist is an elaborate set of assumptions concerning party domination. Regardless of the intricacies of the actual situation, critical elites were convinced (by at least the fall of 1975) that the new production units were dominated by the PCP. The words of a man who lost property outside Montemor illustrates the scope of the image:

> Who benefited from [the founding of the new production units]? Obviously, the PCP. It gained economic and political control of large regions of the Alentejo. . . . It led perfectly honest workers, perfectly respectable family men, to act as if they were thieves.[19]

Another, younger, landowner from Redondo made a similar, if less emotional, evaluation of the worker-controlled farms.

> [Who benefited from the founding of the cooperatives and collectives?] The big winner was the PC. They knew they'd never keep hold of Lisbon, so they concentrated on the Alentejo. A kolkhoz here, another there, and they control half the county.[20]

The image of party domination was not confined to landowners or even to people on the right. Mário Soares himself was convinced that the Alentejo was an occupied territory. The transcript of a November 1975 television interview illustrates the Socialist leader's beliefs. Discussing the founding of the cooperatives and collectives, Soares stated:

> Expropriations [sic] were hardly ever carried out by workers. They were carried out in two ways . . . by individuals who came from other places, who had nothing to do with the rural workers . . . [and] by the unions, . . . which are controlled by the PC. . . . [W]hen people are not Communists (and the rural workers are not Communists), they even have difficulty getting in.[21]

If the comments on the PCP's role have any unifying theme, it is one of coercion. Allegedly, party militants coerced farmworkers into seizing land

---

Government's . . . nor the Communist party, which attempts to be the singular party of the working class." Mário Soares, Willy Brandt, and Bruno Kreisky, *Liberdade para Portugal* (Amadora: Livraria Bertrand, 1976) p. 68.

[19] António Vacas de Carvalho, *O Fracasso de um Processo: A Reforma Agrária no Alentejo* (Lisbon: Author's Edition, 1977), p. 27.

[20] Personal interview, Redondo, October 1981.

[21] *Portugal Socialista*, November 12, 1975. Soares' reference to expropriations is, judging from the context, a reference to occupations.

and relatedly coerced them into joining organizations (like the unions) in order to get work. Once inside the new production units, the farmworkers were coerced into adopting certain forms of behavior.

Lopes Cardoso himself seemed to share the conviction that the PCP was dominating the South. He too spoke of the party's control of the Alentejo and stated unequivocally that "the majority of the collective production units are controlled by the Farmworkers' Union and, indirectly, by the PC."[22]

Though there was seemingly widespread agreement about the Communist party's association with the new production units, there was little agreement on how the association should affect public policy. Cardoso and the left wing of the Socialist party favored a make-do approach. As the minister explained in a series of interviews:

> This is an agrarian reform that was not carried out by the government, an agrarian reform that was . . . initiated and carried out by rural workers [and] obviously by unions and by certain political forces. . . . We must think and plan *in terms of this reality and not in terms of more or less idealized situations.* It is obvious that . . . this is not the agrarian reform that the Socialist party would have carried out had it had the opportunity, [but we shall] attempt to make the agrarian reform viable, *taking into account the form in which it has developed until today.*[23]

Cardoso believed that the situation on the worker-controlled farms was not ideal, but he also believed that improvements were feasible. "Errors" could be "corrected," "injustices could be undone," "the agrarian reform could be given a different image."[24] Cardoso admitted that errors had been made, but he was reluctant to place the blame on either the workers themselves or on the Communist party specifically. "If anyone is responsible for the errors," he wrote, "it is the successive [provisional] governments who . . . either abdicated their responsibilities, or were not able to carry them out."[25] His ministry would strive to "consolidate and move ahead with the agrarian reform" because it was the only means by which the laborers of the Alentejo could obtain "a minimum of independence and dignity in their work."[26]

While Cardoso emphasized the beneficial aspects of the new production units, farmers' groups emphasized their negative aspects, focusing continuously on their association with the Portuguese Communist party.

[22] See Cardoso, *Luta*, pp. 45-46.
[23] Ibid., pp. 129-130. Emphasis added.
[24] Ibid., p. 142.
[25] Ibid., p. 141.
[26] Ibid.

The private farming community in particular took on a new importance as the sixth provisional government moved toward the consolidation of a representative democracy. The freedom of the press, the freedom of association, and the individual liberties that the Socialist party seemed so eager to ensure brought new opportunities to private farmers' groups—and to all the party's enemies within them.

Cardoso faced a farming community that had become more militant and better organized than ever before. Most importantly, ALA, which had represented farmers' interests since the 25th of April, had been transformed into a new and more dynamic organization called the CAP, the Confederation of Portuguese Farmers. While the ALA had confined itself to private lobbying and closed-door bargaining, the CAP assumed the image of a mass organization capable of dramatic action and considerable public disruption. Within twelve months of its founding, the CAP proved instrumental in the ousting of Cardoso, the ending of the articulation process, and the gradual reversal of the tide of workers' control.

CAP's success was due as much to party relations as to class relations. The organization's major asset was its ability to exploit both the division between Socialists and Communists and the divisions within the Socialist party itself. It did this through the skillful use of its organizational resources. Contrary to what a bipolar view of society might lead us to expect, money was not the most important of these. The CAP proved successful because it appeared to represent significant *numbers* of people. People were its most important resource, people who could be called upon to vote in a certain way or to behave in a certain way, in a strike, in a demonstration, or in a massive public protest like the incident in Rio Maior.

Rio Maior, the scene of the most dramatic antigovernment demonstration, was in fact the CAP's real birthplace. In organizing the November demonstration, Manuel Casqueiro and his associates linked a national network of smaller farmers' groups and thus forged the framework for what appeared to be a broad-based national farmers' association. Photographs and films of the demonstration at Rio Maior showed a cross-section of Portuguese rural society and were ubiquitous in the media. There were scores of men and women with the clothing and hairstyles of the petite bourgeoisie, but there were hundreds of men and women whose faces bore the marks of a life of outdoor labor. *Bonés*—the flat caps worn almost exclusively by farmworkers and peasants—were in great abundance. Wealthy *agrários* were no doubt present, but they were far outnumbered by the small-holding peasantry who represented the very backbone of the rural nation.

The CAP's critics could charge that its poorest peasant supporters were merely being "manipulated" by "wealthy reactionaries," but the peasantry still appeared by the hundreds—and even the thousands—for organized protests, and this was an invaluable political resource. The CAP was to prove successful precisely because of its heterogeneity—that is, because it did *not* appear to be an association of wealthy landowners but a mass protest group instead.[27]

The target of the CAP's early protests was not the sixth provisional government but the Ministry of Agriculture itself. This was a wise tactical maneuver. Placards and handbills made clear distinctions between the government as a whole and the ministry. Signs reading "With the Government: Against the MAP" and "With the Government: Against Cardoso" focused attention on the minister as an individual. A CAP press release drew the distinction in the clearest terms.

> The farmers are unlettered, but they are not stupid. They do not confuse the sixth provisional government and its attempts at democratization with the dictatorial policies of its minister [Cardoso].[28]

The CAP seemed to be making a concerted effort to point to contradictions within not only the government but within the Socialist party itself. A communication written by Manuel Casqueiro is illustrative:

> When Mário Soares asserts that the Agrarian Reform Law should be discussed publicly and democratically and Lopes Cardoso gives us the impression that it has already been approved, although never discussed, whom shall we believe? Of the two, who represents the true spirit of the 25th of April and of democracy?[29]

The CAP's comments on one of the elder statesmen of the party play on the same theme. "Professor Henrique de Barros, from the same party as the minister of agriculture, defends theses that are oftentimes diametrically opposed [to those of the minister]."[30] Henrique de Barros was praised as a skilled and a "genuine democrat," while Cardoso was accused of "creating a communist machine."

Since the issue of workers' control had become confused with the issue of party control, Cardoso's attempts to defend the agrarian reform were easily viewed as attempts to defend the Communist party. This was a real

---

[27] Lopes Cardoso was fully aware of the implications of the CAP's composition. He said of the organization's leaders: "They are trying to use the masses of small farmers as a form of pressure so that they can defend their *own* interests. . . . What have [these landowners] done in the past fifty years to benefit the small farmers?" See ibid., p. 111.

[28] Confederação de Agricultores de Portugal, *CAP: Recortes de uma Luta* (Viseu: Edições CAP, 1977), p. 84.

[29] Ibid., pp. 82-83.

[30] Ibid., p. 87.

asset for the leaders of the CAP, for it meant that their struggle could be couched in nationalistic terms. Opposing the ministry, one defended Portugal not simply from bad policy but from Soviet domination. As rumors of Soviet agents and massive arms caches circulated throughout the countryside, the themes of farmers' unity, anticommunism, and national defense began to fuse. The CAP's founding statement presented the themes in relatively mild language:

> Nearly 60,000 farmers, united together in Rio Maior, conscious that there exists an imminent risk to their survival and to the very independence of the nation, repudiate the partisan manipulation of the agricultural sector.[31]

The tone grew more heated in other contexts. In Castelo Branco, the CAP declared, "If we don't unite, we shall be ruined and our country shall be too."[32] In Santarém, the CAP declared "a war against the Marxists." In Lisbon, the CAP declared a fight "against dictatorship," "against Communist laws," and against "the Lisbon Commune."[33] Within the "Commune," Cardoso was the most salient target for attack. It was he who was guilty of "demagogic actions"[34] and sought the "total collectivization of land."[35]

Coming from a far-right fringe group, these statements and charges might have been dismissed and forgotten, but the CAP was not a fringe group. The organization became an institutionalized national actor in a remarkably short time. Three weeks after the triumphant meeting at Rio Maior, it was a national organization (complete with its own slogans, posters, and key rings). Manning the barricades at Rio Maior, farmers of all types began to recognize "the extraordinary power that lay in their hands."[36] Casqueiro and the founders of the CAP convinced first the farming community itself and then the nation that the whole population depended on the men and women of the countryside. As Casqueiro was to recall later:

> It was necessary to demonstrate to the people that "the Lisbon Commune" would not have any viability, that it would be totally in the hands of the "green belt" (as the region in which we had great implantation would be known). We proved that Lisbon, without us, would be nothing.[37]

[31] *Expresso*, December 17, 1975.
[32] CAP, *Recortes de uma Luta*, p. 104.
[33] Manuel Casqueiro, speech at Rio Maior, October 10, 1976, mimeographed.
[34] *O Dia* (Lisbon), January 11, 1975.
[35] *Expresso*, December 17, 1975.
[36] Ibid., December 17, 1975.
[37] CAP, *Recortes de uma Luta*, p. 64.

TABLE 7.2
Percentage Change in Socialist Party Votes
April 1975 to April 1976

Northern Districts		Central Districts		Southern Districts	
Aveiro	− 4.4	Castelo Branco	− 16.7	Beja	− 16.2
Braga	+ 16.8	Coimbra	− 14.0	Évora	− 23.2
Bragança	− 12.4	Leiria	− 13.3	Faro	− 8.2
Guarda	− 14.2	Santarém	− 17.3	Lisbon	− 20.8
Porto	− 5.0			Portalegre	− 24.5
Viana do Castelo	− 2.1			Setúbal	− 21.8
Vila Real	− 10.4				
Viseu	+ .3				
Average change − 3.9		Average change − 15.3		Average change − 19.1	

Hyperbole aside, the CAP did prove that it had the human and material resources to disrupt order in dramatic ways. In addition to openly organizing citizens' militias, the CAP presented the government with ultimatums that were bolder than any presented by the left. A press release complaining of a delay in land devolution is typical in its content and tone:

> We have tried to avoid using force because of the particularly unstable period that Portugal is experiencing. But our patience is running out, and if the government does not begin giving back our land by next Monday, we are prepared to unleash a struggle and take it to its ultimate consequences, even though the elections are around the corner.[38]

Threatening to march on Lisbon, to stop producing food, or to disrupt the entire nation on the eve of the elections, the CAP became a force that could only be ignored at great cost.

The Socialist party was willing to support Cardoso and his attempts at articulation until the costs became too high. The first major stimulus to change was the April 1976 electoral race. Table 7.2 illustrates the magnitude of the Socialist party's vote loss in the nation's three geographic regions. The party's decline in support was greatest in the agricultural districts of the center and South. In central districts, the party lost around 15 percent of its 1975 vote, while in southern districts, it lost 19 percent. There were clear signs that the PSP was losing the most important elements

[38] Garin, *Reforma Agrária*, p. 268.

of its rural constituency. In the center and South, the party seemed to be losing the support of both private farmworkers and farmers.

The Socialist party's loss in the South was attributed by many to Communist party domination. It was widely believed that Communist party militants were somehow controlling the farmworkers' vote through the offer and denial of employment. A Socialist party staff member explained his perceptions in an interview:

> When the [Communist] party got control of the occupied lands, they took control of the workers, too. [The system they established] was very simple. Become part of the union, vote for *the* party, and you'll eat well. Declare that you're a Socialist, refuse to follow [party] orders, and you're in the street.[39]

Seen from this perspective, the party's vote loss merely served to justify the relationship the CAP so often played upon: "Worker-controlled farms were really no more than islands of party control." Most significantly, they seemed to threaten the constituency of the Socialist party itself.

The party's vote loss was not the only factor that pushed the Socialists away from the articulation process. Other factors deriving from party politics served as stimuli as well. Important among these were the divisions within the Socialist party itself. The CAP did not have to fabricate contradictions in party members' statements on the issue of the agrarian reform. There were very real divisions within the party on this issue, and they existed at the very top of the party hierarchy. Key among these were the differences between Soares and Cardoso. Though Cardoso deemed it "very strange" that the CAP should express such "violent distrust" of him and such "confidence" in Mário Soares,[40] the response was actually quite predictable. Soares and Cardoso were in agreement on the need for a massive agrarian reform but were not in agreement on either its content or its timing. The PSP platform of December 1974 left many issues unresolved. It read:

> In the regions of the latifúndia, the fundamental objective of the agrarian reform will be to transfer possession of the land to those who work it. [This shall be done] through the *expropriation of large properties* that shall in turn be turned over *either to individual farmers or to cooperatives of rural wage workers.*[41]

What was a *large* property? Was the definition provided by the expropriations law a reasonable one? Although Cardoso never criticized the fifty

---

[39] Personal interview, Lisbon, January 1978.
[40] Cardoso, "A Defesa Intransigente," p. 53.
[41] Partido Socialista, *Declaração de Princípios,* p. 11; emphasis added.

thousand points limitation, other members of his party did. Soares argued that the limitation should be set by the democratically elected representatives of the people. After the legislature convened in July, Henrique de Barros criticized the limitation outright in a highly publicized newspaper article. Arguing that farmers with "extremely modest" incomes would be subject to expropriation, de Barros went on to ask:

> Is a latifundiário . . . a man who has earned, at the end of a harvest, after triumphing over the multiple crises emerging in any agricultural year, a monthly income of around [three hundred dollars]?[42]

De Barros thought not and argued against the law for taking the property of farmers "who were nothing like latifundiários."[43]

The content of the debate was not confined to disagreements about the size of the affected properties. The fate of the expropriated properties was also at issue. The party program asserted that expropriated lands should be turned over to "individual farmers *or* to cooperatives of rural wage workers," but the lands that Cardoso expropriated rarely, if ever, went to individuals. Complicating issues even further, most PSP leaders argued that the collective entities that *did* receive expropriated lands were not cooperatives at all. Henrique de Barros discussed the issue in the Socialist party newspaper. He criticized the undemocratic nature of the new production units and, implicitly, the PCP:

> [The] men of the southern countryside have ended up with a new boss. . . . The Socialist party can and should fight so that the agrarian reform can be truly democratic and so that the new, *so-called cooperatives* are faithful to the liberating ideas of the cooperative movement.[44]

Assailing the "so-called" cooperatives in these terms, Henrique de Barros seemed to be in agreement with the leadership of the CAP. In fact, there appeared to be agreement on two major issues: "the undemocratic" nature of the worker-controlled farms and the unfairness of the existing property limitation.

Electoral pressures and disagreements within the Socialist party itself eventually combined with other factors to stifle Cardoso's articulation plans. In the national arena, the most important factor was the landslide election of Ramalho Eanes as president on June 27, 1976. Eanes' victory was virtually assured by the fact that he had the endorsement of a broad range of important political groups. The PSP was the first party to support

---

[42] CAP, *Recortes de uma Luta*, p. 88.
[43] Ibid.
[44] *Portugal Socialista*, December 1, 1975.

him, but other parties and groups soon followed suit. Unfortunately for Cardoso, these groups were from the right rather than from the left. The PPD, the CDS, and even the CAP itself furnished Eanes with wholehearted endorsements.

Eanes was clearly from the ranks of the more moderate military officers. Unlike most of the military men who had assumed national leadership after the April coup, he had had nothing to do with the revolution itself. He was not a member of the MFA (and had in fact been thousands of miles away in Angola when the coup took place). He was an acceptable candidate for the right for a variety of reasons. Sociologically he was typical of the mainstream of the northern electorate. He was from a modest family in the rural area of Castelo Branco and was serious, taciturn, and religious. Politically he had demonstrated his "independence" from Communist and left-wing pressures on at least three public occasions. First, when he re- signed from an administrative position at the national broadcast station in protest against leftist harassment.[45] Second, when he signed the Document of the Nine. And more recently, on the 25th of November, when he engineered the defeat of the left-wing coup.

During the campaign and in the immediate aftermath of his election, Eanes made several statements that implied a reversal of the articulation process. His statements on the agrarian reform were rare but always in keeping with a moderate image. He alluded to the party-dominated, un- democratic nature of the new production units in a tone not unlike Henrique de Barros, stating that the agrarian reform should be "a means of liberating men and *not merely the exchange of one boss for other bosses.*"[46] Though he never attacked the PCP directly, he did say that "groups within the PCP have acted undemocratically and in a counterrevolutionary way."[47]

Most importantly, Eanes argued openly for a change in the focus of government policy. It should move away from the highly mobilized work- ers, who had already received attention, and toward rural groups who were slower to mobilize. He stated:

> Until now, only those working-class groups that are well-organized have managed . . . to have their demands satisfied. There are other groups, removed from power centers or less organized, who have not seen their situation bettered. . . . The government should concern itself fundamentally with these [latter] groups.[48]

The implications for the highly mobilized workers of the new production units were negative, while the implications for the neglected rural peasantry

[45] Paulino Gomes, *Eanes Porque o Poder?* (Lisbon: Intervoz, 1976), p. 14.
[46] Ibid., p. 90.
[47] Ibid., p. 16.
[48] Ibid., p. 92.

were positive. The continued articulation of the worker-controlled farms, implying the continued allocation of scarce credit and technical resources, began to appear less and less likely.

It also appeared less likely that Eanes would tolerate continued disorder in the southern countryside. Much to the delight of the politically exhausted Portuguese electorate, he emphasized the need for order within the state and within the government itself. In a statement that was clearly directed at the left-wing groups who were alleged to be dominating the rural South, he vowed to prevent minorities from maintaining "powers parallel" to those of the state. Minority parties would no longer be allowed to "promote confusion" and "sow bitterness."[49] The government would ensure that this was the case. It would present "a *truly national* program" (avoiding the special regional focus of the past), and it would be "cohesive" and homogeneous.[50] The emphasis on homogeneity was a particularly ominous sign for Cardoso because he was decidedly in the left wing of the party, far from Soares (who would most certainly be prime minister) and far from the latter's most trusted advisers.

The explicit and implicit content of Eanes' remarks were of special importance because of the extraordinary powers invested in the office of the president itself. Portugal had adopted a semipresidential governing system, meaning that the president had considerable powers vis-à-vis both the cabinet government and the Republican Assembly.[51] Most relevant for the future of worker-controlled farms were the following facts: 1) that no minister could be named without the president's approval; 2) that no law could be passed without the president's endorsement; and 3) that no presidential veto on legislation limiting property could be overridden with less than a two-thirds majority.[52] Even if Cardoso did manage to maintain his position in the Ministry of Agriculture, he could not draft any legislation that the president himself would not approve.

Economic and Strategic Disadvantages

If the election of Eanes made the prospect of articulation unlikely, economic and strategic factors made it nearly impossible. The partisan image of the

[49] Ibid. My emphasis.

[50] Ibid.

[51] Portugal designed a semipresidential system wherein the president sets election dates, convenes the National Assembly out of session, and dissolves the assembly after votes of no confidence in the prime minister. He can also dissolve the assembly at any time with the approval of the Council of the Revolution. In addition to having the sole power to name ambassadors, ratify treaties, and declare war, the president also has the right to declare a state of siege for thirty days—without assembly approval.

[52] The other laws to which the two-thirds rule applies are those related to external relations, national defense, and elections.

worker-controlled farms had panicked the capitalist democracies, especially the United States. The results of Senator Claiborne Pell's "fact-finding mission" indicate what U.S. government officials were thinking at the time. Returning in February of 1976, Senator Pell wrote:

> The setting up of cooperative farms was done in the early days of the revolution under Communist leadership and [sic] became bases for Communist activity throughout Portugal. They became areas for storing arms and staging areas for shock troops that the Communists dispatched to Lisbon and other urban areas. At one point, the Alentejo, under the strong influence of the Communists and other extreme left groups, became virtually a state within a state.[53]

Pell's report was similar in tone and content to the handbills of the CAP, and, like the latter, it was marred by exaggerations and outright errors. But the important fact politically was that Pell's impressions were widely held and used as a basis for U.S. foreign policy. The prospect of a Communist "state within a state" (complete with arms and shock troops) was disturbing anywhere in Europe, but especially disturbing in a NATO nation that hosted an American military base and stood at the mouth of the Mediterranean. Any government that tolerated (much less supported) the worker-controlled farms would be perceived as condoning a situation harmful to United States' interests. The consequences of such a move could be negative.

What would the consequences be? There was certainly the possibility of a destabilization program similar to the one that the United States had recently conducted in Chile. Rumors of CIA activity were common but never publicly authenticated. Economic consequences are easier to discuss and were certainly substantiated in themselves. Two years of provisional governments and political uncertainty had played havoc with Portugal's economy. The nation needed foreign loans and foreign capital to meet the needs of its newly demanding citizenry. Investments had dropped 40 percent in 1975 alone, while consumption rose 15 percent. People seemed unable or unwilling to save. The national rate of savings plummeted from 23 percent of the GNP in 1973 to only 4 percent in 1975.[54] Like the citizenry, the government was spending more and more, with a state budget

---

[53] Lester A. Sobel, *The Portuguese Revolution, 1974-1976* (New York: Facts on File, 1976), p. 11. Sobel's text contains a long quotation from the Pell report. The latter is shocking in its inaccuracy.

[54] Miguel Reis, *Governo Soares: O Exame de S. Bento* (Agência Portuguesa de Revistas, n.d.), p. 45.

deficit soaring from 3.7 million contos in 1973 to an estimated 40 million contos in 1976.[55]

Eanes drew a connection between the nation's economic crisis and the prospect of democratic stability. If the economic crisis "is not overcome," he asserted, "we will not have democracy. . . . We will have a dictatorship of the left or the right." He believed that the crisis demanded dramatic and urgent action. "The experts," he said, "give us six months."[56]

The leaders of the first constitutional government hoped that the Western democracies would play a major role in the solution of Portugal's economic problems. But it was clear from the outset that assistance from the West would be forthcoming only if the Portuguese state maintained its pluralist image and its hostility to communism. Loans from abroad took on the image of rewards for democratic behavior. Each was accompanied by a statement of congratulations on the triumph over communism. The foreign minister of West Germany announced a $250 million loan, saying that Germany was "pleased and impressed" that the Portuguese people had prevented "the installation of a new dictatorship."[57] The European Economic Community announced a $187 million loan in recognition "of Portugal's return to pluralist democracy," and the United States announced an $85 million loan in recognition of Portugal's successful attempts to "restore democratic government."[58]

There was thus a clear connection between Portugal's domestic policies and its desirability as a loan recipient. The possibilities of foreign investment would also be pegged to the degree of security that domestic policies could ensure. The economic and political consequences of a wholehearted attempt at articulation would therefore be very negative. Socialist support for the development and expansion of what were thought to be islands of Communist control would panic the other members of the NATO alliance and decrease the likelihood of both foreign assistance and foreign investment.

Continued attempts to integrate the cooperative farms with the new liberal democratic state were also affected by Portugal's petition to become a member of the EEC. Even before the 25th of April, the Socialists had placed great emphasis on the benefits of strengthened ties to Western Europe. Indeed, the party's motto, À Europa Connosco, To Europe with Us, was reflective of the theme.

[55] Ibid., p. 49. A key factor explaining the nation's economic crisis was the influx of between 600,000 and 800,000 Portuguese colonists returning to the mainland after decolonization. One conto equals 1,000 escudos.

[56] Gomes, *Eanes Porque o Poder?* p. 86.

[57] Sobel, *The Portuguese Revolution*, p. 137.

[58] Ibid., p. 116.

The Socialists realized, though, that successful integration in the EEC necessitated greater emphasis on modernization and economic efficiency. How would the worker-controlled farms fit in with these demands? A great debate developed around the issue, and the partisan image of the new production units was, once again, key. Because the credibility of the Communist party itself was so low, the leaders of the worker-controlled farms were never successful in convincing either critical elites or the general public that the cooperatives and collective farms were in fact efficient targets for the use of the state's material resources. Though the new production units spent a great deal of time and money collecting and then publicizing concrete data on farm investments and production, the validity of their figures was invariably attacked. Even if government or non-Communist party officials believed that the sector did, in fact, produce as much as was claimed, they argued that production costs were too high to make the ventures efficient. As a left-wing Socialist party activist told me in an interview:

> I, personally, know some [worker-controlled farms] that worked like machines. People did not want to believe that they were being well run, but many were. And production increased, maybe more than on any private farm anywhere—but what was the cost? So many hours of labor and so much public money. So many millions [of escudos]! Was it worth it? I think the money should have gone elsewhere.[59]

The path toward the EEC involved an explicit reordering of priorities that left the new production units near the bottom of a long list. A broad range of people inside and outside the first constitutional government believed that the rural sector of the economy was overpopulated and that worker-controlled farms were a barrier to modernization because they anchored workers in the primary sector where they should not be. Opponents of this line of reasoning argued that a further shift away from agricultural employment would merely create a larger reserve army of labor in the cities, enhancing not the interests of the nation as a whole but the interests of employers instead. The basic issue was part of a larger debate that had gone on since at least the time of Marx, but it was no less heated despite its age. Those who criticized the new production units were called "fascists." Those who supported continued credits for the units were accused of squandering scarce resources on politically suspect "unemployment subsidies." Cardoso, having initiated the credits in the first place, was in an especially awkward position.

Clearly, the factors that militated against articulation were both numerous

---

[59] Personal interview, Fundação Azevedo Gneco, Lisbon, July 1978.

and potent. It was only a matter of months before plans for articulation would be scrapped and Cardoso himself would resign. The Second National Socialist Party Congress in November 1976 provided a convenient point of transition. Shortly after the November meeting, Cardoso delivered his letter of resignation to the prime minister.

THE END OF ARTICULATION

Within a few days, a young sociologist named António Barreto would be named to Cardoso's post. There were marked differences between the two men. Barreto was not from the left wing of the Socialist party and was not a native of the agrarian reform zone. He was close to Eanes, and he was well-acquainted with Portugal's mostly Western trading partners, for he had been secretary for foreign trade. The most important contrast between Cardoso and Barreto was the fact that Barreto met with the approval of the CAP. In an editorial written shortly after Barreto assumed his new position, an organization spokesman praised the new minister's "courage" and suggested that his presence in the Ministry of Agriculture could "constitute a turning away from the treacherous agrarian policies of Lopes Cardoso."[60]

The CAP's faith in Barreto would soon be borne out, as the new minister made major changes in state policy. Within less than a year, he drafted and signed into law a complex piece of legislation that altered the future of worker-controlled farms in significant ways. The most important changes involved the nature and value of the property that could be legally expropriated. According to the new legislation (or the *Lei Barreto*, as it was commonly known), government expropriations would not affect any land belonging to "autonomous farmers." These, according to the law, were family farmers who relied "almost exclusively" on their own labor, the labor of their immediate family, *or* (and this was the most controversial point) "domestic labor": the labor of persons who were not related by blood but were not simply salaried workers.[61] Any farm owner who could illustrate that he fit this rather vague description would have his land returned. Cooperatives containing these farms would, of course, lose them.

Another major change in government policy involved the actual value of the properties subject to expropriation. Barreto's Law raised the limit on landholdings a full 40 percent: from 50,000 points to 70,000 points. This change affected the size of reserves as well. Anyone who had farmed 70,000 points' worth of land during the year in which a given property

---

[60] *O Agricultor* (Lisbon), November 30, 1976. The comments appear in an opening article entitled "Could Barreto be the Man who Transforms Agriculture?"

[61] See Law 77/77, article 23: 2.

TABLE 7.3
Increase in Areas of Normal Reserves
1975 Legislation versus 1977 Legislation

District	Average Area of Reserves in Hectares		
	1975 Law	1977 Law	% Increase
Beja	280	390	39
Évora	267	374	40
Portalegre	265	371	40
Santarém	197	276	40
Setúbal	306	428	40

SOURCE: Ministério da Agricultura e Pescas, unpublished records from the Instituto Nacional de Investigação Agrícola.

was occupied had a right to a reserve valued at 70,000 points. Taking average soil quality into consideration and translating points to hectares, the new law would increase the size of reserves in the manner indicated in Table 7.3. In concrete terms, a cooperative farm encompassing three occupied properties in the district of Évora, for example, would have lost 801 hectares under the 1975 legislation but would now lose 1,122 hectares, or approximately 2,800 acres. These figures were for "normal" reserves on land that was being farmed at the time of occupation.

The cooperatives stood to lose land to reserves under other conditions as well. For example, anyone who had farmed a tract of land valued at 35,000 points or more at any time in the three years preceding an occupation had the right to a reserve as well, though their values would be pegged to the amount of land actually used. A whole set of landowners who did not fit either the standard or the special categories had the right to reserves also. The group included any landowners who were over sixty-five, under eighteen, widowed, homeless, or "unable to work." Emigrants were also granted automatic reserves.[62]

These were only the minimum values of the lands that would be returned to the private sector. The area of any reserve could be increased at the discretion of MAP. There were several situations that would legally give rise to such an increase, but the most common was the case in which a landowner's "domestic household" contained more than four people. Families with more than two children, or servants, or even servants' dependents,

[62] Ibid., articles 25-27.

would have their reserves increased 10 percent for every extra household member.[63]

This brief description of Barreto's Law leaves much unsaid. Containing seventy-six separate articles, the law contained many provisions that need not be mentioned here. The important point is that the new law left worker-controlled farms severely debilitated.

Though the methods and the rate of the law's enforcement varied in the years following its passage, the law itself was a first, and giant, step toward the dismantling of the new production units. By January 1981, some 569,000 hectares of land would be taken from the worker-controlled farms and returned to private hands.[64] The text of the new legislation virtually assured that the transferred properties would include the most valuable resources of a farm holding. Thus, the new production units lost not only vast quantities of land but often the houses, buildings, machines, and livestock that went along with it. An estimated 111 cooperatives were dismantled, and scores of others were debilitated. A unit in Vendas Novas, for example, lost so much land that it was forced to "graze" its livestock in the town square.

Massive changes in the nation's credit system had devastating effects on worker-controlled farms as well. The "tight money" policies forced on the nation's banking system as a condition for International Monetary Fund loans meant an end to many special credit programs in industry as well as agriculture. Interest rates skyrocketed not because of a sinister plot, as many believed, but because the nationalized banks were conducting "banking as usual" and pegging interest rates to inflation.

The "banking as usual" policy had especially debilitating effects on cooperatives and collectives, for it meant an end to special concessions based on social rather than economic criteria. When a new production unit failed to meet its loan payment obligations, credit was cancelled. "Agricultural credit cannot," Barreto asserted, "be used in a political or partisan way. [The] distortions that were numerous in the past . . . will be put to a definitive end."[65] The new policy meant that within twelve months, more than 50 percent of all worker-controlled farms would lose their right to credits.[66]

---

[63] Ibid., article 28.

[64] Comissão Organizadora, *5ª Conferência da Reforma Agrária* (Évora, 1981), mimeographed, p. 7.

[65] Ministério da Agricultura e Pescas, *O Crédito ao Sector Primário: A Criação do I.F.A.D.A.P.* (Lisbon: MAP, 1977), p. 18; from a speech entitled "The Future of the Portuguese Begins with Farming and Fishing."

[66] This is an estimate furnished by the Emergency Agricultural Division of the Ministry of Agriculture.

It was not neccesssary for the Socialist party to target the cooperatives on explicitly political grounds, for the decision to treat the units like any other borrowers had sufficiently devastating effects in itself and could easily be rationalized in economic terms. Many cooperatives had, in fact, been unable and/or unwilling to repay their government loans on time. Despite the general increase in productivity, many of these units had taken on more members than they could easily support. Resources, predictably, went to salaries rather than loans. This was especially understandable when it became clear that the former owners would soon recoup their land. Workers did not want to pay for investments that they would soon lose.

The changes in the credit system made it clear that Cardoso's attempts at articulating the cooperatives and the state had clearly been reversed. To the extent that landowners gained and workers lost, the reversal was indeed an example of ''capitalist recuperation'' and another battle in the struggle between the two polar classes. But the failure of articulation cannot be reduced to these simple terms alone. The upper class would never have gained what it did if it had been forced to rely exclusively on its own resources. It was only by taking advantage of the competition between the Socialists and the Communists and, relatedly, the partisan image of workers' control, that the upper class was able to tap the resources of other groups and use these to triumph.

How did this happen? In a first stage of the revolution, partisan competition on the left contributed to the failure of the peasant leagues. These were the only class organizations that might have provided an alternative to an interest group dominated by the *agrários*. Socialist and especially Communist party attempts to lead these organizations weakened their scope and representativeness, leaving the peasantry with no organizations that were exclusively their own. The possibilities of a peasant-*agrário* alliance were thus enhanced.

At a second stage of the revolution, the partisan image of the worker-controlled farms incited the small- and medium-sized farmers to panic and to join with the wealthy landowners against the agrarian reform. Had the land occupations (and later, the agrarian reform itself) been associated with no party at all, or with a Socialist party that made convincing promises to the peasantry, the alliance between large holders and small holders, *agrários* and peasants, would have been much more difficult to forge.

There were, after all, very real differences between the groups. Many small- and medium-sized farmers recognized that latifundiários had not made proper use of their estates,[67] and most drew a clear distinction between

---

[67] Responses to the author's questionnaire in Portel suggested this. In answer to a question

themselves and the large landowners. Coupled with radical differences in wealth and life style, the contrasts between latifundiários and peasants might have been effectively divisive were the two groups not united against a "common enemy." Ultimately, a mutual distrust of the PCP made unity likely indeed. Playing successfully on the authoritarian image of the PCP and on the Socialist party's perceived inability to control the transfer of property in the South, large landowners convinced small holders and medium holders in general that they too were in danger of losing their land and that their interests too were being neglected by the PSP.

Just as the partisan image of workers' control enabled the large landowners to tap the political resources of the middle and small peasantry, so did it enable them to tap the political resources of foreign powers. The new production units were seen as a threat to NATO security not because they were cooperatives or collectives but because they were considered bastions of Communist control. Landowners and the U.S.-allied defense establishment had convergent interests mainly, if not only, because of the partisan image of workers' control.

Searching for the support of the numerically powerful small and medium farm community, pressured by anti-Communist forces abroad, and unable to compromise with its competition on the left, Portugal's Socialist party turned against the agrarian reform. The articulation of participation structures at the national level and the base thus proved impossible—not because the Socialists were opposed to workers' control but because a rival party seemed so closely associated with it.

The passage of the 1977 Agrarian Reform Law illustrated that the postrevolutionary state was unwilling to accept the legacy of the revolutionary period unchanged. Legitimating the devolution of thousands of hectares of land, the new law seemed to be the state's final word on the future of workers' control in agriculture. In fact, the conflict between the state and the workers of the Alentejo was merely entering another new phase.

The *Lei Barreto* was not the state's final word because the state itself was undergoing rapid change.[68] The state was too unstable to ensure that the agrarian reform law would immediately be enforced, and the Ministry of Agriculture itself was the scene of great turmoil. Even before the new legislation was passed, Barreto became the target of virulent public hostility. In Lisbon and throughout the South scores of walls and hundreds of placards and banners read "Barreto—Hit the Road!" "Barreto—Fascist!" and "Barreto and CAP—Get out of MAP!" Barreto became the

that asked for an explanation of local poverty prior to the revolution, 52.5 percent of the farmers questioned placed the blame directly on landowners. See Table 6.10.

[68] For an idea of the extent of change in the government itself, see the Chronology of Constitutional Governments in Appendix II.

personification of the counterrevolution and met more and more hostility within his own party as 1977 wore on. When the first constitutional government fell in December 1977 and Barreto publicly proclaimed that he was unwilling to serve in another Socialist cabinet, many party militants breathed a sigh of relief. The PSP had lost 50 percent of its supporters in a special election in Évora the month before, and party militants were eager that the debacle not be repeated.

When a second constitutional government was formed by a Socialist-Center Democrat coalition in January 1978, the portfolio for agriculture was given to a political independent named Luís Saias. Like his immediate predecessor, Saias was the target of great public hostility, but this time the hostility was to come from the right rather than the left.

Backed by Soares (who maintained his position as prime minister in the new government), Saias adopted a go-slow policy on the implementation of Barreto's Law. Estimating that twenty thousand to thirty thousand workers would be left unemployed if the law were enforced immediately, Saias publicly expressed his desire to minimize the "social costs" of the new legislation.[69] Accordingly, he slowed the repossession of property considerably and withdrew the riot police who had been dispatched to cooperatives to enforce the law. CAP reacted immediately and demanded that Saias be dismissed. When Soares refused, the CDS ministers resigned from his cabinet, broke the coalition, and brought down the government.

Why had the Socialist leadership changed positions? The answer lies in the changed nature of the party struggle on the left. Competition and animosity between the Socialists and Communists continued, but the nature of the conflict had changed. It was no longer a battle between a Socialist party seeking to better an already dominant position and a Communist party threatening simultaneously to erode the Socialists' constituency and provoke a right-wing reaction. By 1978, the right had already reacted, the Communist party was clearly on the defensive, and the Socialists, associated with a series of unpopular austerity measures, had little immediate chance of maintaining, much less expanding, support.[70] Once again, the issue of worker-controlled farms had divided the state and transformed the government.

[69] For an English language report of this, see Economist Intelligence Unit, *Quarterly Economic Review of Portugal* (Third Quarter, 1978), p. 4.

[70] The refusal to cater to CAP and the CDS had been brought on by a changed mood within the PSP. There was a widespread if not pervasive feeling that Barreto had gone too far. As a Socialist deputy told the author, "We accepted him without knowing what he would do, and when we opened our eyes, it was already done." "Suddenly," explained another, "our . . . party [was] the party of the most unpopular man in Portuguese history. Even Salazar was more popular than Barreto."

The Socialists stayed out of government for the next five years (from 1978 to 1983), but the 1977 Agrarian Reform Law remained—and remains, as of this writing—unchanged. The Center Democrat/Popular Democrat coalition (AD) that gained control of the state after the Socialists were forced from office applied the law with much more zeal than its originators. In the first year of AD administration, private citizens recouped a full 324,000 hectares from worker-controlled farms—an amount far exceeding the 245,000 recouped in the previous four years. The rapid devolution of land meant a decline in the number of collectives and cooperatives. A full sixty units were destroyed in 1980, exceeding, once again, the fifty-one cooperatives that had disappeared prior to the election of the AD.[71]

THROUGHOUT the Alentejo now the quiet of the village streets is occasionally shattered by convoys of jeeps and trucks rumbling toward another devolution of land. At nightfall the cafes ring with stories of how much was taken, of who said what, and of who will be left jobless. There are tales of occasional individual heroics, but the workers are no longer offering physical resistance to the seizures of land. There is a pervasive feeling that the National Guard will shoot to kill and that the land will be taken at any price.[72]

It is too early to speculate on whether the recently elected Socialist government will reverse this trend, but one can certainly see the political logic behind the devolutions of the past. Both the AD and the PSP were motivated in part by the desire to dismantle what continues to be seen as both a bastion of the PCP and one of the few remaining strongholds of working-class radicalism. That they have been wholly successful in this task is highly questionable.

There is no doubt that the worker-controlled farming sector has been severely debilitated since the passage of the 1977 law. The loss of land, livestock, and machinery is a crippling blow. But it is not a lethal blow. Both government officials and union leaders estimate that at least one-third to one-half of the original cooperatives will survive the implementation of the law. Providing secure employment and a relatively egalitarian work environment to thousands of laborers, the farms will remain, for many, tangible proof of the promise of workers' control. These units will stand

---

[71] Federação das Cooperativas Agrícolas, Distrito de Évora, unpublished records, and Ministério de Agricultura, unpublished records. Figures are estimates.

[72] It is difficult to describe with certainty what is being done with the land the cooperatives have lost. A survey conducted in 1981 suggests that approximately 85 percent of it is being held by former landowners and that some 15 percent is being held by small farmers, medium farmers, or small craftsmen. *5ª Conferência da Reforma Agrária*. Official figures from the Ministry of Agriculture were not available at the time of this writing.

as a concrete legacy of the days when rural laborers took the revolution into their own hands.

The units that have ceased to operate, or will do so soon, will also leave their legacy in the rural South. Like Catarina Eufémia herself, each of these cooperatives will be remembered as a victim of a tragic conflict between rural workers and the Portuguese state. Thus, at both a concrete and symbolic level, the experience of workers' control leaves a legacy that fortifies hostility to the postrevolutionary order. For the people of the Alentejo, the revolution within the revolution leaves resources from which future proponents of radical change can readily draw. For scholars, the revolution within the revolution leaves the means for a better understanding of rural mobilization, the reorganization of labor, and the building of democratic socialism. In the conclusion that follows I discuss these three interrelated themes.

EIGHT

Conclusion: Lessons from the Portuguese

THIS study began with a report of two men who risked and lost their lives in the defense of a worker-controlled farm. The chapters that followed illustrated how such workers came to control the land in the first place, how the control of property affected their own lives, and finally how their new enterprises affected and were affected by the postrevolutionary state. The human drama that lies at the foundation of this study is, essentially, that of a struggle for change in power and property relations. Like most dramas, the study has shown its characters across time and in a variety of settings. In each of these, a different body of literature has been brought in to illuminate the unfolding of events. The literature is diverse because the drama itself is so multifaceted and because no single phase can properly be understood in isolation. What has been learned so far? What has the Portuguese case suggested that might be applicable in other contexts and useful in directing future research?

THE PROBLEM OF ARTICULATION

The problem of articulation discussed in the last chapter is a general one. Portugal's experience with workers' control is not unique. Russian, German, and Chilean history provide us with other cases in which important networks of workers' control at the base level emerged within a system of state-level democracy that was dominated (albeit precariously) by socialist parties. Similar problems with articulation emerged in each case, and though the problems were resolved in different ways, political parties played a major role in each solution.

Russia 1917

The problems of articulation in the aftermath of the February Revolution were extremely complex due to the range and mutability of the structures and parties involved. But peering through the detailed chronology of events, and focusing on what remained constant throughout the two-part postrevolutionary period (that is, after February and then again after October) one sees a situation that is in certain respects very similar to the Portuguese. In Russia, as in Portugal, there were two distinct loci of power:

one a formal locus in the structure of the national government and another decentralized locus of power in a network of soldiers' and workers' soviets. Throughout the two-phase postrevolutionary period, there was a situation of dual power, or dyarchy. From February to the Bolshevik Revolution in October, the articulation problem involved the soviets and the turbulent provisional governments. From November until January of 1918, the problem involved the soviets and the ill-fated Constitutional Assembly.

In both phases of the revolution, there was great debate about where the primary locus of power should be. Indeed, there was even some debate about where primary power actually lay. Lenin, describing the soviets in April 1917, saw "a still weak and embryonic but all the same . . . growing *second government*."[1] Guchkov, minister of war in the provisional government of the same period, argued instead that the soviets had "the actual power, such as troops, railroads and communications." In his opinion, the provisional government existed "only by the soviets' permission" and had, in effect, "no real power" of its own.[2] Guchkov's perceptions were probably more accurate. The soviets certainly had better control of the forces of coercion (as the storming of the Winter Palace would soon illustrate). They also had a more prominent role as a forum for partisan dispute and party struggle.

In Russia, as in Portugal, political parties were closely linked to structures for workers' control. "Soon" after their formation, the soviets "became the battleground for various political tendencies."[3] The battle was not between the two polar classes, but among parties of the working class. "The best minds in the socialist parties were to be found in the [s]oviets: the parties' struggle for influence was decided here and not in the dumas."[4]

The struggle for influence in the most important soviet was ultimately decided in the favor of the Bolsheviks. Though the party began with relatively few soviet representatives, the Bolsheviks won a majority position in the Petrograd soviet by the month of July. Bolshevik ascendancy in the units of workers' control in the capital city made the problems of articulation more acute, for now the two halves of the dual power situation were in the hands of two distinct and highly competitive party groups. The Bolsheviks in the soviets stood on one side, while a coalition of socialist and moderate parties in the provisional government stood on the other.

Lenin's assault on the Winter Palace in October can be seen as an attempt

---

[1] Bertman D. Wolfe, *An Ideology in Power* (New York: Stein and Day, 1969), p. 139; emphasis added.

[2] Oskar Anweiler, *The Soviets: The Russian Workers, Peasants, and Soldiers Councils, 1905-1921* (New York: Pantheon, 1974), p. 128.

[3] Ibid., p. 112.

[4] Ibid., p. 139; emphasis mine.

to resolve the problem of articulation. By doing away with the provisional government, Lenin no longer had two elements to be articulated. But the articulation problem emerged again on November 12 when the elections for the Constitutional Assembly were held. Though Lenin was "not happy about allowing the election" to take place,[5] he was unwilling to risk party and public disruption to stop it. He pinned his hopes on a Bolshevik victory, but this never materialized. Lenin's party polled 9.8 million votes, but the Socialist Revolutionaries polled 20.7 million, an absolute majority.

Thus the problem of articulation emerged once again in stark relief, but this time Lenin found a permanent solution; the Constitutional Assembly was closed on January 5, 1918, after its first and only meeting. Lenin's "weak second government" thus became the *only* government, and the problem of articulation disappeared. Within a few months Lenin turned "viciously" against the soviets themselves, but this is not directly relevant to the present discussion.[6]

What is relevant is the fact that in Russia, as in Portugal, a situation of dual power became convoluted with a situation of fierce party competition and degenerated to a point where one partisan element destroyed the other. The problem of articulation was eliminated rather than resolved, and the principal actors were not the bipolar classes but the Bolsheviks and the Socialist Revolutionaries—the political parties of the working class and the peasantry.

Germany 1918

A similar problem of articulation emerged in Germany in the aftermath of World War I. In Germany, as in Russia, a situation of dual power arose with a precarious provisional government on the one hand and a complex network of workers' and soldiers' councils on the other.

Ironically, the councils had seized power, while the provisional government had had power thrust upon it. The council movement began in the port city of Kiel when a group of sailors mutinied and organized a "soldiers' council," similar in organization and purpose to the original Russian soviets. "Within a few days,"[7] in a movement that "spread like

---

[5] Robert V. Daniels, *Red October: The Bolshevik Revolution of 1917* (New York: Scribner, 1967), p. 212.

[6] Maurice Brinton, *The Bolsheviks and Worker Control* (Detroit: Black Rose Books, 1975), p. ix.

[7] A. J. Ryder, *The German Revolution of 1918* (Cambridge: Cambridge University Press, 1967), p. 3.

an avalanche,'' thousands of sailors, soldiers, and workers organized hundreds of other councils throughout Germany.[8]

The nascent council network presented a dilemma to Friederich Ebert as he received the reins of government from Prince Max. As the monarchy abandoned Germany to a hastily declared republic, there were reportedly only two spheres of authority in the nation. One was the military command on the Western Front; the other was the intricate web of workers' and soldiers' councils.[9] As the flight of Prince Max made patently clear, Ebert's government would have to establish an authority of its own.

The government's authority would have to be articulated with the authority of the workers' councils if the former were to survive. Certain factors suggested that articulation was indeed possible. Most important was the fact that the same parties were ascendant in both halves of the dual power balance. The Social Democrats had the ascendancy in the national government, for their leader, Friederich Ebert, had been appointed head of state by Prince Max. The party also had the ascendancy in most of the workers' and soldiers' councils, for it was the favorite party of most council organizers. Coordination of SPD affiliates in the council and national governments might have provided the means of articulation that a genuine democratic socialism required, but the councils were doomed to disappear instead.

The problem was largely one of party competition. The councils were supposed to be nonpartisan agencies of workers' government. In fact, discussion of their functional role was consistently "overshadowed by the clash between Social Democrats and Independents."[10] The rivalry between the two major left-wing parties was closely linked to the issue of workers' control. The Independents felt strongly that workers' councils were the key to the future of German democracy and that parliamentary government alone would degenerate into authoritarianism. Accordingly, they refused to enter a coalition government with the Social Democrats unless Ebert agreed that the soldiers' and workers' councils would maintain "sovereign power."[11] Ebert's response was positive, but it was one of acquiescence rather than agreement, for he was highly distrustful of the council system.

His suspicions were predictable. First of all, the Social Democrats did

---

[8] F. L. Carsten, *Revolution in Central Europe* (Berkeley: University of California Press, 1972), p. 33.

[9] A. J. Ryder, *Twentieth-Century Germany: From Bismarck to Brandt* (New York: Columbia University Press, 1973), p. 188.

[10] Carsten, *Revolution*, p. 136.

[11] Gordon Craig, *Germany, 1866-1945* (New York: Oxford University Press, 1978), p. 404.

not control *all* of the workers' and soldiers' councils. Many of the councils in the most important industrial centers were controlled by rival parties. In Hamburg, Bremen, Leipzig, Dresden, Halle, and other smaller cities, the council movement was dominated by Independents and eventually even Spartacists. Ebert did not expect these units to act in concert with the Social Democratic party and balked at giving them "sovereignty."

Ironically, a second reason for suspicion derived from the actions of the councils that were nominally Social Democratic. In many cases, the Social Democrats who held leadership positions within the councils were far to the left of the Social Democrats who held leadership positions at the national level. This became evident when councils from all over Germany convened at a national congress in December 1918. Though more than three hundred of the five hundred council delegates were Social Democrats,[12] the councils' resolutions countervened basic elements of the party's official policy.

While Ebert and his party's national hierarchy argued that any changes in military authority or property relations should be postponed until the meeting of a constitutional assembly, the council leaders boldly called for the immediate socialization of key industries and the democratization of the army—a democratization wherein officers would be elected and military action would be subject to council rule. For Ebert—the man who defined socialism as "organization"—these policy proposals were wholly unacceptable. Coupled with strikes, seizures, and sieges of public buildings, council actions provoked mounting frustration within the SPD. In late December, Ebert complained in a cabinet meeting of looking "foolish in the eyes of the world" and, then, reneging on his promise to the Independents, declared: The councils "are advisory authorities and nothing else. . . . A sharp delimitation [of power] is necessary."[13]

At the root of Ebert's frustration was a third and most important reason for suspicion—namely, the actions of the Bolsheviks in nearby Russia. Ebert, like most Social Democrats, was shocked and saddened by Lenin's summary dissolution of Russia's Constitutional Assembly. Party leaders were determined that the scenario would not be repeated in Germany. For them, the council system provided an open invitation for "antidemocratic" parties on the left. Fighting Bolshevism meant fighting the councils, which is precisely what the Social Democrats eventually did.

The councils that were controlled by SPD loyalists relinquished their powers "without demur" in the aftermath of the national elections

---

[12] William Carr, *A History of Germany, 1815-1945* (New York: St. Martin's Press, 1969), p. 192.

[13] Carsten, *Revolution*, p. 133. The first quotation cited follows the second in the original text.

in January 1919.[14] The many councils that refused to disband in Hamburg, Bremen, central Germany, the Ruhr, and, of course, Bavaria were forcefully destroyed under SPD orders.[15]

Once again, articulation proved impossible. The failure to articulate democracy at the national level with democracy at the base was due in some measure to pressures from the military and the propertied classes, but significant pressures also emerged from competition between the parties that aligned themselves with the working class. The whole reformist revolution was, as Barrington Moore put it, "a bitter duel for the allegiance of the industrial working classes."[16] In Germany, as in Russia and Portugal, the structures of workers' control provided the setting for the duel.

Chile 1970

The Allende government in Chile battled with problems of articulation that were similar to those just discussed. Once again, a national government headed by one party group confronted units of workers' control linked to another. Allende won control of the national executive in the presidential elections of October 1970 through a coalition of Communist and Socialist parties called Unidad Popular. His position was especially precarious because moderate and right-wing groups still dominated congress and the judiciary, but he was determined to initiate the democratic transition to socialism that he had promised in his campaign.

A massive agrarian reform was a critical part of Allende's socialist vision, but his commitment to liberal democracy compelled him to work within the confines of existing legislation. An agrarian reform law passed by Christian Democrats was already in effect, and Allende decided to concentrate on the full implementation of this legislation until a future Socialist Congress could be elected and pass more radical laws. This gradualist approach proved unacceptable to the MIR and even to elements within Allende's own Socialist party. Seeking to quicken the pace of socialization, MIR

[14] Carr, *History of Germany*, p. 291.

[15] In a graphic illustration of the importance of party politics in the destruction of the workers' councils, Erhard Auer, Social Democrat from Bavaria, remarked in a February 12, 1919, cabinet meeting: "Through the penetration of the Spartacists into the workers' and soldiers' councils, the situation has become untenable." Allan Mitchell, *Revolution in Bavaria, 1918-1919: The Eisner Regime and the Soviet Republic* (Princeton, New Jersey: Princeton University Press, 1965), p. 258.

[16] Barrington Moore, Jr., *Injustice: The Social Basis of Obedience and Revolt* (New York: M.E. Sharpe, Inc., 1978), p. 285.

militants and sympathizers set out to stimulate property occupations and to institute a framework for dual power and the beginnings of a new st te.[17]

In industrial and mining areas, the MIR encountered strong opposition from unions and workers affiliated with the parties of the Unidad Popular, but they met with much success in the rural South in an area with a high concentration of Mapuche Indians. The Mapuche had long-standing grievances against local landowners. The Indians were underpaid and underemployed, but they also believed that they had ancestral claims on the latifúndia. The MIR-Mapuche alliance had an immediate effect on property relations. As a result of MIR activities, land occupations increased 180 percent during Allende's first year of office. The group provided transportation, organization, and sometimes arms for occupations.[18]

The peasant councils that grew out of the occupations presented a dramatic dilemma for the Unidad Popular. For ideological reasons, the UP could not restrain peasant councils with force. The government did not "believe even remotely in the repression of workers and farmers."[19] Yet the coalition was painfully aware that the wildcat occupations jeopardized the success of the Allende regime. Disturbances in rural areas would lead to a drop in food production and a deleterious increase in agricultural imports. Disturbances would also lead to a backlash among property owners of all kinds, including the medium and small producers from which the UP sought support.[20] True to its ideological commitments, the Unidad Popular chose to battle the movement for workers' control with words alone. The Communist provincial governor, the Socialist minister of agriculture, and even Allende himself traveled to the area to plead for council cooperation, but the occupations and the council movement continued unrestrained.[21]

---

[17] Kyle Steenland, *Agrarian Reform under Allende* (Albuquerque: University of New Mexico Press, 1977), p. 6.

[18] Arturo Valenzuela, *Chile* (Baltimore: The Johns Hopkins University Press, 1978), p. 53.

[19] Ibid., p. 68.

[20] Cristobal Kay, "Agrarian Reform and the Transition to Socialism in Chile, 1970-1973," *The Journal of Peasant Studies* (July 1975), p. 422.

[21] A Communist provincial governor named Fernando Teillier traveled to the area of the MIR seizures, cautioned that the farms seized were too small to take, and urged that the seizures stop. Jacques Chonchol, minister of agriculture, also traveled south and asked that the occupations cease, "since they hindered the government, making it vulnerable to attacks from the right." Finally, Allende himself visited the area and made the same argument. The occupations continued anyway. See Steenland, *Agrarian Reform* p. 83. Exminister Chonchol confirmed the existence of this dual power situation in a conversation with me in Paris in June 1981.

Steadfast in its refusal to resort to physical force, the Allende coalition left the opposition councils intact and merely tried to preempt new waves of occupations by expropriating land as rapidly as possible. This policy only provoked the reaction that the regime had sought to prevent. The middle-sized producers joined the ranks of the latifundiários, production plummeted, food shortages stimulated urban disorder, and the need for increased imports wreaked havoc with the balance of payments.

Whether, in the long run, the forebearance of the Allende regime would have resulted in a stable articulation of national and popular democracy will never be known, for the national democracy itself was destroyed in a right-wing coup in September 1973.

WHILE the three cases just reviewed differ from each other and from the Portuguese in several ways, their similarities are marked. Each represents an example of failed articulation in which party conflict played a major role. In each case, left-wing national governments faced structures of workers' control in which rival left-wing parties had the ascendancy. The problems of structural control and party competition were resolved in different ways. In Russia, the party that had the ascendancy in the structures of workers' control destroyed the national democracy. In Germany, the party with the ascendancy in the national democracy destroyed the structures of workers' control. In Chile, the coalition leading the national democracy allowed the structures of their left-wing opposition to continue, and both forms of democracy were demolished by a right-wing coup.

With the Bolsheviks battling the Socialist Revolutionaries, the Social Democrats battling the Independents (and the Spartacists), and, finally, the Unidad Popular battling left-wing Socialists and the MIR, the conflict was always fought on the left, and the issue was always the loyalty and control of the peasantry and the working classes. In this respect, the cases are identical to the Portuguese.

In all four cases, the cogs of representative democracy failed to "mesh" with the cogs of workers' control. The problems of articulation are thus far more perplexing than the literature on democratic socialism would lead us to believe. Moreover, the problems cannot be reduced to a bipolar model of class conflict. In none of these cases did the upper class manage to prevent articulation single-handedly. In the Russian case, the upper class itself was destroyed. In the other cases, the upper class managed to endure and to block the path to socialism, but it did so with the support and resources of other groups. There can be no doubt that power lay with the forces of capital, but power also lay with peasants, shopkeepers, and skilled workers who could swing elections, fill the streets in protests, or wreak

havoc with the economy. These were resources which could not be ignored—least of all by left-wing parties in power.

The SPD, the Unidad Popular, and the Portuguese Socialists recognized
that their positions in national government were precarious. They needed
to stabilize their economies, restore public order, and gain a stronger
electoral mandate if they were to continue in power. The resources of social
groups outside the upper classes were required for these goals, and it was
the desire to attract and maintain these resources that forced the left-wing
parties to move against workers' control. To the extent that structures of
workers' control were dominated by elements from a rival party, they
escaped government control and jeopardized the ruling parties' goals.

Aware of the precedent set by the Bolsheviks, the SPD moved against
the workers' councils before its own goals were overturned. The Unidad
Popular failed in its attempt to do the same and was itself ruined, along
with the Chilean national democracy as a whole. Just as the Bolshevik
victory was salient in the minds of the Social Democrats in Germany, so
was the Chilean debacle salient in the minds of Portuguese Socialists.
Refusing the risky option of articulation, the PSP moved against the worker-
controlled farms. Workers' control began to disintegrate, but the national
democracy itself was preserved. Thus, as the preceding chapter illustrated,
the social revolution receded but the gains of the political revolution
remained.

The generalization that emerges from this section of analysis is that
parties matter. Party conflict can be as important as class conflict. The
duration, the integration, and ultimately the consequences of workers'
control are greatly affected by the party image of the controlled structure.
Just as this can be illustrated comparatively with cases from Russia, Germany, and Chile, so can it be illustrated within Portugal if we compare
the fate of worker-controlled farms with that of worker-controlled industrial
firms.

Portugal 1975

As I mentioned in the preface of this study, agricultural property was not
the only property occupied during the revolution. There were occupations
of industrial properties as well, and a small sector of worker-controlled
factories and service firms grew up as a result. Though only 3 percent of
all nonagricultural firms fell into this category, the number of workers
involved totaled thirty thousand.

Though both examples of workers' control involved the extralegal seizure of productive property by wage workers, the agricultural and nonag-

ricultural sectors were treated quite differently by the postrevolutionary Socialist party governments. In one case, we had an outright assault on the sector through dismantling legislation. In the other case—with nonagricultural properties—we had a combination of modest support and benign neglect.[22]

The worker-controlled industrial and service firms did not receive the low-cost credits and administrative assistance they desired, and their spokesmen complained bitterly that the Socialist party governments did not give them the support they required. However, the PSP did give the sector scarce resources and created two special institutes to promote its growth.[23] These institutes worked imperfectly, but the worker-managed sector in industry expanded rather than contracted in the aftermath of the revolution. Despite bankruptcies and repossessions by original owners, the number of worker-controlled firms in Portugal actually increased by four hundred between the end of 1975 and 1978. As the previous chapters illustrate, the opposite occurred in agriculture.

The explanation for contrasting policies is complex, but much of it boils down to differences in the party image of the two worker-controlled sectors. The worker-controlled factories and service firms were not perceived as bastions of the Communist party. Dispersed throughout the nation in all but two of its eighteen districts, the firms were not a party enclave and could not be described as such. Moreover, the Socialist party itself had a real presence in many of the most important enterprises. Vocal party militants sat on the management councils of many firms, and party notables gave the sector and the whole concept of *autogestion* in industry a great deal of verbal support. There were Communist party activists in many firms and on many management boards, but the sector itself was identified with no particular party. The small businessmen who lost these firms in the heady days of 1975 could not easily use party rivalry to get their property returned because the fight against workers' control in factories and service firms could not be fused with a fight against communism.

[22] More detailed discussions of either the comparative cases or of workers' control in Portuguese industry would lead us too far from the argument here. For more on workers' control in industry see Nancy Gina Bermeo, ''Worker Management in Industry: Reconciling Representative Government and Industrial Democracy in a Polarized Society,'' in Lawrence S. Graham and Douglas L. Wheeler, eds., *In Search of Modern Portugal: The Revolution and Its Consequences* (Madison: University of Wisconsin Press, 1983). The article discusses how the sector emerged and why the Socialist party could only give it modest support.

[23] One institute dealt with industrial and service cooperatives; the other dealt with ''self-managed enterprises.'' The latter were firms that (unlike cooperatives) were not legally owned by the workers themselves. Workers in these firms were in a most disadvantageous position and were most likely to encounter difficulties keeping their enterprises open.

There was, as a result, no "Rio Maior" for this sector: that is, no massive cross-class public display of opposition to property seizures in small firms.

With a mixed party image, worker-controlled factories and service firms were spared the equivalent of the 1977 land devolution law and were the beneficiaries of modest (though for many, inadequate) government support. This sector grew while its equivalent in agriculture diminished in size.

It would have been difficult to predict these different outcomes with the literature on workers' control as it stands today because party competition is the critical explanatory variable. As scholars who are concerned with the establishment of democratic socialism turn away from abstract analyses and embark on concrete case studies, the importance of parties as the organizational links between changed structures at different levels of society will become clear.

THE emphasis on party competition as a central problem in the articulation process emerged from my conviction that experiments with workers' control should be viewed in both their local and national contexts. Indeed, if the various conclusions of this study can be condensed into a single assertion it is this: that our generalizations about revolutionary challenges and changes must emerge from holistic analyses in which the dialectical relations between one level of structural change and another can be appreciated.[24] If, as I have suggested, no single *phase* in the drama of workers' control can be understood in isolation neither can any *level* of the drama be understood alone. We must be aware of both a temporal and a vertical structural dynamic if the process of workers' control is to be properly assessed.

On a theoretical level, this implies the integration of several literatures. On an empirical level, it calls for the coordination of both microlevel and macrolevel analysis. Unfortunately, this integrative approach is not often taken, and our understanding of challenges to property and power relations has suffered accordingly. Both the literature on rural proletarian mobilization and the literature on the consequences of workers' control suffer from the same problem. Rarely is a holistic approach taken in either of these subject areas. As a consequence, the studies that aimed at explaining why property relations are challenged and what the effects of a reorganization of property might be were of only limited utility in the Portuguese case.

[24] Evelyne Huber Stephens also appreciated this point. Indeed her study of self-management in Peru opens with a four-country comparison which argues that the effects of self-management vary greatly across systems. See Evelyne Huber Stephens, *The Politics of Workers' Participation: The Peruvian Approach in Comparative Perspective* (New York: Academic Press, 1980), esp. pp. 1-37.

The Consequences of Workers' Control

In trying to assess what the consequences of workers' control might be, I encountered an impressive array of positive forecasts. Workers' control might lead to fully participatory, egalitarian management, increased productivity, increased political participation, increased social consensus, and increased radicalization. Turning from theory to the Portuguese reality, I found a more complex situation. Two predictions proved accurate, one proved questionable, and two proved erroneous. Worker-controlled farms were in fact more productive than the units they replaced and worker-managers were, in fact, "radicalized" by the workers' control experience. Cooperative members were also much more likely than nonmembers to participate in elections, parties, campaigns, and demonstrations, but their activities were confined almost exclusively to the defense of the worker-controlled farms themselves.[25] Because the predicted increase in participation took this unprecedented, highly partisan form (bearing out the radicalization hypothesis presented by other theorists), the second half of the participatory society hypothesis was not confirmed: an increase in participation led not to an increase in social consensus and a strengthening of democracy but to a level of polarization that came perilously close to armed conflict.[26]

The fact that the maximalist version of participatory management was never actually established merely exacerbated the already tense situation. The limited pool of potential leaders and the workers' deference to the more experienced (and more militant) cooperative members opened the way for charges of "manipulation from above." Unable to observe the democracy within the farms, or the workers' fervent and informed support for the existing distribution of responsibilities, outsiders mistook solidarity for political naiveté. Thus, the positive effect that workers' control initially had on productivity was easily overshadowed by its disruptive political consequences, fueling the partisan battles that would eventually prevent articulation.

The consequences of workers' control in Portugal would have been more

[25] Cynthia McClintock made similar observations in her excellent study of agricultural cooperatives in Peru. She writes that cooperative members did indeed become more participatory but that "the focus of new attitudes was the self-managed enterprise itself." See McClintock, *Peasant Cooperatives and Political Change in Peru* (Princeton, New Jersey: Princeton University Press, 1981), p. 320.

[26] Though McClintock illustrated that the Peruvian cooperative units were more competitive and less conscious of responsibilities to nonmembers than their Portuguese counterparts, she, too, noted a certain sort of radicalization in that the Peruvian workers' new-found participatory skills were often directed *"against* rather than for the state." See ibid., p. 322; emphasis mine.

easily predictable with a holistic approach. Looking beyond individual production units and at host societies instead, one could predict where egalitarian management was feasible and where it was not. In societies with low levels of literacy and a history of authoritarianism (in which deliberate depoliticization diminished opportunities for organizational experience), only a limited number of workers could have the skills that management required. Unlettered workers would willingly and wisely defer to this group—since family ties and structures for recall and monitoring performance prevented abuses of privilege.

As it was unreasonable to expect egalitarian management in a case such as Portugal, so it was unreasonable to expect that increased political participation would go far beyond activities associated with the defense of workers' control itself. The absence of a holistic approach was the source of the problem here as well. Those who argued (and hoped) that workers' control would lead to a "participatory society" neglected both historical and structural factors. Most worker-controlled enterprises have histories. Some, such as the Israeli kibbutzim, emerge from nothing, but most emerge from open, class-based struggle. If national political structures allow the classes that lose the struggle to operate freely—that is, to pressure the enterprises through parties, credit establishments, lobbies, and the media—the struggle for control will continue and of necessity absorb the organizational energies of the workers involved. It is not coincidental that Gramsci (having witnessed the occupation of the factories in Italy) associated workers' councils with radicalization and not merely with participation. He had seen what the defense of workers' control could do first hand and would not have been surprised by the radicalization of the Portuguese.

Ironically, much of the success of workers' control in Portugal derived from this need to defend the experiment. If the Portuguese case can be judged more positively than its counterparts elsewhere this is probably why. The extraordinary political solidarity of the cooperative members, the low incidence of managerial corruption, and the workers' willingness to accept low levels of compensation are due in large measure to the unity born of external threat. If landowners had not been so quick to try to restore the old order, the new units might have been troubled with more internal conflict.

The success of the experiment was also due to the appropriate presence and absence of outside actors. If the cooperatives *had* been run by "outside agitators," there might well have been less sharing of power and more corruption. Fortunately, it is harder to bully or cheat a brother than a stranger, and this sort of behavior was minimized. Though base-level activities were run by community members, there is no doubt that outsiders in national organizations assisted the cooperatives in a variety of ways.

Intersindical and the Communist party indirectly provided accounting, marketing, and legal services that the people of the countryside could not have provided themselves, and there is no doubt that these services contributed to what little stability the cooperatives achieved. There is also no doubt that the association with the Communist party had negative consequences as well.

THE EMERGENCE OF WORKERS' CONTROL

The mention of enterprise history brings us to the etiological questions that motivated the first phase of this study: How did workers' control emerge? Why did landless cultivators seize the properties of others and challenge a system of domination that had been in place for generations? For these questions, I turned to the literature on peasant mobilization, and here, too, I was led astray by the absence of holistic analysis. The "classics" reviewed in Chapter One have much to recommend them, and they are certainly superior to many of the other works discussed here in their simultaneous attention to both theory and empiricism. The problem lies not with the *quality* of their empirical work but with its scope, for many of the scholars who have shaped our views on peasant mobilization have used materials from macrolevel studies. Many of these have been carried out with great skill, but they have understated the importance of the dialectic between structures at the national level and structures at the base.

Part of the problem comes from methodological necessity. The classics on peasant revolution by Wolf, Paige, Scott and Popkin have focused on peasants' individual motivation. But none of these studies are based on first hand conversations and interviews with the peasants themselves. All are macrolevel in terms of data: though Scott focused on regions and Popkin focused on selected villages, history and political turmoil made contact with the villagers themselves impossible. Through no fault of their own, these authors are forced to focus on individual human actors through a long-distance lens.

The danger in taking the long-distance view is that the peasantry becomes isolated conceptually. The most salient contemporary debate in the literature rests on whether "the peasantry" revolts offensively, as Popkin maintains, or defensively, as Scott maintains. As Popkin describes it, the debate derives from the fact that moral economists focus on decline and crisis and view "peasant political and religious protests as last-gasp, *defensive* reactions," while he insists that peasant protests are collective actions [that] depend, not on any drop in welfare, but simply "on the ability of a group or class to organize and make demands.''[27] Both of these views portray the peasantry more as a group *against* society than a group *within* society. As such, the debate revolves around which of the two reified actors moves first.

Seen from a holistic perspective, the Portuguese case suggests that these ''first-cause'' debates are not particularly helpful, nor are their elements as discordant as is sometimes assumed. Protests *are* collective actions that ''depend on the ability of a group or class to organize and make demands,'' but collective action is more likely to be *successful* when the crises that Scott describes occur.

In Portugal, the success of the rural revolt depended not just on organization and force of numbers but on the force of resistance from the state. The men and women of the Alentejo seized land because they saw that their subsistence was threatened, but they also acted because they recognized that a state weakened by crisis might not move against them. It was a crisis at *two* levels of society that explained events. There was an imbalance in the Alentejo itself brought on by the return of enlisted soldiers, the collapse of the civil construction industry, the defensive decapitalization of large estates, and the closing of emigration opportunities, but all but the last of these factors derived directly from the crisis of the state in Lisbon. The discord within the coercive apparatus and the general confusion at the ministerial level enabled the landless to act with less risk of repression derived from the same state crisis. It is only by studying rural revolt within the context of a larger national crisis—working constantly at two levels of analysis—that this interconnectedness can be appreciated. Likewise, the means by which rural revolts affect national politics can only be appreciated with a holistic approach.[28]

Of course, any generalization about ''peasant'' revolt must be qualified, for the term *peasant* embraces such a wide range of cultivators. Unfortunately, the rural proletarians who occupied center stage in the Portuguese drama are possibly the least understood of all the peasant groups. Our knowledge, of rural proletarians has ''grown slowly and, in sharp contrast to peasant studies'' in general, has not developed ''a core of theorists identified with the category.''[29] Moreover, some of the major works on

---

[27] Samuel Popkin, *The Rational Peasant* (Berkeley: University of California Press, 1979), p. 35; emphasis added.

[28] Theda Skocpol takes a holistic approach in *States and Social Revolutions* (Cambridge: Cambridge University Press, 1979), where she argues that an understanding of revolution requires an analysis not only of state and agrarian structures but of international factors as well.

[29] Thomas Greaves, ''The Andean Rural Proletarians,'' in June Nash and Juan Corradi,

peasants and revolution such as Eric Wolf's *Peasant Wars of the Twentieth Century* state from the outset that the term peasant "does not include" the landless.[30]

This inattention has led to misconceptions. Many of the works that do generalize about rural proletarians describe a group that bears little resemblance to the people of the Alentejo. Sidney Mintz, who is deservedly the best known student of peasants in the Caribbean, informs us that "rural proletarians do not play a vanguard role."[31] Likewise, Samuel Popkin alerts us to the "almost *universal* finding that agricultural laborers are harder to organize or less likely to protest" than other sorts of cultivators.[32] When they do revolt, rural proletarians are thought by many to behave just as small-holding peasants would, carving out their own parcels of land and working independently. From Mexico where "[the struggles] . . . of the wage earners . . . have an essentially peasant [small-holder] character,"[33] to Brazil, where "plantation wage-workers define their demands in terms of land ownership,"[34] a similar picture emerges. Yet, this is a picture of only a part of the rural proletariat. The landless workers of Portugal *were* as a sort of "vanguard," and their cooperatives were *not* the product of an individualistic drive for small holdings.

How can we explain their seemingly unique role? Is it so unique after all? Here again simultaneous microlevel-macrolevel analysis serves us well. Portugal's farmworkers behaved differently because their history and structural position were different. Just as it is unwise to generalize about peasants per se, so it is unwise to generalize about all rural proletarians. Jeffrey Paige grasped this in his study of migrant workers and sharecroppers in export agriculture. The Portuguese case points to yet another type of revolutionary farmworker.[35]

The landless workers of southern Portugal constitute what should be

---

eds., *Ideology and Social Change in Latin America*, vol. 1, *The Emergence of Worker Consciousness* (New York: Authors' Edition, 1975), p. 31.

[30] Eric R. Wolf, *Peasant Wars of the Twentieth Century* (New York: Harper and Row, 1973), p. xiv.

[31] Sidney Mintz, "The Rural Proletariat and the Problem of Rural Proletarian Consciousness," in June Nash and Juan Corradi, eds., *Ideology and Social Change in Latin America*, vol. 1, *The Emergence of Worker Consciousness* (New York: Authors' Edition, 1975), p. 64.

[32] Popkin, *The Rational Peasant*, p. 250. Emphasis mine.

[33] Silvia Terán, "Formas de Conciencia Social de los Trabajadores del Campo," *Cuadernos Agrários* (October-December 1976), pp. 20-36, as quoted in Alain de Janvry, *The Agrarian Question and Reformism in Latin America* (Baltimore: The Johns Hopkins University Press, 1981), p. 267.

[34] Lygia Sigaud, "A Idealização do Passado numa Area de Plantation," *Contraponto* (November 1977), as quoted from its Portuguese version in ibid., p. 267.

[35] See Jeffrey M. Paige, *Agrarian Revolution* (New York: Free Press, 1975).

called a *mature* rural proletariat. They can be distinguished from some, though not all, of their counterparts elsewhere by two criteria. First, they have been landless for generations and, second, they have of necessity been involved in two proletariats: one in the rural world of the Alentejo and another in urban areas in Portugal and abroad. The first quality made them less likely to parcelize the land,[36] while the second made them more likely to seize it.

Scott writes that migration "works against economic and political co-operation at the village level,"[37] and this might indeed be true—until the migrants come home with union experience, new sophistication, new information, and no jobs.[38] Men of this description led the revolution in the Portuguese countryside and constitute today the very backbone of the cooperative farms. Their biographies point to the danger of abstracting village life from national life. Their actions point to the need to rethink previous assumptions about the political capabilities of rural proletarians elsewhere, for the phenomenon of the mature rural proletariat is not confined to Portugal.

In Italy and southern Spain these groups have long existed, and as one would predict, they have engaged in massive land occupations on several occasions. The rural proletariat of Italy rose up and took control of estates in Bologna, Puglia, Sicily, and the Roman Campagna in the interwar years and then seized properties again at the end of World War II. Rural proletarians in Spain seized thousands of acres of land during the First Republic and then again more recently under the democratized post-Franco regime.[39]

The mature rural proletariat is not a construct appropriate to southern Europe alone, for there are reasons to expect the group to expand elsewhere. In Latin America, where the "rural proletariat [often] constitutes the largest and most substantial group of all,"[40] the process of "maturation" continues

[36] It is significant that the wage workers to which Sigaud refers were only recently proletarianized.

[37] James Scott, *The Moral Economy of the Peasant* (New Haven, Connecticut: Yale University Press, 1976), p. 213.

[38] Gerrit Huizer, after a broad survey of peasant mobilization in Latin America, also notes the connection between urban union activity and rural militancy. See his valuable but too often forgotten *Peasant Revolt in Latin America* (Baltimore: Penguin, 1973).

[39] The best English language discussion of the rural proletariat in Spain is Edward Malefakis, *Agrarian Reform and Peasant Revolution in Spain: The Origins of the Civil War* (New Haven, Connecticut: Yale University Press, 1970). For brief discussions of the seizures in interwar Italy, see Anthony L. Cardoza, *Agrarian Elites and Italian Fascism: The Province of Bologna, 1901-1926* (Princeton, New Jersey: Princeton University Press, 1982), pp. 249, 282, and 294. See also Frank Snowden, "On the Origins of Agrarian Fascism," *European Journal of Sociology* 13 (1972), and Sidney G. Tarrow, *Peasant Communism in Southern Italy* (New Haven, Connecticut: Yale University Press, 1967).

[40] Mintz, "The Rural Proletariat," p. 61.

daily: promises of land reform go unfulfilled, urban employment continues uncertain, farms become capitalist enterprises, the number of landless laborers increases, and year after year farmworkers drift farther and farther from their landowning past.

The advance of capitalist development has suggested to some that the era of peasant revolts is drawing to an end. Even as sophisticated a scholar as Alain de Janvry now argues that "the locus of class struggle is increasingly being displaced away from the countryside and into the cities."[41] The struggle for workers' control in Portugal suggests that this may not be so. The actions of the landless laborers of the Alentejo and the maturation of rural proletariats elsewhere suggest not the decline of rural revolt but rather the potential for more rural proletarian struggle.

[41] Alain de Janvry, *The Agrarian Question and Reformism in Latin America* (Baltimore: The Johns Hopkins University Press, 1981), p. 267.

222

APPENDIX I

Questionnaire, 1980

1. First of all, what is your main occupation at the present time?
     Dayworker
     Permanent wage worker
     Seareiro
     Renter
     Small farmer
     Medium farmer
     Other

2. And before the 25th of April, what was your main occupation?

3. Where did you live before the 25th of April?
     Where I live today
     On the land I farmed
     Here, but in another house
     In Lisbon
     Abroad
     Other (specify)

4. Where are you employed now?
     UCP/agricultural cooperative
     Private farm
     Self-employed
     Other

5. Have you ever been a part of a UCP or Cooperative?
     Yes
     No

   Why did you leave?
     I did not like the working conditions
     I earned more elsewhere
     I did not get along with the others in the cooperative
     I was fired/let go
     Other (specify)

6. Have you ever worked outside the farming sector here in Portugal?
     Yes
     No

When?
    Before the 25th of April
    Between the 25th of April and 1976
    After 1976

Where?
    Lisbon
    City of Évora
    Here in this county
    Other (specify)

How long?
    Months
    Years

What did you do?
    Civil construction
    Factory work
    Other (specify)

Was your position funded by the state or through a private company?
    State
    Private company

Why didn't you continue working in this job?

7. Have you ever worked abroad?
    Yes
    No

How many times?

What did you do?

For how long?
    Months
    Years

Why didn't you continue working abroad?

8. Thinking about when you began to work and about your situation today, do you think that your situation today is better or worse than what you were hoping for?
    Much better
    Better
    The same
    Worse
    Much worse

9. And is your standard of living better or worse than it was before the 25th of April?

Much better
Better
The same
Worse
Much worse

And in the next five years do you think your standard of living will be better or worse than it is today?
Much better
Better
The same
Worse
Much worse

10. Here, in your town (area), what social classes exist?

11. And in which of these classes would you include yourself?

12. Would you like to do other work?

What?

13. People talk a lot about small and medium farmers. I would appreciate it if you could help me define these terms.

What is the maximum number of hectares of unirrigated land a small farmer can have and not be called a medium farmer?

And what is the maximum number of hectares a medium farmer can have and not be called a large farmer?

What is the maximum number of hectares of irrigated land a small farmer can have?

And what is the maximum number of hectares of irrigated land a medium farmer can have?

14. There is often disagreement between the people who rule and the people who don't (in the country, in the village, at work). Speaking of the period before the 25th of April, do you know of cases of people from here in the village (or nearby) who have suffered for publicly criticizing those who ruled?
Yes
No

What happened to these people?

Speaking once again of the period before the 25th of April, do you know people who suffered for criticizing the latifundiários?
Yes
No

What happened to these people?

225

15. Before the 25th of April, did you speak with people who earned much more than you?
    Yes, frequently
    Yes, at times
    Yes, rarely
    No, never

    And the conversations you had with these people were
    Friendly
    Purely professional
    Hostile

    And today do you speak with people who earn much more than you?
    Yes, frequently
    Yes, at times
    Yes, rarely
    No, never

    And the conversations that you have with these people are
    Friendly
    Purely professional
    Hostile

16. Are there people who earn more than you whom you would appeal to if you had a serious problem and needed help?
    Yes
    No

    To whom would you appeal?

17. Here in the town/village there are various people with different professions. Do you think that in general your interests are the same as, very similar to, similar to, different from, or very different from the interests of the members of the production cooperatives?

    And from those of the workers who work for landowners?

    And from those of the seareiros?

    And from those of the renters?

    And from those of the small farmers?

18. In your opinion, do you think it would be good to eliminate class differences in Portugal?
    Yes
    No

    In your understanding, do you think it would be possible to eliminate class differences in Portugal?

Yes
No

In your understanding, do you think that there was a possibility of eliminating class differences in Portugal after the 25th of April?
Yes
No

When?

19. There are various ways of explaining the poverty before the 25th of April. In your opinion, which of these sentences would best explain the poverty in your area? Choose only one sentence.
The land is very poor.
The technical support for farming the land effectively was missing.
The land was poorly divided.
The majority of the land belonged to people who did not want to farm it.
The latifundiários had big profits but did not want to pay well.

20. When was the first time you heard of the land occupations?

21. The idea of the occupations came from whom?
From the workers themselves
From the people in the unions
From the Armed Forces' Revolution
From the political parties

[*If he indicates more than two, ask the next question.*]

Which of these groups had a more important role in the occupations?

22. Did you participate in any occupation?
Yes
No
No response

For participants

In how many?

Of all these sentences, which two best explain the reason why you participated in the occupations?
I wanted permanent employment.
I thought that the land should belong to those who work it
I wanted to participate in the Revolution.
I did not believe that the government would start an agrarian reform.
I wanted to help end the latifundiário system.
I thought I would be able to earn more money.
I was convinced by other people.

The landowner did not deserve the land.

Of the two sentences you have chosen, which better explains why you participated in the occupation?

For nonparticipants

Of all these sentences, which two best explain the reason why you did *not* participate in the occupations?
> I thought that the action was unjust.
> I had no reason to complain about the landowners.
> I did not believe in the Revolution.
> I preferred to wait for the government to initiate the agrarian reform.
> I wanted to participate, but I did not want to place myself in difficulties with the landowners.
> I thought about participating, but I did not have confidence in the people who were leading the occupations.

Of these two sentences, which better explains the reason why you did not participate in the occupation?

23. Do you remember how many people participated in the occupations?
> 10 or less
> Between 11 and 50
> Between 51 and 100
> Between 101 and 200
> More than 200
> Don't remember/Don't know

24. Of the people who participated in the occupation, how many remained to work on the occupied properties?
> 10 or less
> Between 11 and 50
> Between 51 and 100
> Between 101 and 200
> More than 200
> Don't remember/Don't know

25. How was it decided which persons remained to work permanently on the occupied properties?

26. Did other people who had not taken part in the occupation get work on the occupied properties?

How many?

27. Was there help from some organized groups in the occupations with which you are familiar?
> Yes
> No

From which groups?
> Teams from the Dynamization Campaigns
> Members of COPCON
> Unions
> Political parties
> Members of the Regional Agrarian Reform Center
> Other functionaries from the ministry (MAP)

28. After the occupations, was there much discussion about what should be done with the occupied land?
> Yes
> No

29. In your opinion, would it be better or even desirable to have divided the land among all who had occupied it in order to make private properties?
> Yes
> No

30. Was it possible to occupy the land and divide it up?
> Yes
> No

> Of all these sentences, which best explains why this was not possible?
> The soil in this area is too poor to permit the division of the land into small plots.
> There is not sufficient land for all.
> The people prefer to work together on something that belongs to all.
> Those who led the occupations did not want to divide the land.

31. I have here a group of statements one hears about the agricultural cooperatives here in the Alentejo. You might think some are true and others are false. I would appreciate it if you told me which are true and which are false in your opinion.
> With the same land a cooperative always produces more than a private property.
> The people integrated into cooperatives talk too much about politics.
> The members of a cooperative think too much about their personal future and not about the future of the cooperative.
> Poverty in the countryside would be eliminated if all the land belonged to the cooperatives.
> If a member of a cooperative has political ideas different from those of the managers of the cooperative, he does not speak much of his ideas.
> The people with more education are the people who run the cooperatives.
> The cooperatives have too many people, and there is not enough work for all of them.
> The problems that the cooperatives have are all caused by the government.
> If the Communist party did not exist, we would not have cooperatives.
> If the farmers had lived up to the labor contracts, we would not have

cooperatives.

Working on a cooperative or on a private farm is very similar; in both cases, those who control the payroll are those who rule.

There are no conflicts between those who manage the cooperatives and those who work there.

Long before the 25th of April, the workers here wanted to have production cooperatives.

There are many capable individuals leaving cooperatives because they can make more outside.

The workers on the private farms work harder than those on the cooperatives.

32. How many times a year does your cooperative have meetings?
    8-12 times
    5-7 times
    2-4 times
    1 time
    Not at all

    How many of these do you attend?
    None
    Some
    Almost all
    All

    When you go to these meetings, do you participate in the discussions?
    Yes, always
    Yes, sometimes
    Rarely or never

33. Have you ever been on the managerial board of your cooperative?
    Yes
    No

34. When you entered the cooperative, did you contribute machinery, tools, or livestock?
    Yes
    No
    What?

    Did you receive anything for your contribution?
    Yes
    No

35. How are the members of the cooperative paid?
    They all receive the same salary
    There are different salary levels
    They divide the profits equally
    They divide the profits some other way I don't know about

Do you get products from the cooperative for free?
>   Yes
>   No

Can you tell me more or less what would be the value of these products?

36. Are you content with this system of pay?
>   Yes
>   No

37. As you know, there are various types of people in the cooperatives—those who like to go to the meetings and participate in the discussions and those who like to spend their free time with their family or friends instead. With which of these types of people do you identify the most—which of these is most like yourself?
>   I like to go to the meetings and participate in them.
>   I like to go to the meetings, but I don't like to speak in them.
>   I like to spend my free time another way.

38. Suppose that you and two fellow cooperative members had to decide about how an unexpected amount of money should be used on the cooperative. One says that it would be better to spend the money on machinery or cattle or some other thing that would increase the productive capacity of the cooperative. The other says that this money should be used to improve the salaries of the members of the cooperative. With whom do you agree?
>   With the one who wanted to buy machinery
>   With the one who wanted to improve salaries

39. On what types of decisions are the members of the cooperatives consulted directly?
>   Salary
>   Hours of work
>   Investment
>   Sale of products
>   Loans
>   None
>   All

40. [*If not a manager*]

Would you like to be consulted on other decisions?
>   Yes
>   No

Which?

[*The following questions are for all the interviewees.*]

41. On average, how much do you earn on your main job?

42. And how much do you earn in the months of less work?

43. Who runs the cooperatives?
    The union leaders
    Members of the workers' commission
    All the members
    No one
    Other response
    Don't know

44. How are the people who run the cooperatives chosen?
    Secret ballot elections
    Show-of-hand elections
    Self-nomination
    Don't know

45. In your opinion, who has the most power in this parish?
    The mayor of the parish
    The mayor of the town
    The civil governor
    The union
    The landowners

46. What happens today to those people who publicly criticize those in power in the parish?

47. And what happens to those people who publicly criticize those who run the cooperatives?

    And what happens to those people who publicly criticize those who run the private farms?

48. Are you accustomed to speaking about politics with your friends
    Yes
    No

    How often?
    Every day
    A few times a week
    From time to time
    No response

49. Many people, when they speak of politics, use the words left or right. I have a scale here with 10 numbers. On one side of the scale is the word Right and on the other the word Left.

    Left 1 2 3 4 5 6 7 8 9 10 Right

    Please indicate the number that best defines your political position. For example, if you consider yourself very much to the left, indicate number 1. If you consider yourself very much to the right, indicate number 10. If you consider yourself neither to the right nor to the left, indicate number 5. As you see, there are other numbers between these, some on the left side and others on the right side. Which number would you pick in order to define your political position?

50. Do you think that, in the next ten years, Portugal will be:
    More or less as it is now?
    More socialist than today?
    Less socialist than today?
    Not at all socialist?

51. People speak frequently nowadays about the economic problems of Portugal. Do you think that the solution for the economic problems of Portugal is:
    More an agricultural solution than an industrial one?
    More an industrial solution than an agricultural one?

52. If you could take part in land occupations today without being punished by anyone and with persons whom you trust, would you take part?
    Yes
    No

    What would you do with the occupied land?
    Start a cooperative such as the one we now have
    Divide the land into small parcels

    Why wouldn't you participate?

53. To what extent do you agree or disagree with the political actions of *Eanes*? And with those of *Otelo*? And with those of *Cunhal*? And with those of *Sá Carneiro*? And with those of *Soares*? And with those of *Freitas do Amaral* and those of *Vasco Gonçalves*?
    Agree completely
    Agree in part
    Neither agree nor disagree
    Disagree
    Disagree completely

54. For whom did you vote in the elections for the Constitutional Assembly after the 25th of April?

    For whom did you vote in the election for the Assembly of the Republic in 1976?

    For whom did you vote in the last elections for the Assembly of the Republic?

    For whom did you vote in the 1980 election?

55. From the following list of goals, choose the one that you feel is the most important for the government in the next few years.
    Equality

Order and stability
Socialism
Peace
Development
Don't know
No answer

56. Knowing what you know today, do you believe that cooperatives in general have
    Little future
    A difficult future
    A reasonable future
    A prosperous future

57. Did you talk politics with your friends before the 25th of April?
    Yes
    No
    No answer

   How frequently?
    Every day
    A few times a week
    Once in a while
    No answer

58. Do your friends and the people with whom you associate all have the same opinions, or do they have different opinions?
    They all have the same opinions
    Sometimes we have different opinions
    We always have different opinions

59. How often do you follow the news regarding political affairs?
    Frequently
    Several times a week
    Once in a while
    Never

60. In which of the following activities do you take part?
    Hold an office in a political party
    Affiliated with a political party but don't hold an office
    Assist in distributing political literature
    Take part in rallies or demonstrations
    Read, hear, or watch news about political activities in the media

61. In your opinion, do you think you can help to resolve national or regional problems?
    Yes
    No

No answer

How?

62. Before the 25th of April—that is to say, in the years between '70 and '74—was it difficult or easy to find work here in this town?
    Very difficult
    Difficult
    Easy
    Very easy

63. During how many months, and during exactly which months, is there work for you to do?

64. During the times when there is no work here what do you do?
    Stay home
    Find agricultural work elsewhere
    Find nonagricultural work elsewhere

65. Before the establishment of cooperatives, how many months a year were you able to find work?

66. [*If the answer to question 65 is less than the answer to question 63, ask the following question.*]

    Currently you have work for longer periods. Which of these phrases explains why?
    We're doing work now that we didn't do for the latifundiários
    The work is better distributed

    Why is it that the latifundiários didn't do the work?

67. Today your standard of living is
    Better than it was before the 25th of April
    The same as it was
    Worse than it was

68. As I read the following list, please tell me which things you owned before the 25th of April
    Land
    Your own home
    Garden
    Donkeys or horses
    Chickens, rabbits, etc.
    Goats
    Sheep
    Pigs
    Cows
    Agricultural machinery, tractors, etc.

Truck
Automobile
Motorcycle
Bicycle
Television
Radio
Refrigerator
Washing machine
Bank account

69. Do you still have all these things, or are there some things you no longer have? [*Read the items he had before the 25th of April and make a note of those he owns at present.*]

[*For the items he no longer possesses*]: Why do you no longer own these things?
    I contributed it to a cooperative
    I sold it for a good price
    I sold it because I had to
    It was expropriated
    Other reason

70. Are you the owner of something that you didn't have before the 25th of April?
    Yes
    No

What? [*Make a note in the table previously listed.*]

Were these items purchased, given to you, or obtained in another manner?
    Purchased
    Given to me
    Obtained in another manner

71. Do you have a part-time job to add to the salary you earn in your principal job?
    Yes
    No

What is it?

About how much do you earn from these activities?

72. Before the 25th of April, did you have an additional job to supplement your main income?
    Yes
    No

What was it?

About how much did you earn from this?

73. Using this scale of 10 numbers, please indicate the number that, in your opinion, best indicates the political position of

Eanes	1	2	3	4	5	6	7	8	9	10
Álvaro Cunhal	1	2	3	4	5	6	7	8	9	10
Otelo	1	2	3	4	5	6	7	8	9	10
Mário Soares	1	2	3	4	5	6	7	8	9	10
Freitas do Amaral	1	2	3	4	5	6	7	8	9	10
Vasco Gonçalves	1	2	3	4	5	6	7	8	9	10
Sá Carneiro	1	2	3	4	5	6	7	8	9	10

74. [*For dayworkers only*]

Do you remember how much you earned per day in 1973? That is, in the year before the 25th of April?

75. Have you done your military service?
   Yes
   No

Where?
   In the former colonies
   Here in Portugal

76. Where, and in what year, were you born?
   Place
   Year

77. As far as religion is concerned, do you consider yourself:
   Very religious
   Somewhat religious
   Indifferent
   Atheist
   Antireligious

78. Are you married?
   Yes
   No

How many children do you have?

79. Is your wife employed?
   Yes
   No

What does your wife do?

80. Before the 25th of April, was your wife employed?
   Yes

No

What was your wife's occupation?

81. How many people live in your house with you?

How many contribute to the support of the family?

82. Before the 25th of April, how many people lived in your house?

How many contributed to the support of the family?

83. Taking into consideration all those who contributed money to support the family, can you tell me how much is currently earned per month?

84. Taking into consideration all those who contributed money to support the family, can you tell me how much was earned per month before the 25th of April?

85. What education have you had?
    I can neither read nor write
    I can read and write, but I never went to school
    I went to primary school but did not finish
    I finished primary school
    Fifth year or equivalent
    Seventh year or equivalent
    University

86. What was your father's profession?

87. What profession would you choose for your children if you could?
    Worker in a cooperative
    Worker on a private farm
    Factory worker
    Small farmer
    Teacher
    Other

APPENDIX II

Chronology of Constitutional Governments
July 1976 to June 1983

Government	Prime Minister	Tenure[1]	Cabinet Composition
I	Mário Soares	July 23, 1976 December 8, 1977	PSP
II	Mário Soares	January 30, 1978 July 27, 1978	PSP/CDS
III	Alfredo Nobre da Costa	August 28, 1978 September 14, 1978	PPD-PSD/technocrat
IV	Carlos Alberto Mota Pinto	October 25, 1978 June 7, 1979	PPD-PSD/technocrat
V	Maria de Lourdes Pintassilgo	August 1, 1979 January 3, 1980	Independent/technocrat
VI	Francisco Sá Carneiro[2]	January 3, 1980 December 8, 1980	Democratic Alliance: PPD-PSD
VII	Francisco Pinto Balsemão	January 9, 1981 August 11, 1981	PPD-PSD/CDS
VIII	Francisco Pinto Balsemão	September 2, 1981 December 19, 1982[3]	PPD-PSD/CDS
IX	Mário Soares	June 9, 1983	PSP/PPD-PSD

SOURCE: *Facts on File Yearbooks* (New York: Facts on File, 1976-1984).

NOTES: [1] Dates of swearing in and resignation.

[2] Government resignation brought on by death of Sá Carneiro in aircrash, December 4, 1980.

[3] Government continued in caretaker capacity until elections (April 25, 1983) and formation of new government.

SELECTED BIBLIOGRAPHY

Abel, Andrew B. et al. "A Economia Portuguesa: Evolução Recente e Situação Actual." Paper presented at the Conference on the Portuguese Economy, Lisbon, October 10-13, 1976.

Adizes, Ichak. *Industrial Democracy Yugoslav Style.* New York: Free Press, 1971.

O Agricultor. Lisbon.

Alavanca. Lisbon.

Allum, P. A. "The South and National Politics, 1945-50." In S. J. Woolf, ed., *The Rebirth of Italy, 1943-50.* London: Longman, 1972.

Almeida, Carlos, and Barreto, António. *Capitalismo e Emigração em Portugal.* Lisbon: Prelo Editora, 1970.

Almeida, Carlos Fernandes de; Vara, Flávio Henrique; and Martins, Isabel Faria. *Adaptação do Trabalhador de Origem Rural ao Meio Industrial e Urbano.* Lisbon: Ministério da Economia, 1971.

Almeida, Diniz de. *Ascensão, Apogeu e Queda do MFA.* Vols. 1 and 2. Lisbon: Edições Sociais, 1976.

Amaro, Rogério Roque. "A Agricultura Portuguesa Perante a C.E.E." *Análise Social* (April-June 1978).

Antunes, Marinho L. *A Emigração Portuguesa Desde 1950.* Lisbon: Gabinete de Investigações Sociais, 1973.

Antunes, Oliveira. *A I.T.T. Contra o 25 de Abril.* Lisbon: Ulmeiro, n.d.

Anweiler, Oskar. *The Soviets: The Russian Workers', Peasants', and Soldiers' Councils, 1905-1921.* New York: Pantheon, 1974.

Apontamentos sobre o Outeiro: Do Senhor da Terra à Reforma Agrária. SAFIL, 1976.

Arroz, Maria Emília; Ferrão, João; Almeida, Virgínia Ferreira de; Santos, José António dos; Resende, Ana Isabel; Abreu, Diogo; Marin, Ana; Cabeleira, Emília; Correia, Fernando; Ferreira, Júlio L.; and Catita, Ana Cristina. *As Eleições Legislativas—Algumas Perspectivas Regionais.* Lisbon: Livros Horizonte, n.d.

A Terra, Cooperativa Editorial. *A Nossa Vida Dava um Romance—Rendeiros Falam dos Seus Problemas.* Porto: A Terra, 1977.

Avante. Lisbon.

Avrich, Paul H. "The Bolshevik Revolution and Workers' Control in Russian Industry." *Slavic Review* (March 1963).

Azevedo, Cândido de. *Portugal Europa Face Ao Mercado Comum.* Lisbon: Livraria Bertrand, 1978.

Azevedo, Julião Soares de. *Condições Económicas da Revolução Portuguesa de 1820.* Lisbon: Básica Editora, 1976.

Bacalhau, Mário. "The Cooperativism" [sic]. *Portugal Information* (August-September 1976).

Bacalhau, Mário. *Eanes: A Solução?* Lisbon: Heptágono, 1979.

―――. *Os Portugueses e a Política Quatro Anos Depois do 25 de Abril.* Lisbon: Editorial Meseta, 1978.

Badaloni, Nicola. "Gramsci and the Problem of the Revolution." In Chantal Mouffé, ed., *Gramsci and Marxist Theory.* London: Routledge and Kegan Paul, 1979.

Baklanoff, Eric. *The Economic Transformation of Spain and Portugal.* New York: Praeger, 1978.

Balibar, Etienne. *On the Dictatorship of the Proletariat.* London: New Left Books, 1977.

Bandarra, Álvaro, and Jazra, Nelly. *A Estrutura Agrária Portuguesa-Transformada?* Lisbon: Iniciativas Editoriais, 1976.

Baptista, Fernando Oliveira. *Portugal 1975—Os Campos.* Porto: Edições Afrontamento, 1978.

Barker, Rodney. "Guild Socialism Revisited?" *Political Quarterly* (July 1975).

Barnard, F. M., and Vernon, R. A. "Socialist Pluralism and Pluralist Socialism." *Political Studies* (December 1977).

Barreto, António. *Discursos na Construção de um Ministério.* Lisbon: Ministério da Agricultura e Pescas, 1977.

―――. "Land Reform and Revolution in Portugal, 1974/1976." Paper presented at the Third International Conference on Modern Portugal, Durham, New Hampshire, June 1984.

―――. *Memória da Reforma Agrária.* Lisbon: Publicações Europa-América, n.d.

Barros, Afonso de. *A Reforma Agrária em Portugal: Das Ocupações de Terras à Formação das Novas Unidades de Produção.* Oeiras: Instituto Gulbenkian, 1979.

―――, ed. *A Agricultura Latifundiária na Península Ibérica.* Oeiras: Instituto Gulbenkian, 1980.

Barros, Henrique de. *Alguns Problemas da Estrutura Agrária Portuguesa Perante o Cooperativismo.* Lisbon: Author's Edition, 1958.

―――. *Cooperação Agrícola.* Lisbon: Livros Horizonte, n.d.

―――. *A Estrutura Agrária Portuguesa.* Lisbon: Editorial República, 1972.

Bastos, João Carlos Pereira. *Cooperativas Depois de Abril.* Coimbra: Centelha, 1977.

Bermeo, Nancy Gina. "As Occupações de Terra: Un Estudo de Caso." In Michel Drain, ed., *La Réforme Agraire Portugaise.* Paris: Centre National de la Recherche Scientifique, 1984.

―――. "Worker Management in Industry: Reconciling Representative Government and Industrial Democracy in a Polarized Society." In Lawrence S. Graham and Douglas L. Wheeler, eds., *In Search of Modern Portugal: The Revolution and Its Consequences.* Madison: University of Wisconsin Press, 1983.

Bettelheim, Charles. *The Transition to Socialist Economy.* Hassocks, Sussex: Harvester Press, 1975.

Bica, António. *Agricultura e Reforma Agrária em Portugal*. Porto: Editorial Inova, 1974.

Birot, Pierre. *Portugal*. Lisbon: Livros Horizonte, n.d.

Blackburn, Robin. "The Test in Portugal," *New Left Review* (September-December 1974).

Blumberg, Paul. *Industrial Democracy: The Sociology of Participation*. New York: Schocken Books, 1973.

Boletim MFA. Lisbon.

Borkenau, Franz. *The Spanish Cockpit*. Ann Arbor: University of Michigan Press, 1963.

Brasileiro, Álvaro Favas. "A Cooperativa Agrícola Muchão do Inglês (Alpiarça)." In Michel Drain, ed., *La Réforme Agraire Portugaise*. Paris: Centre National de la Recherche Scientifique, 1984.

———. "A Luta dos Trabalhadores Rurais Durante o Fascismo e Depois do 25 de Abril 1974." In Michel Drain, ed., *La Réforme Agraire Portugaise*. Paris: Centre National de la Recherche Scientifique, 1984.

Brettell, Caroline B. "Emigration and Its Implications for the Revolution in Northern Portugal." In Lawrence S. Graham and Harry M. Makler, eds., *Contemporary Portugal: The Revolution and Its Antecedents*. Austin: University of Texas Press, 1979.

Brinton, Maurice. *The Bolsheviks and Worker Control*. Detroit: Black Rose Books, 1975.

Brito, Carlos, ed. *Pequeno Guia Parlamentar*. Lisbon: "Avante!" 1978.

Brito, Rogério. "Reforma Agrária e Contra-Reforma Agrária no Concelho de Grândola," in Michel Drain, ed., *La Réforme Agraire Portugaise*. Paris: Centre National de la Recherche Scientifique, 1984.

Bruneau, Thomas C. "Church and State in Portugal: Crises of Cross and Sword." *Journal of Church and State* (Autumn 1976).

———. *Politics and Nationhood: Post-Revolutionary Portugal*. New York: Praeger, 1984.

———. "The Portuguese Coup: Causes and Probable Consequences." *World Today* (July 1974).

Buci-Glucksmann, Christine. "State, Transition and Passive Revolution." In Chantal Mouffé, ed., *Gramsci and Marxist Theory*. London: Routledge and Kegan Paul, 1979.

Bustorff, Jochen M. *Diário no Alentejo*. Porto: Edições Afrontamento, 1983.

Cabral, Manuel Villaverde. "Agrarian Structures and Recent Rural Movements in Portugal." *The Journal of Peasant Studies* (July 1978).

———. *O Desenvolvimento do Capitalismo em Portugal no Século XIX*. Porto: A Regra do Jogo, 1976.

———. "O Fascismo Português Numa Perspectiva Comparada." In *O Fascismo em Portugal*. Papers from the Colloquium at the Faculdade de Letras of Lisbon, March 1980. Lisbon: A Regra do Jogo, 1982.

———. "Situação do Operariado nas Vésperas da Implantação da República." *Análise Social* (April-June 1977).

Cabral, Manuel Villaverde, ed. *Materiais para a História da Questão Agrária em Portugal, Século XIX e XX*. Porto: Editorial Inova, 1974.

Caldas, Eugénio de Castro. *A Agricultura Portuguesa no Limiar da Reforma Agrária*. Oeiras: Instituto Gulbenkian, 1978.

Caldeira, Reinaldo, and Silva, Maria do Céu, eds. *Constituição Politíca da República Portuguesa 1976*. Lisbon: Livraria Bertrand, 1976.

Cardia, Sotomayor; Gama, Jaime; Alegre, Manuel; and Reis, António. *Forças Armadas e Democracia*. Lisbon: Edições Portugal Socialista, 1976.

Cardoso, António Lopes. "A Defesa Intransigente com a Correcção dos Erros (Inevitáveis?) Cometidos." *Cadernos de o Jornal* (August 1976).

———. *A Liberdade Defende-se Construindo o Socialismo. O Socialismo Constroi-se Defendendo a Liberdade*. Beja: Edição da Federação de Beja do Partido Socialista, 1976.

———. *Luta Pela Reforma Agrária*. Lisbon: Diabril, 1977.

———. *A Nova Lei da Reforma Agrária*. Lisbon: Livros Horizonte, 1977.

Carneiro, Francisco Sá. *Por uma Social-Democracia Portuguesa*. Lisbon: Publicações Dom Quixote, 1975.

Carr, William. *A History of Germany, 1815-1945*. New York: St. Martin's Press, 1969.

Carrillo, Santiago. *Eurocommunism and the State*. Westport, Connecticut: Lawrence Hill and Co., 1978.

Carsten, F. L. *Revolution in Central Europe*. Berkeley: University of California Press, 1972.

Carvalho, António Vacas de. *O Fracasso de um Processo: A Reforma Agrária no Alentejo*. Lisbon: Author's Edition, 1977.

Carvalho, J. M. *Da Reforma Agrária ao Melatunismo*. Lisbon: Colecção Politikar, 1976.

Carvalho, Odete Esteves de. "Alguns Indicadores de Desigualdades na Distribuição do Rendimento em Portugal nos Últimos Anos." Paper presented at the International Conference on the Portuguese Economy, Lisbon, October 10-13, 1976.

———. *Distribuição e Redistribuição dos Rendimentos em Portugal*. Lisbon: Ministério do Trabalho, 1976.

Carvalho, Otelo Saraiva de. *Alvorada em Abril*. Lisbon: Livraria Bertrand, 1977.

———. *O Povo é Quem Mais Ordena*. Lisbon: Assírio e Alvim, 1977.

Castrim, Mário. *História da Intersindical*. Lisbon: Proença, 1978.

CGTP/Intersindical. "La Réforme Agraire au Portugal." Paper presented at the World Conference on Agrarian Reform and Rural Development, Rome, July 1979.

Chamberlain, William Henry. *The Russian Revolution, 1917-1921*. New York: Grosset and Dunlop, 1965.

Clark, Martin. *Antonio Gramsci and the Revolution that Failed*. New Haven, Connecticut: Yale University Press, 1977.

Claudín, Fernando. *Eurocommunism and Socialism*. London: New Left Books, 1978.

Clegg, Ian. *Workers' Self-Management in Algeria*. New York: Monthly Review Press, 1971.

Cohn-Bendit, Daniel, and Cohn-Bendit, Gabriel. *Obsolete Communism: The Left-Wing Alternative*. New York: McGraw Hill, 1969.

Cole, G.D.H. *Chaos and Order in Industry*. New York: Frederick A. Stokes Co., 1920.

————. *Guild Socialism Restated*. London: L. Parsons, 1920.

————. *Labour in the Commonwealth*. London: Headly Bros., 1918.

Colectivo das Edições Avante. *A Banca ao Serviço do Povo*. Lisbon: "Avante!" 1975.

————. *"Dossier" Eleições: Em que Sentido se Desloca o Eleitorado Português?* Lisbon: "Avante!" 1977.

————. *Em Defesa da Reforma Agrária*. Lisbon: "Avante!" 1977.

————. *Livro Negro do MAP*. Lisbon: "Avante!" 1977.

————. *O PCP e a Luta Sindical*. Lisbon: "Avante!" 1975.

Collin, Claude. "Enquête sur les Coopératives Agricoles au Portugal," *Les Temps Modernes* (November-December 1976).

————. "Révolution et Contre-Révolution dans les Campagnes Portugaises." *Les Temps Modernes* (October 1975).

Comissão Revolucionária de Apoio à Reforma Agrária. *CRARA Contra "Lei Barreto."* Lisbon: Associação de Apoio à Reforma Agrária, 1977.

————. *Uma Legalidade Revolucionária*. Amadora: CRARA, 1976.

————. *Os Sindicatos na Vanguarda da Luta*. Amadora: CRARA, n.d.

Comissão Organizadora. *5ª Conferência da Reforma Agrária*. Évora, 1981. Mimeographed.

Comisso, Ellen Turkish. *Workers' Control under Plan and Market*. New Haven, Connecticut: Yale University Press, 1979.

Confederação dos Agricultores de Portugal. *CAP: Recortes de uma Luta*. Viseu: Edições CAP, 1977.

Conlin, Sean. "Participation versus Expertise." *International Journal of Comparative Sociology* (September-October 1974).

Correia, Pezarat. "A Influência das Forças Políticas Militares e Sindicais no Período Inicial da Reforma Agrária: O Papel Específico do Exército." Paper presented at the French-Portuguese Roundtable on the Portuguese Agrarian Reform, Paris, June 15-17, 1981.

————. "Reforma Agrária: Uma Destruição Metódica." *O Jornal*, June 29, 1979.

Correia, Ramiro; Soldado, Pedro; and Marujo, João. *MFA e Luta de Classes*. Lisbon: Ulmeiro, n.d.

Costa, C. L. Sa'; Lino, M.; Teixeira, O.; Cascais, R.; Ventura, F.; and Fonseca, V. *As Eleições no Portugal de Abril*. Lisbon: "Avante!" 1980.

Costa, Leonel, and Roldão, Victor. *As Organizações Políticas e o Controlo Operário*. Lisbon: Instituto Nacional de Investigação Industrial, 1975.

Cotta, Freppel. *Economic Planning in Corporative Portugal*. London: P.S. King and Son Ltd., 1937.

Craig, Gordon. *Germany, 1866-1945*. New York: Oxford University Press, 1978.

Crawfurd, Oswald John Frederick [John Latouche]. *Travels in Portugal*. New York: Putnam's Sons, 1975.

Cunhal, Álvaro. *Contribuição para o Estudo da Questão Agrária*. Vols. 1 and 2. Lisbon: "Avante!" 1976.

———. *Relatório da Actividade do Comité Central do VI Congresso do PCP*. Lisbon: "Avante!" 1975.

———. *A Revolução Portuguesa: O Passado e o Futuro*. Lisbon: "Avante!" 1976.

Cutileiro, José. *A Portuguese Rural Society*. Oxford: Clarendon Press, 1971.

Da Costa, Fernando Ferreira. *As Cooperativas na Legislação Portuguesa*. Lisbon: Petrony, 1976.

Dahl, Robert. *After the Revolution?* New Haven, Connecticut: Yale University Press, 1968.

Daniels, Robert V. *The Conscience of the Revolution*. Cambridge, Massachusetts: Harvard University Press, 1965.

———. *Red October: The Bolshevik Revolution of 1917*. New York: Scribner, 1967.

Da Silva, Antunes. *Terras Velhas Semeadas de Novo*. Lisbon: Livraria Bertrand, 1976.

Davies, John Paton. "Revolution of the Red Carnations." *New York Times Magazine*, July 13, 1975.

O Dia. Lisbon.

Diário de Notícias. Lisbon.

Diário Popular. Lisbon.

Dornbusch, Roger; Eckhaus, Richard S.; and Taylor, Lance. "Analysis and Projections of Macroeconomic Conditions in Portugal." Report from an OECD-sponsored mission to Portugal, December 15-20, 1975, Lisbon, 1976.

Drain, Michel. "La Réforme Agraire Portugaise." *Méditerranée* (1979).

———, and Domenech, Bernard. *Occupations de Terres et Expropriations dans les Campagnes Portugaises*. Paris: Centre National de la Recherche Scientifique, 1982.

Eaton, J. "The Relevance of Mondragón to Britain." *Political Quarterly* (October 1978).

Economist Intelligence Unit. *Quarterly Economic Review of Portugal* (1968-1979).

Espinosa, Juan, and Zimbalist, Andrew. *Economic Democracy: Workers' Participation in Chilean Industry*. New York: Academic Press, 1978.

Estrela, Ana de Vale. "A Reforma Agrária Portuguesa e os Movimentos Camponeses: Uma Revisão Crítica." *Análise Social* (April-June 1978).

Expresso. Lisbon.

Fallaci, Oriana. "I Care Nothing for Elections." *New York Times Magazine*, July 13, 1975.

———. "Disintegrating Portugal: An Interview with Mário Soares," *New York Review of Books*, November 13, 1975.

Faye, Jean Pierre. *Portugal: The Revolution in the Labyrinth*. Nottingham: Spokesman Books, 1976.

Feder, Ernest. *The Rape of the Peasantry*. Garden City, New York: Doubleday and Co., 1971.

Fernandes, Blasco. *Para uma Reforma Agrária em Portugal*. Lisbon: Prelo, 1969.

Ferreira, Serafim. *MFA: Motor da Revolução Portuguesa*. Lisbon: Diabril, 1975.

Ferreira, Vitor Matias. *Da Reconquista da Terra à Reforma Agrária*. Lisbon: A Regra do Jogo, 1977.

Ferro, António. *Salazar: Portugal and Her Leader*. Translated by H. De Barros Gomes and John Gibbons. London: Faber and Faber, 1935.

Fields, Rona M. *The Portuguese Revolution and the Armed Forces Movement*. New York: Praeger, 1975.

Figueiredo, António de. *Portugal: Fifty Years of Dictatorship*. New York: Holmes and Meier, 1976.

Figueiredo, Carlos. "Limites das Formações Económicas Diferenciadas: Caso da Reforma Agrária." *Economia e Socialismo* (February 1979).

Forrester, Joseph James. *Portugal and Its Capabilities*. London: John Weale, 1856.

Freitas, Eduardo de. "Alguns Dados Referentes à Reforma Agrária no Distrito de Évora." *Análise Social* (April-June 1977).

————; Almeida, J. Ferreira de; and Cabral, Manuel Villaverde. *Modalidades de Penetração do Capitalismo na Agricultura*. Lisbon: Presença, 1976.

Gallagher, Tom. "Peasant Conservatism in an Agrarian Setting: Portugal 1900-1975." *Iberian Studies* (Autumn 1977).

————. *Portugal: A Twentieth-Century Interpretation*. Manchester: Manchester University Press, 1983.

Garin, João. *Reforma Agrária: Seara de Ódio*. Lisbon: Edições do Templo, 1977.

Gaspar, Jorge, and Vitorino, Nuno. *As Eleições de 25 de Abril: Geografia e Imagem dos Partidos*. Lisbon: Livros Horizonte, 1976.

Gay, Peter. *The Dilemma of Democratic Socialism*. New York: Columbia University Press, 1952.

Gervásio, António. "Direcção da Organização Regional do Alentejo e Algarve." In Partido Comunista Português, ed., *Congresso Extraordinário do PCP*. Lisbon: "Avante!" 1974.

Gilmore, David. D. *The People of the Plain*. New York: Columbia University Press, 1980.

Gomes, Paulino. *Eanes Porque o Poder?* Lisbon: Intervoz, 1976.

Gomes, Soeiro Pereira. *Praça de Jorna*. Lisbon: Partido Comunista Português, 1976.

Gorz, André. *Strategy for Labor*. Boston: Beacon Press, 1964.

Governo Constitucional. *Programa do Governo Apresentação para Apreciação—Debate—Encerramento do Debate*. Lisbon: Imprensa Nacional—Casa de Moeda, 1976.

Governo Constitucional, II. *Programa do II Governo Constitucional*. Lisbon: Imprensa Nacional—Casa da Moeda, 1978.

Governo Provisório da República Portuguesa. *Programa Política, Económica, e Social*. Lisbon: Imprensa Nacional—Casa da Moeda, 1975.

Graham, Lawrence S., and Makler, Harry M., eds. *Contemporary Portugal: The Revolution and Its Antecedents*. Austin: University of Texas Press, 1979.

————, and Wheeler, Douglas L., eds. *In Search of Modern Portugal: The Revolution and Its Consequences*, Madison: University of Wisconsin Press, 1983.

Gramsci, Antonio. "Selected Writings from *L'Ordine Nuovo*." In Branko Horvat, Mihailo Markovic, and Rudi Supek, eds., *Self-Governing Socialism*. Vol. 1. White Plains, New York: International Arts and Sciences Press, 1975.

————. *Selections from the Prison Notebooks*. Edited and translated by Quintin Hoare and Geoffrey Nowell Smith. White Plains, New York: International Arts and Sciences Press, 1975.

Great Britain. Department of Overseas Trade. *Report on the Trade, Industries, and Economic Conditions in Portugal*. London: His Majesty's Stationery Office, July 1924, September 1934.

Greaves, Thomas. "The Andean Rural Proletarians." In June Nash and Juan Corradi, eds., *Ideology and Social Change in Latin America*, vol. 1, *The Emergence of Worker Consciousness*. New York: Authors' Edition, 1975.

Green, Gil. *Portugal's Revolution*. New York: International Publishers, 1976.

Habermas, Jürgen. *Legitimation Crisis*. Boston: Beacon Press, 1973.

Hammond, John L. "Electoral Behavior and Political Militancy." In Lawrence S. Graham and Harry M. Makler, eds., *Contemporary Portugal: The Revolution and Its Antecedents*. Austin: University of Texas Press, 1979.

Harvey, Robert. *Portugal: Birth of a Democracy*. New York: St. Martin's Press, 1978.

Heady, Earl O. *Análise do Desenvolvimento Agrícola e Da Reforma Agrária em Portugal*. Lisbon: Ministério da Agricultura e Pescas, 1977.

Hobsbawm, Eric J. *Primitive Rebels*. New York: W.W. Norton and Co., 1959.

Horvat, Branko; Markovic, Mihailo; and Supek, Rudi, eds. *Self-Governing Socialism*. White Plains, New York: International Arts and Sciences Press, 1975.

Huberman, Leo, and Sweezy, Paul. *Cuba: Anatomy of a Revolution*. New York: Monthly Review Press, 1960.

Huizer, Gerrit. *Peasant Revolt in Latin America*. Baltimore: Penguin, 1973.

Hunnius, Gerry, Garson, G. David; and Case, John, eds. *Workers' Control: A Reader on Labor and Social Change*. New York: Random House, 1973.

Inkeles, Alex, and Smith, David. *Becoming Modern: Individual Change in Six Developing Countries*. Cambridge, Massachuttes: Harvard University Press, 1974.

The Insight Team of the Sunday Times. *Insight on Portugal: The Year of the Captains*. London: André Deutsch, 1975.

Institute of Social Studies, The Hague, Netherlands. "Field Trip Report: Portugal, March 1977."

Instituto Nacional de Estatística. *Estatísticas Agrícolas Distrito de Beja, 1960-1974*. Évora: INE, 1976.

————. *Estatísticas Agrícolas Distrito de Évora, 1960-1974*. Évora: INE, 1976.

————. *Estatísticas Agrícolas Distrito de Portalegre, 1960-1974*. Évora: INE, 1976.

————. *Estatísticas Agrícolas do Continente*. Lisbon: INE, 1970-1977.

————. *Inquérito às Explorações Agrícolas do Continente*. Lisbon: INE, 1968.

Janvry, Alain de. *The Agrarian Question and Reformism in Latin America*. Baltimore: The Johns Hopkins University Press, 1981.

Jeanneret, Teresa; Moraga, Leopoldo; and Ruffing, Lorraine. *Las Experiencias Autogestionarias Chilenas*. Santiago: Universidad de Chile, 1976.

Johnson, Ana Gutierrez, and Whyte, William Foote. "The Mondragón System of Worker Production Cooperatives." *Industrial and Labor Relations Review* (October 1977).

O Jornal. Lisbon.

Jornal Novo. Lisbon.

Kay, Cristobal. "Agrarian Reform and the Transition to Socialism in Chile, 1970-1973." *The Journal of Peasant Studies* (July 1975).

Keep, John L. H. *The Russian Revolution: A Study in Mass Mobilization*. New York: W.W. Norton and Co., 1976.

Knight, Peter. "New Forms of Economic Organization in Peru: Toward Workers' Self-Management." In Abraham Lowenthal, ed. *The Peruvian Experiment*. Princeton, New Jersey: Princeton University Press, 1975.

Koebel, W. H. *Portugal: Its Land and People*. London: Archibald Constable and Co., Ltd., 1909.

Kogan, Norman. *A Political History of Postwar Italy*. London: Pall Mall Press, 1966.

Kolaja, Jiri. *Workers' Councils: The Yugoslav Experience*. London: Tavistock Publications, 1965.

Kolakowski, Leszek. *Main Currents of Marxism*, vol. 3, *The Breakdown*. Oxford: Oxford University Press, 1978.

Kramer, Jane. "Letter from Lisbon." *New Yorker*, September 23, 1974.

Laffon, Virginie. "Dificuldades e Realizações dos Trabalhadores numa Unidade Colectiva de Produção no Baixo-Alentejo: Freguesia de Amareleja." Paper presented at the Third International Conference on Modern Portugal, Durham, New Hampshire, June 1984.

————. "Les Premiers pas de la Réforme Agraire dans une Freguesie du bas Alentejo." In Michel Drain, ed., *La Réforme Agraire Portugaise*. Paris: Centre National de la Recherche Scientifique, 1984.

Lewin, Moshe. *Russian Peasants and Soviet Power*. New York: W.W. Norton and Co., 1975.

Lima, Albano. *Movimento Sindical e Unidade no Processo Revolucionário Português*. Lisbon: "Avante!" 1975.

————. *Sindicatos e Acção Sindical*. Lisbon: "Avante!" 1976.

Lindblom, Charles E. *Politics and Markets*. New York: Basic Books, 1977.

Linz, Juan. "Patterns of Land Tenure, Division of Labor and Voting Behavior in Europe." *Comparative Politics* (April 1976).

Livermore, H. V. *A New History of Portugal*. Cambridge: Cambridge University Press, 1976.

Lourenço, Eduardo. *Os Militares e o Poder*. Lisbon: Arcádia, 1975.

Lourenço, Joaquim. "Princípios da Reforma Agrária na Constituição de 1976." *Economia* (January 1977).

————, and Siguiera de Carvalho, Nuno, eds. *Participação dos Associados na Gestão de Cooperativas Agrícolas.* Oeiras: Instituto Gulbenkian, 1974.

Lowenthal, Abraham, ed. *The Peruvian Experiment: Continuity and Change under Military Rule.* Princeton, New Jersey: Princeton University Press, 1975.

Lucena, Manuel de. *A Evolução do Sistema Corporativo Português*, vol. 1, *O Salazarismo*, and vol. 2, *O Marcelismo.* Lisbon: Perspectivas e Realidades, 1976.

Lukes, Steven. "Dual Power in Portugal." *New Statesman*, September 19, 1975.

————. *Power: A Radical View.* London: Macmillan, 1974.

A Luta. Lisbon.

McClintock, Cynthia. *Peasant Cooperatives and Political Change in Peru.* Princeton, New Jersey: Princeton University Press, 1981.

Macedo, Jorge Braga de, and Serfaty, Simon, eds. *Portugal since the Revolution: Economic and Political Perspectives.* Boulder, Colorado: Westview Press, 1981.

Makler, Harry. "A Case Study of the Portuguese Business Elite, 1964-1966." In Seymour Sayers, ed., *Portugal and Brazil in Transition.* Minneapolis: University of Minnesota, 1968.

————. *A Elite Industrial Portuguesa.* Lisbon: Instituto Gulbenkian, 1969.

Malefakis, Edward. *Agrarian Reform and Peasant Revolution in Spain: The Origins of the Civil War.* New Haven, Connecticut: Yale University Press, 1970.

————. "Peasants, Politics, and Civil War in Spain, 1931-1939." In Robert Bezucha, ed. *Modern European Social History.* Lexington, Massachusetts: Heath, 1972.

Mansfield, Michael Joseph. *Portugal in Transition: A Report to the Committee on Foreign Relations, United States Senate.* Washington, D.C.: U.S. Government Printing Office, 1975.

Mansinho, Maria Inês. "A Liquidação dos Grêmios da Lavoura no Alentejo e Algarve." *Análise Social* (July-September 1979).

Maravall, José M. "The Limits of Reformism: Parliamentary Socialism and the Marxist Theory of the State." *British Journal of Sociology* (September 1979).

————. "Spain: Eurocommunism and Socialism." *Political Studies* (June 1979).

Marques, A. H. de Oliveira. *História de Portugal.* Lisbon: Palas Editores, 1981.

————. *História da la República Portuguesa: As Estruturas de Base.* Lisbon: Iniciativas Editoriais, 1978.

————. "The Portuguese 1920s: A General Survey." *Revista de História Económica e Social* (January-June, 1978).

Marques, J. A. Silva. *Relatos da Clandestinidade—O PCP Vista por Dentro.* Lisbon: Edições Jornal Expresso, 1976.

Martinez-Alier, Juan. *Labourers and Landowners in Southern Spain.* London: George Allen and Unwin Ltd., 1971.

Martins, Herminio. "Portugal." In Margaret Archer Salvador, ed., *Contemporary Europe: Class, Status and Power.* London: Weidenfeld and Nicolson, 1971.

Martins, J. Silva. *Estruturas Agrárias em Portugal Continental.* Lisbon: Prelo Editora, 1973.

Marzani, Carl. *The Promise of Eurocommunism.* Westport, Connecticut: Lawrence Hill and Co., 1980.

Maxwell, Kenneth. "The Hidden Revolution in Portugal." *New York Review of Books,* April 17, 1975.

———. "Portugal: A Neat Revolution." *New York Review of Books,* June 13, 1975.

———. "Thorns of the Portuguese Revolution." *Foreign Affairs* (January 1976).

Medeiros, Fernando. *A Sociedade e a Economia Portuguesa nas Origens do Salazarismo.* Lisbon: A Regra do Jogo, 1978.

Mercier, Pierre, and Rocha, Nuno. "Mário Soares: The Road Ahead for Portugal." *Vision* (September 1976).

Miguel, Francisco. *Uma Vida na Revolução.* Oporto: A Opinião, 1977.

Miliband, Ralph. *Marxism and Politics.* Oxford: Oxford University Press, 1977.

———. *The State in Capitalist Society.* London: Weidenfeld and Nicolson, 1969.

O Militante. Lisbon.

Mill, John Stuart. *Principles of Political Economy.* London: Longmans, Green and Co., 1926.

Ministério da Administração Interna. *Eleição Intercalar para a Assembleia da República—1979.* Lisbon: Ministério da Administração Interna, 1979.

———. *Eleição para a Assembleia da República—1976.* Lisbon: Ministério da Administração Interna, 1976.

Ministério da Agricultura e Pescas. *O Crédito ao Sector Primário: A Criação do I.F.A.D.A.P.* Lisbon: MAP, 1977.

———. *Lei das Bases Gerais da Reforma Agrária.* Lisbon: MAP, 1977.

———. *Lei Orgânica do Ministério da Agricultura e Pescas.* Lisbon: MAP, 1977.

———. *Por uma Reforma Agrária Democrática e Constitucional.* Lisbon: MAP, 1977.

———. *A Reforma Agrária.* Lisbon: MAP, 1977.

Ministério de Trabalho. "Statement on Labour Legislation. Lisbon: Secretária de Estado da Comunicação Social." 1976. Mimeographed.

Mintz, Sidney. "The Rural Proletariat and the Problems of Rural Proletarian Consciousness." In June Nash and Juan Corradi, eds., *Ideology and Social Change in Latin America,* vol. 1, *The Emergence of Worker Consciousness.* Authors' Edition, 1975.

———. *Worker in the Cane.* New York: W.W. Norton and Co., 1974.

Miranda, Jorge. *Fontes e Trabalhos Preparatórios da Constituição.* Vols. 1 and 2. Lisbon: Colecção Estudos Portugueses, 1978.

Mitchell, Allan. *Revolution in Bavaria, 1918-1919: The Eisner Regime and the Soviet Republic.* Princeton, New Jersey: Princeton University Press, 1965.

Mondadori, Alberto, ed. *Dossier sul Portogallo—A Cura di Dante Bellamio.* Rome: Edizione Avanti, 1963.

Moore, Barrington, Jr. *Injustice: The Social Basis of Obedience and Revolt.* New York: M.E. Sharpe, Inc., 1978.

Mouro, Joaquim Barros. *A Contra-Reforma Agrária*. Coimbra: Coimbra Editora Limitada, 1978.

———, and Mouro, Manuel Barros. *Reforma Agrária: Legislação, Notas, Comentários*. Vila Nova de Famalicão: Centro Gráfico, 1976.

Movimento de Esquerda Socialista. *Sobre a Questão Agrária*. Lisbon: MES, 1977.

Mujal-León, Eusebio. "The P.C.P. and the Portuguese Revolution." *Problems of Communism* (January-February 1977).

Mulder, Mauk. "Power Equalization Through Participation?" *Administrative Science Quarterly* (March 1971).

Murias, Manuel Beca. *Reforma e Contra Reforma Agrária*. Lisbon: O Jornal, 1976.

Nash, June, and Corradi, Juan, eds. *Ideology and Social Change in Latin America*, vol. 1, *The Emergence of Worker Consciousness*. New York: Authors' Edition, 1975.

Navarro, António Modesto. *Memória Alentajana*. Amadora: Orion, 1977.

Nunes, Avelas. "Em Defesa da Reforma Agrária—Por uma Estratégia de Desenvolvimento que Respeite a Constituição." *Economia* (April-May 1977).

Olesczuk, Thomas. "Convergence and Counteraction: Yugoslavia's Anti-technocratic Campaign." *Comparative Political Studies* (July 1980).

Oliveira, Cesar. *M.F.A. e Revolução Socialista*. Lisbon: Diabril, 1975.

Opello, Walter C., Jr. "The Second Portuguese Republic: Politico-Administrative Decentralization since April 25, 1974." *Iberian Studies* (Autumn 1978).

Organization for Economic Cooperation and Development. *Economic Survey: Portugal*. Paris: OECD, 1963-1980.

Osterud, Oyvind. *Agrarian Structure and Peasant Politics in Scandinavia*. Oslo: Scandinavian University Books, 1978.

Ottaway, David, and Ottaway, Marina. *Algeria: The Politics of a Socialist Revolution*. Berkeley: University of California Press, 1970.

Paige, Jeffrey M. *Agrarian Revolution*. New York: Free Press, 1975.

Pais, José Machado; Lima, Aida Maria Valadas de; Baptista, José Ferreira; Jesus, Maria Fernanda Marques de; and Gameiro, Maria Margarida. "Elementos para a História do Fascismo nos Campos: A 'Campanha do Trigo,' 1928-1938 (II)," *Análise Social* (April-June 1978).

Partido Comunista Português. *As Eleições para a Assembleia Legislativa*. Lisbon: PCP, 1976.

———. *O PCP e a Luta Pela Reforma Agrária*. Lisbon: "Avante!" 1975.

———. *Por uma Constituição Revolucionária*. Lisbon: "Avante!" 1975.

———. *Programa e Estatutos do PCP—Aprovados no VII Congresso (Extraordinário) Realizado em 20/10/74*. Lisbon: "Avante!" 1974.

———. *A Saida da Crise*. Lisbon: "Avante!" 1977.

Partido do Centro Democrático Social. *O CDS e o Segundo Governo Constitucional*. Agueda: CDS, 1978.

Partido Social Democrata. *Análise Crítica ao Programa do II Governo*. Lisbon: Gabinete de Estudos Nacional do Partido Social Democrata, 1978.

————. *Política Agrária do Partido Social Democrata.* Loures: Serviço de Informação e Relações Públicas, 1978.

Partido Socialista. *Autogestão-Perguntas em Aberto.* Lisbon: Partido Socialista, n.d.

————. *Declaração de Princípios: Programa e Estatutos do Partido Socialista-Aprovado em Dezembro do 1974.* Lisbon: Partido Socialista, 1975.

————. *Dez Anos para Mudar Portugal: Proposta PS para os Anos 80.* Lisbon: Partido Socialista, 1979.

————. *Política Económica de Transição.* Lisbon: Edições Portugal Socialista, n.d.

————. *Relatório do Secretário Geral, Mário Soares—Segundo Congresso Nacional.* Lisbon: Edições Portugal Socialista, 1976.

————. *Os Socialistas na Assembleia da República.* Vols. 1 and 2. Lisbon: Edições Portugal Socialista, 1976, 1977.

————. *Vencer a Crise. Salvar a Revolução.* Lisbon: Edições Portugal Socialista, 1975.

————. *Vencer as Eleições para Reconstruir Portugal.* Lisbon: Edição do Centro de Documentação do Partido Socialista, 1976.

Pateman, Carole. *Participation and Democratic Theory.* Cambridge: Cambridge University Press, 1970.

Pell, Claiborne. *Portugal and Spain in Search of New Directions: A Report to the Committee on Foreign Relations, United States Senate.* Washington, D.C.: U.S. Government Printing Office, 1976.

Pereira, J. Azevedo. *Associações Agrícolas.* Lisbon: Clássica Editora, n.d.

Pereira, João Martins. *O Socialismo, a Transição e o Caso Português.* Lisbon: Livraria Bertrand, 1976.

Pereira, José Pacheco. "Atitudes do Trabalhador Rural Alentejano Face à Posse da Terra e ao Latifúndio." In Afonso de Barros, ed., *A Agricultura Latifundiária na Península Ibérica.* Oeiras: Instituto Gulbenkian, 1980.

————. *Conflitos Sociais nos Campos do Sul de Portugal.* Lisbon: Publicações Europa América, 1982.

————. "O PCP na I República: Membros e Direcção." *Estudos Sobre a Comunismo.* November 1983.

————. "Problemas da História do P.C.P." *O Fascismo em Portugal.* Paper from the Colloquim at the Faculdade de Letras of Lisbon, March 1980. Lisbon: A Regra do Jogo, 1982.

Pereira, Mário. *Fundamentos e Objectivos do Plano de Fomento Agrário.* Lisbon: Instituto Nacional de Estatística de Portugal, 1955.

Perrie, Maureen. "The Russian Peasant Movement of 1905-1907: Its Social Composition and Revolutionary Significance." *Past and Present* (November 1972).

Pery, Gerardo A. *Geographia e Estatística Geral de Portugal e Colónias.* Lisbon: Imprensa Nacional, 1875.

Pimlott, Ben. "Were the Soldiers Revolutionary? The Armed Forces Movement in Portugal, 1973-1976." *Iberian Studies* (Spring 1978).

Pintado, V. Xavier. *Structure and Growth of the Portuguese Economy*. Geneva: European Free Trade Association, 1964.

Pinto, J. Madureira. "Problemas da Análise das Colectividades Rurais." *Análise Social* (October-December 1977).

Pinto, Maria José Nogueira. *O Direito da Terra*. Lisbon: Publicações Europa-América, n.d.

Pinto, Mário, and Moura, Carlos. *As Estruturas Sindicais Portuguesas: Contributo para o Seu Estudo*. Lisbon: Gabinete de Investigações Sociais, 1973.

Pires, Carlos Borges. *Condições de Vida e de Alimentação das Famílias dos Trabalhadores Rurais da Freguesia de Albernôa*. Oeiras: Instituto Gulbenkian, 1979.

————. "As Cooperativas de Produção Agrícola da Freguesia de Albernôa." 1981. Manuscript.

Pisani, Francis. *Torre Bela*. Coimbra: Centelha, 1978.

Plastrik, Stanley. "The Enemy is Democracy." *Dissent* (Winter 1976).

————. "Portugal's Dangling Revolution." *Dissent* (Fall 1975).

Popkin, Samuel. *The Rational Peasant*. Berkeley: University of California Press, 1979.

Porch, Douglas. *The Portuguese Armed Forces and the Revolution*. Stanford, California: The Hoover Institution Press, 1977.

Portugal Socialista. Lisbon.

Poulantzas, Nicos. *The Crisis of the Dictatorships: Portugal, Greece, Spain*. London: New Left Books, 1976.

————. *Political Power and Social Classes*. London: New Left Books, 1975.

————. *State, Power, Socialism*. London: New Left Books, 1980.

————. "Towards a Democratic Socialism." *New Left Review* (May-June 1978).

Pusic, Eugen, ed. *Participation and Self-Management*. Vols. 1-6. Zagreb: Institute for Social Research, 1972.

Raby, David L. "Populism and the Portuguese Left: From Delgado to Otelo." Paper presented at the meeting of the International Conference Group on Modern Portugal, Durham, New Hampshire, June 21-24, 1979.

Raptis, Michel. *Revolution and Counter-Revolution in Chile*. London: Allison and Busby, 1974.

Rau, Virginia. *Estudos de História Económica*. Lisbon: Edições Ática, 1961.

Redfield, Robert. *The Little Community: Peasant Society and Culture*. Chicago: University of Chicago Press, 1967.

Reis, António. *O Marxismo e a Revolução Portuguesa*. Lisbon: Edições Portugal Socialista, 1978.

Reis, Jaime. "A 'Lei da Fome': As Origens do Protecçionismo Cerealífero, 1889-1914." In Afonso de Barros, ed., *A Agricultura Latifundiária na Península Ibérica*. Oeiras: Instituto Gulbenkian, 1980.

Reis, Miguel. *Governo Soares: O Exame de S. Bento*. Agência Portuguesa de Revistas, n.d.

Ribeiro, Orlando. *A Evolução Agrária no Portugal Mediterrâneo: Notícia e Comen-*

tário de uma obra de Albert Silbert. Lisbon: Centro de Estudos Geográficos Universidade de Lisboa, 1970.

———. *Introduções Geográficas à História de Portugal*. Lisbon: Imprensa Nacional—Casa de Moeda, 1977.

Riegelhaupt, Joyce Firstenberg. "Peasants and Politics in Salazar's Portugal: The Corporate State and Village 'Nonpolitics.' " In Lawrence S. Graham and Harry M. Makler, eds., *Contemporary Portugal: The Revolution and Its Antecedents*. Austin: University of Texas Press, 1979.

Roca T., Santiago. *La Autogestión en América Latina y el Caribe*. Lima: Ediciones CLA-IICA, 1981.

Rodrigues, Avelino; Borga, Cesário; and Cardoso, Mário. *Abril nos Quartéis de Novembro*. Lisbon: Livraria Bertrand, 1979.

———. *O Movimento dos Capitães e o 25 de Abril*. Lisbon: Morães, 1974.

Rodrigues, Edgar. *Breve História do Pensamento e das Lutas Sociais em Portugal*. Lisbon: Assírio e Alvim, 1977.

Rosa, Eugénio. *O Fracasso da Política da Direita*. Lisbon: Seara Nova, 1978.

———. *Portugal: Dois Anos da Revolução na Economia*. Lisbon: Diabril Editora, 1976.

———. *A Reforma Agrária em Perigo*. Lisbon: Editorial Caminho, 1977.

Rus, Veljko. "The Limits of Organized Participation." In Eugen Pusic, ed., *Participation and Self-Management*. Vol. 2. Zagreb: Institute for Social Research, 1972.

Rutledge, Ian. "Land Reform and the Portuguese Revolution." *The Journal of Peasant Studies* (October 1977).

Ryder, A. J. *The German Revolution of 1918*. Cambridge: Cambridge University Press, 1967.

———. *Twentieth-Century Germany: From Bismarck to Brandt*. New York: Columbia University Press, 1973.

Salazar, António de Oliveira. *Doctrine and Action: Internal and Foreign Policy of the New Portugal, 1928-1939*. London: Faber and Faber, 1939.

———. *A Questão Cerealífera: O Trigo*. Coimbra: Imprensa da Universidade, 1916.

Santillán, Diego Abad de. *Organismo Económico da Revolução: A Autogestão na Revolução Espanhola*. São Paulo: Brasiliense, 1980.

Santos, Fernando Piteira dos. "O Fascismo em Portugal: Conceito e Prática." In *O Fascismo em Portugal*. Papers from the Colloquim at the Faculdade de Letras of Lisbon, March 1980. Lisbon: A Regra do Jogo, 1982.

Saraiva, José Hermano. *História Concisa de Portugal*. Sintra: Europa-América, 1978.

Scott, James. "Hegemony and the Peasantry." *Politics and Society* (Fall 1977).

———. *The Moral Economy of the Peasant*. New Haven, Connecticut: Yale University Press, 1976.

Secretário de Estado Adjunto de Primeiro Ministro para Assuntos Políticos. *Vencer a Crise-Preparar o Futuro*. Lisbon: Secretária de Estado da Comunicação Social Direcção da Divulgação, 1977.

Secretário de Estado da Comunicação Social. *O Instituto António Sérgio do Sector Cooperativo*. Lisbon: Secretária de Estado da Comunicação Social, 1976.

Serra, Andreu Claret. *Hablan los Capitanes*. Barcelona: Ariel, 1975.

Silva, Carlos da. "Acercas da Génese das Relações de Produção Características do Latifúndio em Portugal—Tentame de Enquadramento dos Factores da Sua Formação." In Afonso de Barros, ed., *A Agricultura Latifundiária na Península Ibérica*. Oeiras: Instituto Gulbenkian, 1980.

Silva, Luiz Augusto Rebello da. *História de Portugal*. Vols. 1-4. Lisbon: Imprensa Nacional, 1869.

————. *Memória Sobre a População e a Agricultura de Portugal desde a Fundação da Monarchia até 1865*. Lisbon: Imprensa Nacional, 1868.

Silveira, Joel Frederico da. "Alguns Aspectos da Política Económica do Fascismo: 1926-1933." In *O Fascismo em Portugal*. Papers from the Colloquim at the Faculdade de Letras of Lisbon, March 1980. Lisbon: A Regra do Jogo, 1982.

Simões, António Cortes, and Moreira, Manuel Belo. "Seis Meses nos Centros da Reforma Agrária (Évora e Setúbal)." Paper presented at the French-Portuguese Roundtable on the Portuguese Agrarian Reform, Paris, June 15-17, 1981.

Skocpol, Theda. *States and Social Revolutions*. Cambridge: Cambridge University Press, 1979.

Sobel, Lester, A. *The Portuguese Revolution, 1974-1976*. New York: Facts on File, 1976.

Spínola, António. *Portugal and the Future*. Johannesburg: Perksor, 1974.

Stavenhagen, Rodolfo, ed. *Agrarian Problems and Peasant Movements in Latin America*. Garden City, New York: Doubleday and Co., 1970.

Steenland, Kyle. *Agrarian Reform under Allende*. Albuquerque: University of New Mexico Press, 1977.

Stepan, Alfred. *State and Society: Peru in Comparative Perspective*. Princeton, New Jersey: Princeton University Press, 1978.

Stephens, Evelyne Huber. *The Politics of Workers' Participation: The Peruvian Approach in Comparative Perspective*. New York: Academic Press, 1980.

Sweezy, Paul, and Bettelheim, Charles. *On the Transition to Socialism*. New York: Monthly Review Press, 1977.

Tarrow, Sidney G. *Peasant Communism in Southern Italy*. New Haven, Connecticut: Yale University Press, 1967.

Teixeira, Blanqui. "A Terra a os Que Nela Trabalham." In Partido Comunista Português, ed., *Congresso Extraordinário do PCP*. Lisbon: "Avante!" 1974.

Therborn, Goran. *What Does the Ruling Class Do When It Rules?* London: New Left Books, 1980.

Thompson, Dennis. *The Democratic Citizen*. Cambridge: Cambridge University Press, 1970.

Torres, Flausino. *Portugal: Uma Perspectiva da Sua História*. Porto: Afrontamento, 1970.

25 de Novembro. Lisbon: Terra Livre, 1976.

União Democrática Popular. *O Que É a UDP?* Lisbon: Voz do Povo, n.d.

Valenzuela, Arturo. *Chile*. Baltimore: The Johns Hopkins University Press, 1978.

Vanek, Jaroslav. *The Participatory Economy.* Ithaca, New York: Cornell University Press, 1971.

———. *Self-Management: The Economic Liberation of Man.* Baltimore: Penguin Books, 1975.

Ventura, António. *Subsídios para a História do Movimento Sindical Rural no Alto Alentejo, 1910-1914.* Lisbon: Empresa de Publicidade Seara Nova, 1976.

Verba, Sidney, and Shabad, Goldie. "Workers' Councils and Political Stratification." *American Political Science Review* (March 1978).

Vester, Michael. "Moral Economy and Traditional Culture as a Motivating and a Blockading Force of the Agrarian Reform in Portugal, 1975-1984." Paper presented at the Third International Conference on Modern Portugal, Durham, New Hampshire, June 1984.

Viera, M., and Oliveira, V. *O Poder Popular em Portugal.* Coimbra: Centelha, 1976.

Vylder, Stefan de. *Allende's Chile: The Political Economy of the Rise and Fall of the Unidad Popular.* Cambridge: Cambridge University Press, 1976.

Ward, Benjamin. "Marxism-Horvatism: A Yugoslav Theory of Socialism." *American Economic Review* (June 1967).

Wheeler, Douglas. *Republican Portugal: A Political History, 1910-1926.* Madison: University of Wisconsin Press, 1978.

Wiarda, Howard J. *Corporatism and Development: The Portuguese Experience.* Amherst: University of Massachusetts Press, 1977.

———. "The Portuguese Revolution: Towards Explaining the Political Behavior of the Armed Forces Movement." *Iberian Studies* (Autumn 1975).

Wolf, Eric R. *Peasants.* Englewood Cliffs, New Jersey: Prentice Hall, 1966.

———. *Peasant Wars of the Twentieth Century.* New York: Harper and Row, 1973.

Wolfe, Bertram D. *An Ideology in Power.* New York: Stein and Day, 1969.

World Bank. *Land Reform.* Washington, D.C.: World Bank, 1975.

———. *Portugal: Agricultural Sector Survey.* Washington, D.C.: World Bank, 1978.

———. *Portugal: Current and Prospective Economic Trends.* Washington, D.C.: World Bank, 1978.

———. *Portugal, Staff Appraisal Report: Small and Medium Scale Industry Development Project.* Washington, D.C.: World Bank, 1979.

———. *Unemployment in Portugal: Causes, Prospects, and Policy Options.* Washington, D.C.: World Bank, 1979.

Wrong, Dennis. *Power: Its Forms, Bases, and Uses.* New York: Harper Colophon Books, 1980.

Young, George. *Portugal Old and Young: An Historical Study.* Oxford: Clarendon, 1917.

Zukin, Sharon. *Beyond Marx and Tito.* London: Cambridge University Press, 1975.

INDEX

accountants, 111
AD. *See* Center Democrat-Popular Democrat Coalition
Afonso III, 9
agrários. *See* landed elite
agricultural workers' unions. *See* farmworkers' unions
ALA (Free Association of Farmers). *See* landowners' associations
Alandroal, 128
Alcáçer do Sal, 174
Alentejo: comparison with northern Portugal, 21-23; emigration from, 28-33; in First Republic, 11-13; land occupations in, 5, 54-55, 65, 77-78, 80-81; party competition in, 41, 171-172, 175-178, 189-190; prerepublican history, 9-11; prerevolutionary social structures, 21-23; under Salazar-Caetano, 13-21; secularity, 26-27
Algeria, 110, 135, 146-147
Allende, Salvador, 210-212
Alliance of the United People (APU), 163n
Almond, Gabriel, 133
Amaral, Freitas do, 233, 237
Antunes, Captain Melo, 52-53
APU. *See* Alliance of the United People
Armed Forces Movement, 3, 4, 38-39, 60-61, 66, 71, 74-75, 79, 97, 171, 175; and agrarian reform, 52-53, 67
army, xv, 3, 38-40, 67-69, 79-80. *See also* Armed Forces Movement; colonial wars; demobilization; military service
articulation, xvii. *See also* parties and the problem of articulation
Aveiro: city of, 74; diocese of, 27; district of, 22-23, 29-30, 189
Azevedo, Pinheiro de, 4, 79

Balsemão, Francisco Pinto, 239
Baptista, Fernando, 61, 181
Barker, Rodney, 132
Barreto, António, 197, 199, 201-202
Barreto's Law, 197-199, 201-203
Barros, Henrique de, 53, 187, 191-192
Beja: city of, 155, 174; county of, 116; diocese of, 27; district of, 12, 17, 22-23, 29-30, 41, 44-45, 47-48, 74, 78-79, 87-88, 114, 117, 119, 136-137, 171, 177, 180, 189, 198; land occupations in, 5-6, 35-36, 54-55, 64-65, 73, 76-78, 155

Bica, António, 175, 178
Blumberg, Paul, 107, 134
Bolivia, 147
Bolsheviks, 206-207, 209, 212-213
Braga: diocese of, 27; district of, 22-23, 29-30, 173n, 189
Bragança: diocese of, 27; district of, 22-23, 29-30, 173n, 189

Cabral, Manuel Villaverde, 29n, 37
Caetano, Marcelo, 20, 32, 57
Campos, Ezequiel de, 13
CAP (Confederation of Portuguese Farmers). *See* landowners' associations
Caravela, João, xiii
Cardoso, Fernando Henrique, 165
Cardoso, Lopes, 77-78, 178-193, 196-197, 200
Carlos, Adelino Palma, 4
Carneiro, Francisco Sá, 152, 233, 237, 239
Carrillo, Santiago, 166n
Carvalho, Otelo Saraiva de. *See* Otelo
Casas do Povo. *See* corporatist institutions
Casqueiro, Manuel, 174-175, 186-188
Casquinha, António, xiii
Castelo Branco, 22-23, 27, 29-30, 44, 46, 74, 78, 176, 188-189, 192; land occupations in, 6
Catholic Church, 26-27, 115
CDS. *See* Social Democratic Center
Center Democrat-Popular Democrat Coalition (AD), 203
Central Intelligence Agency (CIA), 194
Chile, 109-110, 128n, 135, 147, 168, 194, 210-213
Chonchol, Jacques, 211n
Claudín, Fernando, 165, 169
Cohn-Bendit, Daniel and Gabriel, 166n
Coimbra: diocese of, 27; district of, 22-23, 29-30, 173n, 189; university of, 14
Cole, G.D.H., 106, 132
collectives: defined, 111. *See also* worker-controlled farms
collectivization, 4
colonial wars, 3, 25, 27, 33
Communist party (PCP), xv, xvi, 40-44, 61, 65, 72, 74-77, 87-88, 96, 143, 148, 152-153, 171, 174, 186-187, 192, 214; association with worker-controlled farms, 183-185, 190, 201, 218, 229;

Library of Congress Cataloging-in-Publication Data

Bermeo, Nancy Gina, 1951-
The revolution within the revolution.

Bibliography: p.
Includes index.
1. Agriculture, Cooperative—Portugal. 2. Agriculture and state—Portugal.
3. Land reform—Portugal. 4. Portugal—Politics and
government—1974-   . I. Title.

HD1491.P8B47 1985   334'.683'09469   85-42675
ISBN 0-691-07688-X (alk. paper)

Nancy Gina Bermeo is Assistant Professor
of Politics at Princeton University.